INVENTING
AIDS

INVENTING AIDS

CINDY PATTON

ROUTLEDGE   New York and London

Published in 1990 by

Routledge
An imprint of Routledge, Chapman and Hall, Inc.
29 West 35 Street
New York, NY 10001

Published in Great Britain by

Routledge
11 New Fetter Lane
London EC4P 4EE

British Library cataloguing in publication data is available.

Library of Congress Cataloging-in-Publication Data

Patton, Cindy, 1956—
    Inventing AIDS/Cindy Patton.
        p.   cm.
    Includes bibliographical references and index.
    ISBN 0-415-90256-8. — ISBN 0-415-90257-6 (pbk.)
    1. AIDS (Disease)—Social aspects.   2. AIDS (Disease)—Social aspects—United States.   I. Title.
RC607.A25P39   1990
362.1'969792—dc20

Contents

Acknowledgments

This book came about through a process at once public and collaborative, and intensely lonely and private. During the three years I worked on this book, I was engaged in community organizing, held a job in the "AIDS service industry," lectured, debated, and taught about AIDS. I have institutional debts to Amherst College, which gave me a Copeland Fellowship in 1988 and where I taught part-time from 1989 through the completion of the book. In addition to the financial support, I want to acknowledge the generosity of staff, especially Joyce Soucier and Margaret Grossbeck, and the Women's and Gender Studies Department's allotment of a student assistant. I also thank the students in my "Representing AIDS" seminar, and particularly Raisa Lawrence and Siobhan Burns, for their patient and thoughtful challenges to my opinionated presentation of material.

I am also appreciative to the AIDS Action Committee, of which I was an early member, and which brought me on staff as Manager of Community Education for nine months in 1989. This also gave me a financial boost and allowed me to try out some of my programming ideas with the excellent education and community resource development staff. In particular, Chris LaCharite, Wanda Allen, Steven Colarusso, Sandy McLeod, Robert Colon, the guys in Safe Company, my boss David Aronstein, and my longtime friend, Larry Kessler, were challenging and supportive, and overlooked my extensive conference and lecture absences.

The ideas, though ultimately my responsibility, were forged from countless conversations, arguments, shared experiences, proferred citations, and vague concepts filtered through my own, very personal confrontations with self-doubt and loss of faith in the project in the face of, as my friend Michael Lynch so beautifully put it, "these waves of dying friends."[1] Countless individuals contributed to the specific content of the book, only a few of whom I will be able to single out for acknowledgement here. Jan Zita Grover, Douglas Crimp, Meurig Horton, Paula Treichler (who also provided invaluable comments on a draft manuscript), Liz Wolf, Larry Gross, Peg Byron, Amber Hollibaugh, Richard Goldstein, Hector Carrillo, Steve Epstein, Tom Waugh, Cindy Zegers, Carol Lafavor, Alfred Machela, Benny Henricksson, Hasse Ytterberg, and Jeffrey Weeks all contributed to the shape and direction of the ideas.

There are also a smaller number whose contribution was to sustain my hope that I might have something worthwhile to say, individuals whose contribution was and is to build a life with me at that fragile point where who I am and what I am trying to say can no longer be separated.

My greatest debt is to Eve K. Sedgwick, who unwaveringly supported me during this book process, getting me space on panels in order to put early versions of the work out, and ultimately, along with Hal Sedgwick, constituting a central core in my "extended pretended family." I can only say that as a witness to (and, I hope, participant in) Eve's painstaking and provocative interrogation of life, I have begun to see how to live with integrity one's life as a writer and as contestatory subject in the whirl of post-modernity.

Over the last year of writing, and especially in the final months of revisions, Judith Frank, my running partner and dear friend, helped me take the risk of speaking my darkest uncertainties. I admire both her professional prowess and the reflexiveness with which she lives her life.

Chris LaCharite and I lived through nine very intense months of projects at the AIDS Action Committee in 1989: as acculturated as I have become to urban gay male life, I often have been painfully aware of my difference as a woman. I have benefited greatly from learning about his lived experience as a gay man, as well as enjoying our numerous shopping adventures.

Erica Carter has been intimately involved with this project from the beginning, although we hardly realized that at the time. She organized the 1988 conference in London at which I presented the first piece of what eventually became this book. She subsequently edited earlier versions of several chapters which were published in *Taking Liberties* London: Serpent's Tail, 1989 ("The AIDS Industry"); in *Critical Quarterly*, 31:1, Autumn, 1989 ("Power and the Conditions of Silence"); and *New Formations*, Summer, 1990, ("Inventing African AIDS"); performed a last minute salvage operation on an interview which appeared in *Feminist Review*, Spring, 1990; and ultimately edited this book. Her stunning breadth of knowledge and keen sense of style has profoundly affected this work, and I am indebted to her professionally and personally for her contributions technical and emotional to my work over the past two years.

Siobhan Burns was also an integral part of the technical completion of the manuscript. She labored for hours entering the editorial changes and finding citations, and was still cheerful when I dropped into gloomy silences.

Thanks to Peter Aggleton, who edited an earlier version of "What Science Knows About AIDS," which appeared in his *AIDS: Individual, Cultural, and Policy Dimensions*, Philadelphia: Falmer Press, 1990. And, thanks to Ian Angus, whose comments on "Power and the Conditions of Silence" made it one of the strongest sections of this volume.

The book also benefitted greatly from an international perspective. In particular, I thank Simon Watney and John-Paul Phillipe for giving me their couch and lives over two years worth of trips to London. I am especially indebted to Simon for support, suggestions, disagreement over important points, and willingness to listen to my incredulity at the changing course of AIDS politics.

Beth Zemsky was there for me in innumerable ways, supporting me in moments of doubt and reeling me in when I got too wild. Patricia Hanrahan helped me face the demons. Sher Vieira always insisted on the applicability of elegant ideas, in life and art. Tom Huth has been a steadfast friend, gym partner, and adviser for a decade.

And finally, I want to dedicate the book as a whole to Bob Andrews, who was as at home at Sporters and Chaps as he was at the AIDS Action Committee and *Gay Community News*. The daffodils have bloomed again this spring.

Introduction

The late twentieth century quivers with the extreme microscopic and extreme macroscopic; imaging and communication technologies and the metaphoric frames they place on daily experience leave us more knowledgeable about the distant and the tiny than we seem to be about the proximate and palpable. The notion that there may also be such a thing as medium range experience seems prosaic, yet it is precisely in medium range that class, race, and gender are inscribed on the body through the micro- and macro-politics of occupation and surveillance. Radically different metaphors of power, of community, of resistance are deployed across different sites in the class war surrounding AIDS.

This book works from the paradoxical place of criticizing discourses, and yet proposing new ways of saying. The six autonomous chapters not only view the cultural and administrative shifts occurring in response to the "AIDS crisis" as framed in social service, educational, and popular discourses, but crucially, they interrogate the interests served by the narratives framing AIDS as "crisis." I apply a bifocal lens to the extremes of highly personal experience and the vast cultural shifts in which these are lived, described, resisted.

Representations of AIDS at every level—in the media, in the science, in the cultural assumptions manifest in the effects of institutional process—are multiple and discontinuous. By referring to meanings in different systems, the terms of AIDS discourse also relate to different already-inscribed relations of power. Given the multiple levels and domains of power relations implicated in AIDS discourse, no system or situation can ever be compared by simple analogy to the next, or totalized by structural analysis. It is hazardous indeed to seek a single logic underlying AIDS discourse or policy decisions. For example, gay men, in general, can define sexual self-determination as a community and personal goal which, if government interference is minimized, may be approached through a variety of self-help and grassroots democratic projects. Women, however, do not have the access to sexual decision-making or equality either in sexual partnerships or in the legal, medical, and social support structures which could promote rapid and positive changes to safer sexual practices. Strategies for safe sex organizing among gay men and among women (lesbian, bisexual, or heterosexual) must differ in relation to the sexual/political economy in which men versus women operate. In addition, class, race, and regional factors radically reduce the space for men and women of counter-hegemonic sexualities to discuss and experiment with new sexual norms; this space is at least minimally available to the core of the urban gay male communities.

Representations of AIDS seem inadequate, even sinister, carriers of the deep, unconscious political anxieties that inhabit the terrain which those who engage with the epidemic must negotiate daily. And yet we *must* speak about our experience, participate in public debate, make available medical test results, and render as data the individual social experiences out of which broader scientific and pedagogical strategies may be created. We must use the inadequate metaphors available to construct a cultural space from which those people most affected in the epidemic, as well as those observing its radical ruptures from afar, can make sense of HIV and AIDS and make the necessary personal and social choices and resistances. These inadequate metaphors must be critically employed, if they are to convey—as they must—the meanings of HIV and AIDS in lived experience, and the effects of policy and of the major cultural changes engendered in the epidemic as witnessed in specific times and places.

Any framework offered for understanding "the AIDS epidemic" is laden with historical references and assumptions which relate our lived experience to particular social institutions. Discussions of AIDS as a holocaust, as a CIA biomedical experiment, as an act of holy retribution all promote and justify particular community and policy responses, because each refers to broad forms of social power relations which, in our collective Western history, have deep and equivocal meaning. As different as each of these narrative frames is, they all suggest that the most important aspects of AIDS are larger than any particular human body and require extraordinary responses which may range from heightened concern for ethics and humanitarism, to the cynical witholding of treatment and information.

This book seeks to understand the tensions between the extremes (a tiny virus at one extreme, vast cultural shifts on the other); to understand how systems of power both inhibit and enable communities to organize around AIDS; to understand who is allowed to speak and what is kept from view; and to provide at least a handful of strategies for moving through the vertigo produced by engaging in or being engaged by the HIV epidemic at any of its many levels.

The vertigo of "living with HIV" will be reflected in the structure of this book. I do not follow a traditional course either from system to particulars or from everyday examples to theory. Instead, the chapters are independent, but move between linked systems of knowledge, attempting to identify and trace the edges of silence in discourses that purport to say all there is to say about AIDS. Though I prefer the chapters in the order presented here, readers with differing purposes may choose another reading order. Those not familiar with the technical language of AIDS discourse may wish to start with the explanatory footnotes early in Chapter Two. The chapters, as I envision them, are roughly paired: Chapters One and Two explore some of the broader social formations which frame what is said about "AIDS"—the AIDS service organizations, the medical industry, the media. Here, in the landscape of the HIV epidemic, we will discover vast tracts of barren land, territories whose existence remains unspoken, perhaps even—for the time being—unspeakable. My aim here is not to "give voice to" the hidden voices in the epidemic (though I will indicate where—and who—they might be), but rather to examine why they cannot be heard within the present discourses about AIDS, and in some cases, to suggest whose interests are served in suppressing the knowledges these voices might embody.

Chapters Three and Four discuss in detail the social construction of scientific knowledge and its relation to AIDS policy in areas where strategies against the epidemic seem to be heading in particularly sinister directions. Finally, Chapters Five and Six look at pedagogy and cultural productions which to some extent may open up spaces for the representation of absent bodies and experiences, but which have crucial limitations.

It must be clear that the political project of this book is to inform both local and global resistance to the social repressions accompanying the HIV epidemic. Critically, I question why and when "AIDS" has attracted discursive attention. This should never be misunderstood as an attempt to minimize the effects of the HIV epidemic; rather, I suggest that attention and surveillance, silence and relinquishing of control over one's own meanings are discursive effects symptomatic of relations of power. Untold numbers of people have been dramatically and deeply touched by HIV—as people living with HIV, the loved ones of people living with HIV, people affected by the political backlash of HIV, concerned citizens, curious scientists, involved policymakers. But no simple response to the epidemic can be seen as the "natural" reaction which "ideology" or "fascism" or "homophobia" somehow prevents. Throughout the book, I identify historically specific factors that account for why or with what logics particular institutions and individuals became involved in particular ways of combatting the epidemic. I will seem critical of some progressive or radical moves within the AIDS and community movements; I hope the critical insights I offer improve strategies for resistance. But I will insist throughout that neither dialectical analysis nor "speaking out" (the articulation of previously foreclosed "personal" or "private" experience characteristic of the new left, Black Power, feminist, and gay liberation movements) exhaust strategies of resistance; in the present situation, they may in fact impede them. While these new social movements continue to be vital to AIDS organizing, their strategies must be used critically. Though the current social and political arrangements require coalition politics based in these contemporary movements, highly problematic and stultifying disputes will continue to arise around educational and cultural strategies if we oversimplify the similarities between "communities."

Attempting to find and apply new theoretical frames in such a rapidly changing and, at the immediate and local level, devastating social experience as the HIV/AIDS epidemic may seem like a luxury. Yet the comprehensiveness of the political and cultural repression of people infected by or in any way imagined to be associated with HIV makes each and any maneuver within the policy or community process potentially treacherous. More than other critical policy debates in the post-war era, those which surround the AIDS epidemic seem repeatedly to descend into relativism; in the pluralist moment of the late twentieth century, it seems easier to quantify policy decisions in terms of body counts and dollars than to look more deeply at the workings of society and policy. This lends a particularly critical importance to cultural analysis and to an assessment of the strategies of educational and community-directed processes. I hope that the anxiety and pessimism incurred by letting go of traditional, dialectical, and essentialist modes of analysis are recouped by the optimism that I believe will emerge from new strategies for pedagogy, cultural activism, and local organizing.

1

The AIDS Service Industry:
The Construction of "Victims,"
"Volunteers," and "Experts"

We are experiencing a dawning recognition that while science constructs our reality, it cannot deliver on its promise to save us from our human limitations. This is especially evident in cultural and political responses to AIDS, which are at once a throwback to medieval notions of sin and disease, and a confrontation with a cybernetic future of slow viruses and technologized sex.

In the Age of Reason, feudal and clerical explanations of human difference were reordered by constructing taxonomies of science. Now, the apparent irrationality of responses to AIDS has served to legitimate the reorganization of modern categories of class, race, and sexuality: in particular, the construction of "AIDS knowledge" and the specific educational strategies used to organize and control this knowledge have been mobilized to anchor a new, if dubious claim to objectivity. If we are cynical about the scientific bureaucracy's ability to efficiently produce treatments, computer models, or vaccines relevant to the HIV epidemic, the para-sciences—health education, social policy, even the popular science media—claim a sort of lay objectivity still based in the assumptions of positivist science with its will to predict and control. But para-sciences are driven as much by the metaphors and tropes of the popular imagination as they are organized around the methods of big science (though I will suggest in Chapter Three that big science itself follows the twin masters of technology and metaphor, and has neither a privileged access to reality nor an objective method of inquiry). Big science and the para-sciences appear to be close relatives, since both stand apart from their objects of study and outside the communities they serve. But more than this, para-science in obvious ways and big science in more subtle ways, rearticulate and rationalize power relations as they go about their business of solving bodily problems. Indeed, the language used in science and para-science rests on the same metaphors of self/other, origin/return that structure the myths and stereotypes which make visible institutional patterns of stigmatization and discrimination.

This is not to say the discourses of AIDS are seamless, or that there is no possible resistance. Arising from different sectors of intellectual and social praxis, and expressed in the particular logics and rhetorics of the mass media and of scientific and policy journals, the emerging ideas of class, race, and sexuality reflect contradictory commitments and contested borders: the ideological paradoxes they produce open up strategic possibilities for resisting the racism, classism, sexism, and homophobia written into the AIDS crisis. A progressive response to the HIV epidemic must engage inequities on three levels: within the logics and administration of science and research agendas, within and between politically and socially constituted communities, and in the symbolic meanings and the lived experiences of the HIV epidemic.

I became interested in the rearticulation of such identity categories as race, class, and sexuality while struggling to understand the perceptions of homophobia and racism, sexism and classism which seemed to prevent natural allies from forming coalitions in order to address problems raised by the HIV epidemic. In policy debate, particular groups were persistently pitted against each other—African Americans versus gays, the poor versus women—as if the pairs were mutually exclusive. This suggested that particular ideologies of difference were in play in the political and social crises surrounding HIV. Why, in the vast, though incoherently articulated set of differences that operate within the epidemic, did certain antagonisms so regularly come to the fore? (Or rather, perhaps, to suggest themselves as hot spots for analysis and for political organizing.) How do accusations of racism and homophobia arise between the (largely white) gay-community-based AIDS service groups and health advocacy groups in African American communities? Why does the conflict between gay-community-based groups and the medical industry never take on the same dialogic quality of accusation and counter accusation? The easy answer is that disenfranchised groups share some common organizing strategies, and are therefore able to comprehend and critique their convergent and conflicting interests. The centers of power within our culture may remain mute to such critiques, and probably do not understand the needs and practices of self-determining communities. However, this does not explain why the process of mutual critique among potential allies has persistently failed to produce coalitions or other models of collective effort against the common, if multiply organized problems of the HIV epidemic. Why were gay-community-based groups chronically ineffective in working with groups based in communities of color? Why did the emergence of significant leadership by women in the communities of color and the influx of large numbers of white, middle-class women volunteers into gay-community-based groups fail to move issues specific to women to a position of high priority?

1.1 AIDS Service Organizations and the Limits of Community

The recent inclusion of lesbians and gay men in the Rainbow Coalition; the development of a vocal lesbian and gay people of color movement with strong ties in feminist, gay liberation, and ethnic liberation movements; and the more complex understanding of multiple differences that arose from nearly three decades of organizing on a liberationist model, have surely laid the groundwork for a broad coalition effort to address the range of issues surrounding the HIV epidemic. But such coalition efforts (or "partnerships" in current parlance) have rarely emerged, either locally or nationally—international efforts raise additional problems, which will be examined in Chapter Four. The coalitions which occur are often as result of the overt or covert work of lesbian, gay, or bisexual people of color at the interstices of several historically separate communities.[1] These coalition efforts upset the politically asserted categories of "gay community" or "community of color" because they highlight the complex experience of multiple and conflicting social identities. Thus in the first stages of the epidemic, the perception that people lived in two communities often seemed threatening, since it appeared to fragment the identity of the individual gay person of color.[2] However, the gay communities and the communities of color had to face the fact that their claims to be totalities were invalid if they could not meet the needs of members who were "minorities within minorities." Incorporating a range of identities meant negotiating conflicting social roles and working through the fragmenting effects of differences within communities that needed to present a unified front if they were to gain political power in the larger society. The social stigma of homosexuality, for example, made it difficult for the communities of color publicly to embrace their gay members, even if gay and lesbian social roles were already tacitly accepted in these communities (preachers in the African American tradition, for example).[3] In the largely white gay communities,[4] the use of the plural "communi*ties*," as in "gay communities" and "communities of color," was encouraged, in an attempt to acknowledge the existence of different fractions; yet even these terms fail to reflect the existence of much smaller groupings organized, not around the values of "community," but around particular norms of sexual and drug use practice. The term "community" has political valency in the United States, but fails as an analytic concept; for it cannot illuminate the shifting personal or network allegiances lived by individuals in face-to-face relations. Thus through the 1980s, gay theorists and strategists began to see the term community as increasingly politically problematic, especially when taken out of the U.S. context of civil rights politics.[5] Activists and educators, too, find themselves confronted with the disparity between notions of communities and the realities of sex and drug practices. The notion of "community" required adherence to identity categories; yet AIDS activists were increasingly concerned to delink practices and identity, so that for example men-having-sex-with-men could recognize the risks involved without having to reorganize their identity and claim to be gay.[6]

More insidiously, the term community was doubly coopted. The term "heterosexual community," which began to appear in AIDS discourse in about 1985, suggested that there existed among heterosexuals in general a sexual identity and shared history comparable to those of the "gay community." Likewise, the notion of a "general community" suggested a clear-cut and common normative structure different and separate from that of "minority communities." Both new terms diminished the powerful critiques of mainstream society lodged by the liberation movements, which foregrounded the term community in order to create a sense of unity where discrimination and assimilation had produced fragmentation. The idea of community can bond a group based on a set of qualities and values (race and tradition; sexual orientation and freedom from oppressive gender roles) set against a broader society which attempted to homogenize their unique difference. Used in the context of the new social movements, the idea of community recalls an important moment in contemporary politics and thematizes the power of collective action. In the context of collective activism around empowering service provision and changing sexual norms, by contrast, the idea of community loses its specificity and becomes cooptable. We seem unwilling to abandon the idea of community, complexly rooted as it is in a brand of North American turn-of-the-century philosophical pragmatism infused into new left politics through C. Wright Mills, and into black cultural politics through W. E. B. DuBois; and yet the mobilization of "community" as a rhetorical strategy continues to cause problems in our political analysis.[7] We might be better served if we understand community as a *political* formation specific to a society conceived as blocks of similarities, requiring clear articulation as a unit (community, minority) in order to attain political leverage. By contrast, the symbolic structures framing the HIV epidemic only partially derive from the political formations constituted at this particular historical juncture. The meanings of sexuality or drug use are engendered within networks of face-to-face communication and within cultural productions (counter-cultural practices, the media, art, rituals of partnering, styles of dress) which *cut across* the "communities" articulated for the purpose of engaging in the political languages of civil rights and claims for apportionment of social resources.

1.2 AIDS Service Organizations and the Limits of Identity

I take up the issue of power and the political alignments in AIDS activism in Chapter Six; here, I want to turn more specifically to the emergence of AIDS service organizations (ASOs). By the mid-1980s, rather than multi-cultural or other cross-difference coalitions, it was the original, gay-community-based AIDS groups which achieved hegemony.[8] The differing agendas and approaches which had marked early AIDS groups were homogenized by focusing on the single condition of the AIDS diagnosis: the mission of nearly every early group was caring for people with AIDS, educating the public in order to promote compassion and decrease irrational fear, and educating those at risk of contracting HIV. The orientation toward treating AIDS fundamentally as a disease and not a social problem meshed well with the existing public health approach to disease, and laid the groundwork for several states to include AIDS-related discrimination under existing disability law, which was sometimes also interpreted to cover people perceived to be at risk for AIDS (most often, gay men). A landmark 1987 Supreme Court decision found that a Florida school teacher who was suspended from her job because of perceived attitudes toward tuberculosis had been discriminated against, setting a precedent for including in anti-discrimination laws protection for anyone perceived to be "contagious."

An attempt at coalition outside of but related to the ASOs is the People Living With AIDS (PWLA) movement.[9] Here, the "coming out" experience of gay liberation is mobilized as a model for people with AIDS, who, it is believed, can create an identity and group unity by claiming the common experience of living with AIDS. Yet the PLWA movement has experienced many of the same difficulties as its predecessor identity movements: in reality, many different aspects of identity shape the experience of living with AIDS/HIV. Differences in class, race, gender, and sexuality, in drug use, in diagnostic protocols, and in the concentration of cases across regions produce divergent models of identity (or non-identity); thus many people diagnosed with AIDS do not immediately relate to "coming out" about their diagnosis, since they may never enjoy the benefit of freedom from "hiding" or repression which is the implicit reward for openness in the coming out model. For a poor, urban, single mother, AIDS may feel like more of the same; her experience of AIDS may not easily be rendered in the rhetoric of "living with AIDS" or the often referenced reorganization of life priorities which comes with the distress of diagnosis in people whose lives held more promise before their diagnosis. With important exceptions, the PLWA movement has therefore largely attracted individuals who can acculturate to the coming out model. The recruitment of women and injecting drug users alongside gay men in order to broaden the understandings and efforts of the National Association of People with AIDS has created a hybrid between a gay liberation/identity model and the lobby/self-help model of such health-related groups as the Multiple Sclerosis Society or the Hemophilia Foundation, which similarly create micro-cultures of diverse people sharing a common medically-related experience.

Interestingly, the perceived need for an autonomous People Living With AIDS movement arose from a self-help and community empowerment ideology which was not so different from the organizing principles of AIDS service organizations in their initial grassroots phase. The PLWA movement was launched in 1983[10]—before the major AIDS service organizations (ASOs) took on their institutionalized forms. The PLWA movement was initially a self-help movement which ran parallel to the emergent ASOs, but it quickly grew into a coalition of local groups which were dissatisfied with the increasing bureaucratization of the AIDS service organizations, despite the obvious affinites between the two movements— both were formed and are still largely led by culturally similar groups (of gay men) and neither has been successful in overcoming gender or racial/ ethnic differences. One clear source of conflict between the gay-based ASOs and gay people living with AIDS was the split between "helping others" and community self-empowerment that began to emerge with the institutionalization of AIDS service organizations. Where once there was an easy slippage between helping oneself and helping one's community, the other-oriented model of the ASOs forced gay PLWAs into a "patient" role which they had always hitherto rejected. The role paradox within the AIDS service organizations was in part due to the difficulties of negotiating cultural differences and divergent interests among the demographic groups affected by AIDS. In addition, staff/"patient" roles eased adjustment to the reality that members and staff of these organizations were themselves being diagnosed with AIDS and testing HIV antibody positive.

In addition to the gay-community-based ASOs and the PLWA movement, there were other small, community-based groups addressing AIDS in the African American, Latin, Haitian, and Asian communities and to some extent among American Indians in urban areas and on reservations. These groups developed both from existing multi-service agencies and from cultural affirmation projects. Fewer AIDS-specific projects emerged in these communities because historically they had used multiservice, community-empowerment, "full plate" approaches as the best strategy for addressing the multiple and complex factors that create individual problems.[11] Because the dominant approach to AIDS was to consolidate many services in one AIDS-specific agency, government planners, the media, and funders often failed to recognize how communities of color organized against AIDS by extending existing church or community programs. In 1987, Hunter College sociologists began studying the AIDS-related efforts in communities of color in New Jersey and New York. They found considerable and in some cases long-standing HIV and AIDS-related education and support work, most of which was construed as an adjunct to existing programs.[12] Instead of being articulated as a wholly new issue into which enormous group resources must be shifted—which was the approach in the gay communities (though not without great concern that AIDS was sidetracking other gay civil rights efforts)—AIDS, though viewed as important, was seen as a phenomenon already understandable through the existing analysis of government neglect, of poverty and of lack of access to health care and education.

Finally, the Narcotics Anonymous (NA) groups, working in concert with drug rehabilitation programs, developed another model for understanding HIV. Here, self-empowerment takes the form of submitting to a "Power greater than oneself,"[13] which is seen as the only force capable of combatting what is viewed as an unchangeable propensity to addiction. Unlike organizations within communities of color, which tend to view drug use in terms of government neglect or social control, NA, which in some cities has a solid membership of people of color, views "addiction" as a disease located in the individual which results both in self-destruction and in the abuse of those close to the "addicted." In the codependency theory on which the NA analysis rests, the people around the addict are seen to support addictive behavior (and therefore to support their own abuse at the hands of the addict) by insulating the addict from the consequences of her/his behavior. To escape addiction, the addict must "hit bottom," while the codependents express "tough love" by letting the addict fall and then "recover." In this framework, HIV infection becomes another consequence, both of addiction *and* of codependent behavior. Addiction is seen as a disease, indeed as the *primary* disease in an HIV-infected "addict." Unlike gay-community-based safe sex campaigns, which seek shifts in group mores to insure better individual decisionmaking, and unlike the communities of color which demand social change in living conditions as the basis for preventing drug use and enabling responsible sexual practices, the NA model seeks change by the individual, who is perceived to be driven by an essential addiction. The classic 12-step theory of Narcotics and/or Alcoholics Anonymous contains no social analysis of the social construction of, or historical changes in ideas about drug use; yet the program does involve speaking publicly, first in the safe confines of the AA or NA group. This is similar to the "coming out" model of gay liberation, except that it inverts the process: the drug user rearticulates her/his social identity (as "irresponsible addict") as a *medical* identity—as sufferer from the disease of addiction. By contrast, the homosexual rearticulates a medical identity (drawn from psycho-sexual pathology) as a social role.[14]

From the above, we can see how, in the early days of AIDS organizing, at least four distinct models of grassroots organization emerged. Yet it was largely the groups based in gay community traditions which formed the basis of what was to become an AIDS service *industry* which now stands in an institutionalized relationship to the medical industry and government. The AIDS service organizations[15] in the U.S. are character-ized by a recognizable staff profile (they employ large numbers of gay white male staff with professional experience); by the use of volunteers drawn from the gay community, though increasingly including white heterosexual women; by their view of AIDS as the primary problem; by their increasing separation from other gay groups; by substantial private funding. Its structural similarity to other non-profit health organizations made it difficult for the AIDS service industry to work with smaller groups operating with different approaches. Because the new AIDS industry was more familiar and therefore easier to make accountable to private funders and government agencies, and because gay activists were successful in articulating an analysis of AIDS as a single health issue hampered by social bigotry, the gay-based AIDS groups received the bulk of private funding and, until recently, most of the government *service* contracts. Multi-service groups in the communities of color, by contrast, had to divide existing resources between previous programs and new AIDS-related programs. One solution adopted by the largest AIDS agencies was to engage in coalition fund raising and the redistribu-tion of finances.[16] Yet, while the ASOs have moved toward addressing their gender, race, and class biases in employment practices and service delivery, there has been little attention to changing the unifocal approach to AIDS which results in fundamental conflicts between these and the smaller groups. The two hundred or so small groups based in the commu-nities of color now form the National Minority AIDS Council. Blood product consumer concerns are addressed almost exclusively within the national and regional hemophilia societies. Drug-related concerns are sometimes integrated into the ASOs, which work in concert with NA groups, but are also separately handled by local public health depart-ments and drug rehabilitation programs or street outreach programs funded by the National Institute of Drug Abuse.

It is admittedly somewhat artificial to include or exclude certain groups in defining the AIDS service "industry." I have chosen to focus primarily on the ASOs because of their size and autonomy, and because they are perceived both by the government and by smaller AIDS-related organizations to have the characteristics of an industry or "establishment." While the following sections of this chapter offer an overview of the kinds of shifts that produced this "industry," I am not suggesting that this general trajectory is exactly reproduced in any particular group. Important differences across regions and cities, as well as among and between significant individual players are lost in this analysis. A key factor in determining differences between the "industry" and the community of color and injecting drug groups is, for example, the historical relation of these groups to state departments of health; however, I will leave it to others to detail the emergence of AIDS work within government agencies. I should simply point out briefly that as the tasks of caring for people with HIV-related illnesses and providing education were divided up through the 1980s, many departments of public health in urban areas were already providing significant services to communities of color. People of color have, in some cases, gained significant power in the state bureaucracies; yet this continues to raise historical suspicions about the extent and ability of the state to observe and control people of color through the creation of state-mediated services.

I use the idea of an AIDS service industry—which I understand roughly as the private-sector non-profit organizations devoted exclusively to AIDS work—because it implies a set of social relations based on shared norms and styles of organizational behavior institutionalized through patterned power relations, rather than a collusion of the powerful who maintain an "establishment" by coercion or conscious exclusion, or act purely as a conduit for government monies to communities. This is not, of course, the only useful way to analyze the political economy of AIDS work. Shilts (1987) uses a traditional notion of the emergence of a ruling elite that pursues politically-based interests to the exclusion of solutions which he views as of "scientific" benefit and "for the good of all." Bateson and Goldsby (1988) take a very interesting ecological approach which views AIDS work as a cultural response to both disease and shifting mores. My approach is intended to historicize the current practice of AIDS service providers in order to locate the longer-standing social forces which motivate them. After years of work on AIDS-related issues, I no longer believe social differentials in care and education are due to the conscious policies of a ruling elite. Rather, these differentials follow logically from a range of assumptions hidden in common institutional and ideological histories.[17]

The notion of an "industry" is of course a fiction, and runs the danger of over-generalizing and obscuring local differences. Nevertheless, there is value in identifying the hidden policy assumptions and material conditions that construct AIDS as a particular type of problem and legitimate

only a limited set of solutions and administrative structures. It is important to differentiate between the industry, with its rules and norms,
and the people involved as staff or volunteers in particular groups.
Individuals will have a wide range of views of their roles in such organizations, and may feel conflicts with the internal or external aims and objec-
tives of their own organization or the industry as a whole.[18] Understanding individual AIDS workers as embedded in an industry is useful in
uncovering the full implications of homophobia, racism, classism, and
sexism in the handling of AIDS issues and needs in particular communities or groups. Suggesting that AIDS organizations operate within the
limits of an industry which has taken on a life of its own helps locate the
limits of AIDS service groups in the broad political sphere within which
they operate. I propose this model as a means of analyzing the formation
of an AIDS service industry in an attempt to identify strategies for
reforming particular organizations, for correctly targeting efforts to
change the larger assumptions which inform those organizations, and
for locating the effects of broader societal beliefs about AIDS.

The remainder of this chapter examines some of the forces behind the
formation of the AIDS service industry through the mid-1980s and
explores the routes of assimilation of activists into the new industry.
There are points of convergence between the commitments of activists
and of those at the core of the new industry, but there continue to be
significant differences between organizational forms and thought styles
which had broad implications for the direction of community organizing
around AIDS issues in the last half of the decade.[19]

The three U.S. epicenters of the HIV epidemic—New York, Los
Angeles, and San Francisco—set the initial trends in AIDS organizing,
and these styles were consciously picked up and refined by the second-
tier cities like Boston, Chicago, Washington, D.C., Atlanta, and Houston,
which followed closely on the epidemiological heels of the three hardest-
hit cities, but had the opportunity to learn from those cities' successes
and failures.[20]

1.3   From Grassroots to Business Suits

There was a major shift in the fight against AIDS between mid-1985
and mid-1986 in the largest U.S. cities, creating an organizational style
cloned by groups which sprang up later. This shift was *away* from gay
liberation-inspired resistance to a hostile government and indifferent
medical empire, and *toward* an assimilation of activists into a new AIDS
service industry, with its own set of commitments and its own structuring
logic. The forces underlying the shift are complex: in New York, Los
Angeles, San Francisco, and a handful of other hard-hit cities, the gay

community had gained political power through strategies ranging from the appointment of city liaisons, the constitution of a local electoral swing vote, the election of gay officials, and gay inclusion in some anti-discrimination ordinances. These made possible a degree of self-determination in AIDS work for the gay communities, whose historically developed infrastructure included a community funding base, successful organizational styles, some ideological coherence between cities nationally, and positive relations with government and civic powers which provided an least a modicum of credibility in asserting policy agendas, particularly in workplace non-discrimination and in HIV antibody testing issues. However, unlike the Black civil rights movement, gay civil rights efforts never achieved inclusion in national statutes regulating access to public accommodation or social welfare programs. Since the development of a community infrastructure had first occurred in the context of the gay movement, some of the ideological features of gay liberation were implicit in both gay-community-originated AIDS groups and in government policies on AIDS. In particular, the historical fight of gay men against surveillance through such public health practices as registries for sexually transmitted diseases (STDs) and contact tracing, as well as against police surveillance of gay bars and clubs under public health and sanitation laws, created a general consensus that gay men could and should work out their evolving sexual norms within the private confines of their community. State interventions such as the public identification of HIV-Ab+ people, or legal penalties against individuals refusing to practice safe sex—which were argued by some to protect compliant gay men against their seamier brothers—were rejected, although proposals like these for protecting women against male partners who refused to inform them or engage in safe sex were considered justifiable.[21] Gay male culture assumed rough equality between sexual partners—both could be equally responsible for ensuring that safe sex occurred. This assumption promoted a discourse of collective responsibility and choice about safe sex rather than a protectionist and rights-based discourse, a logic more consistent with feminist organizing around issues of violence against women.

Finally, the gay movement, entering the public political arena only in the 1970s, had achieved little formal power. Judged against the post-WWII trajectory of ethnic or racial groups' fight for civil rights in existing legal and administrative bodies,[22] the gay movement was at a relatively early stage of formal political development. Cognizant of the fragile position of homosexuals who lacked civil rights, gay-community-based AIDS groups favored autonomous service provision over the distant hope of government provision of services. It was difficult to press demands for government response as a "gay minority," and there were few structural links to public services with the exception of VD clinics. Equally important to the emergence of non-profit AIDS service groups was the relative economic stability of middle-class gay men, as well as the prominent, if largely unspoken role played by gay men in the arts—these ensured that income was forthcoming from private foundations, community donors, or from benefit performances by musicians and artists. This was understood as community self-determination in the face of government inaction, and produced faith in "empowerment" strategies that were considerably at odds with the ethos in the African American community, which generally viewed social and economic problems to result from government policies (and to a lesser extent, from government inaction) which disenfranchised African Americans. African American community strategies had long been aimed at getting the government to pay for solving the problems that slavery and ensuing economic and social repression had caused. Although cynical about the failure of mass welfare programs, African Americans were much more inclined to view access to public health and control of its agencies as critical to the community's overall empowerment strategy. Thus, African American, Native American, and some ethnic groups would view AIDS services as something the government and society owed their communities as a result of systematic discrimination: AIDS service programs were only part of the solution to a "full plate" of systemic social problems. Although the gay community could have, and in some cases did make the claim that a history of discrimination in STD care, and of the harassment of gays, accounted for the initial rapid spread of HIV in urban areas and the continuing spread among closeted homosexuals outside the core gay communities, AIDS services were more generally viewed as an affair internal to the gay community.

Ironically, this approach dovetailed with the Reagan plan to shift virtually all government services into communities under the guise of Christian charity and volunteerism. Because the gay community had never received government mediated services as an identified minority group with specific claims against social discrimination, the fact that the government might be unloading a responsibility for health care provision was largely forgotten once the major AIDS service groups had consolidated their power. The common perception that government inaction was the result of straightforward, conscious homophobia—that the government failed to act because it was gay men who were most identified with AIDS—obscured the broader convergence of patterns of discrimination caused by Reaganite disfunding strategies. The homophobia argument focused on patterns of funding to the *private* sector—largely gay-community-based groups—with little analysis of the failure to fund drug and poverty programs with AIDS components, programs which Reagan was gutting precisely at the moment when AIDS began exacerbating these longstanding problems. The focus on funding specific AIDS services also meant that small multi-service agencies in communities of color providing some AIDS services or education had difficulty obtaining funding until about 1988, when the Federal Office of Minority Health was ready to fund AIDS programs using the "full plate" approach.

1.4 Medicalization and Community

Of the two groups initially most visibly hit—injecting drug users and gay men—it was gay men who had the most autonomous and highly articulated infrastructure for mobilizing politically around AIDS. Injecting drug users lacked the formal structures of the gay community—especially community newspapers and newsletters key in circulating information and raising political issues[23]—and there was rarely a social identity for drug users to understand themselves as a political constituency.[24] Ironically, the recentness of the "demedicalization" of the homosexual seems to have left its traces in a narrowing of the gay community responses to AIDS—focusing on treatment, care, and individual education. This older medical paradigm rarely figured in the responses of the black community,[25] which had largely "forgotten" the medicalization of race common earlier in the century (and quite explicit in the Tuskegee trials, which were an attempt to duplicate in "negroes" work that had been done on "Scandinavians"). Government epidemiologists and policymakers by contrast promoted the idea of "risk groups," a category which, in equating "Haitians" with "homosexuals" and "IV drug (ab)users" was more obviously racist than homophobic. "Haitian" was the only original marker of "race," yet "race" itself was initially barely seen as even potentially related to AIDS. "Haitian" was used as a risk category because of researchers' beliefs about voodoo religious practices; thus "Haitians" were thought to have a risk practice in a way that "blacks" did not. Later, "black" would be collapsed with drug injection, creating the public perception that all gays were white and all drug users were black. This lack of categoric coherence meant that "Haitians" as a "risk group" was immediately perceived as "political;" the reality that men of color were over-represented within the remaining categories was not perceived as "political" until about 1985 when the gay press first reported the fact that black and latin gay men were overrepresented within the category "homosexual/bisexual."

Government funding patterns from 1985–1988 also promoted the formation of a largely white, covertly gay-commmunity-based AIDS service industry: money went to groups who corresponded to the Public Health Service (PHS) model of AIDS as an epidemic illness, narrowly defined by the acquisition of a virus through specific behaviors—a definition that largely ignores the social and political factors which shape the emerging demographics of AIDS. African American community groups had early recognized the significance of this new disease in their communities, and understood the complex cultural politics of sexuality, poverty, and systemic exclusion from social participation that underlie the patterns of drug use and sexual partnering that facilitate HIV transmission. The PHS, by contrast, viewed AIDS as strictly related to individual decisions about sex or drug use, and funded programs specifically for the care of persons with AIDS or for highly behaviorally oriented education. Disputes certainly arose over whether the gay community should get any "help" from the government, but little was said about the relative appropriateness of conflicting models, nor about the longterm effects of creating programs to meet funding paradigms rather than community needs. To the extent that ASO could present themselves as competent fiscal agents working specifically on "AIDS" they received funds, although the gay community funded the bulk of its educational efforts while the government largely funded service provision and testing. Thus both the internal style of ASOs and the external pressures of government funding patterns and models created AIDS groups whose institutional form has left them ill-equipped to meet either service or educational needs in the black and latin communities (and among women in general). Services to injecting drug users and to people of color have emerged instead out of already existing government or self-help programs.

1.5 Mainstreaming AIDS

A significant perceptual shift, at least in the mass media, occured in 1985 with the death of Rock Hudson. The virtual media blackout which had permitted only a handful of sensational or highly specialized medical articles to be published ended as the public began to perceive that "heterosexuals"—a term that referred not to drug users, who were desexualized by the epidemiologic categories, but to other, "ordinary" heterosexuals—could acquire, indeed had been acquiring HIV. Suddenly, a constituency in the position to *demand* a government response was asking for "the facts" about AIDS. For a brief time in 1985, as government agencies surveyed what had been done, and what was to be done, the large AIDS organizations were perceived as expert because of their experience with AIDS over the previous few years. But as government and media interest increased, gay men came to be viewed largely as a special "lobby" rather than as "experts." As gay-community-based AIDS groups worked more and more with the government, they spoke less directly of sex, and government officials—at least in the more liberal state and local governments—learned not to make embarrassing homophobic remarks.

But this decreasing discussion of homosexuality was not a result of decreased homophobia, as the large AIDS groups argued. Indeed, the political right considered this "de-gaying" of AIDS debate to be a plot to obscure the "real truth" about AIDS. The degaying of AIDS discourse was simultaneous with a heightening in the pitch of class and race anxieties around AIDS. Any perceived decrease in homophobia must be measured against an increase in racist and classist attacks on people associated with AIDS, in a context where racism and classism dovetailed too neatly with the AIDS service industries' newly defined categories and policies.

The emergence of AIDS groups with an identifiable style and a commitment to professional standards and tests of efficacy, coincides with the first major influx of federal government funding for AIDS education and services in late 1985, and with the growing awareness that AIDS cases would continue to be diagnosed at an alarming rate. The AIDS groups realized they needed government funds and the cooperation of public health officials, at least locally, and government officials realized they needed the guidance and support as well as the huge volunteer base of the AIDS groups. But this new industry was not content with this massive, if uncomfortable, consolidation of money and people; it needed also to rewrite the history of the community response to AIDS in order to justify its new methods of coping with the epidemic.

By 1986, the major AIDS organizations had been socialized into and had themselves become vehicles for the socializing of others into a new understanding of the meaning and organization of AIDS which radically separated the ASOs from their liberationist roots. The organizational structure and style which now characterized the ASOs—from hiring patterns to the division of agencies into education and client services, and later into community education and professional or general public education—created institutions in which a range of people constructed a new identity for themselves in relation to their experience of AIDS. The AIDS groups grew closer in sensibility to their partner government agencies, even while they fought over issues like mandatory testing, discrimination, and control of research. The gay-community-originating groups were suspicious of government agencies, since homosexuality was still illegal in over half the states, and the Helms Amendment in 1987 in effect prevented the funding of gay education projects and subjected more than a few agencies to scrutiny and harassment by rightwing politicians. The bulk of ASO funding still came from the gay communities; yet this only served to exacerbate identity conflicts with other groups: if the money came from and many of the services were enjoyed by the gay community, weren't they locked into an identity as gay organizations?

The amnesia surrounding the history of activism between 1981–1985 was initially a product of the emerging AIDS industry; but it has been reinforced by progressives who have begun to locate the beginning of AIDS activism in 1987 or 1988, with the emergence of ACT UP.[26] It is important to reassess the historical significance of the early years and understand both why, and at what cost, the AIDS service industry emerged, *and* who benefits from a reading of the development of these now powerful groups which severs them from their activist roots. It is tempting to hold nostalgic views about the early years of organizing; yet more is at stake than mourning the loss of the clarity and camaraderie of the years before AIDS became an acceptable social issue. Ignoring the context of early organizing renders an overly conservative view of its relation to current agencies, and obscures the contributions ASOs might now make to a more radical address of AIDS issues.

The new industry developed a vision of itself and of AIDS work that stood in sharp contrast to the early community activism, in which there were few distinctions between organizers, activists, people living with AIDS, and sympathetic medical workers. It inscribed a rigid role structure which constructed "victims," "experts," and "volunteers" as the *dramatis personae* in its story of AIDS.[27]

1.6   Who Gets Care? The New Altruism

Care for people with AIDS breaks down on lines that duplicate the existing, irrational delivery of health care and consolidate class and race divisions in the United States. Poor people with HIV-related ailments are cared for—if they get an AIDS-related diagnosis at all—in city hospitals or by their family at home; failing that, they end up in shelters or on the street.[28] While the major AIDS organizations have created group home settings for people living with AIDS who *become* homeless, the task of reaching and working with people who were living in poverty *before* an AIDS-related illness has fallen to groups already serving "the poor." When poor people are taken care of at home, the natural support system is overtaxed; the food and medical needs of the person living with AIDS become the responsibility of her or his relatives, friends, or young children. These unpaid services, and the stress of providing them in the context of a frightening new disease, are not recognized by the AIDS service industry or government. These poor, often African American or Latin relatives and friends are not the people identified within the AIDS service industry as "volunteers." In fact, even among middle-class gay men, the work of friends is now differentiated from the work of "volunteers," the latter being other gay men, or heterosexual women from the white middle class, among whom volunteerism is common.

The AIDS groups which now define volunteerism so narrowly began as grassroots organizations in which unpaid labor was seen as a contribution to community self-determination and liberation. AIDS activists—many of whom had themselves received an AIDS/ARC diagnosis—worked with gay and heterosexual PLWAs in the context of community organizing rather than altruism, and understood their work in terms of political resistance rather than compassion. The distinction between PLWAs and AIDS activists was never sharply drawn: PLWAs were and continue to be activists and activists continue to discover they have HIV or AIDS. The early identification of AIDS activists with the particular problems of PLWAs was both personal and political; AIDS was originally seen as a microcosm of the problems of gay and other oppressed people in general. Thus, the core of lesbians who became involved early on were active not because they perceived a personal risk of HIV/AIDS, but because they saw their community under assault or saw women as particularly vulnerable to medical maltreatment and the political backlash accompanying AIDS. This sense of community resistance created a possibility—which, as indicated earlier, has remained largely unrealized—of forming coalitions with communities of color also affected by AIDS and the AIDS-related backlash.

By 1986, AIDS was an acceptible vehicle for the New Altruism promoted by Reaganism.[29] Reagan cut federal funding of most social service programs, asking states, localities, and private foundations to pick up the bill. This was supposed to be more cost efficient and to instill traditional values like charity and gratitude in "volunteers" and "victims." In reality, it meant those with the time took care of their own.

While the African American community tightened its ranks around its own social agencies and churches, the newly institutionalized AIDS nonprofit organizations tacitly regrouped along race and class divides. The media valorized the gay male volunteer who put aside career and personal fears of AIDS to care for his brothers. Heterosexual white women also volunteered in large numbers, but not because they were depicted as at risk of HIV from their boyfriends or husbands, but because they are the traditional volunteer reservoir. Many women were personally affected by gay male friends with AIDS, but they were not encouraged to understand this experience in the social context of their participation in gay male culture. The weight of the new altruism discouraged them from challenging the sexism they encountered in the division of labor into "volunteers" and "experts" (largely professional men). This influx of women was taken as a sign that the white middle class was educated about AIDS and had overcome its homophobia. But heterosexual white men were almost never AIDS volunteers unless they had a close relative with AIDS: instead, they are now collecting the salaries in areas of AIDS research, public administration, and journalism, as *the experts,* the neutral professionals who are above politics and frequently have no contact with people in the communities most harshly affected by AIDS.

So why, suddenly, in 1985–86, when mainstream society still feared "contagion" through casual contact, did white middle-class women become involved in AIDS groups? What enabled the journalists and white middle-class heterosexual men generally to valorize the unpaid labor of women as altruism rather than fear their AIDS work as a feminist bid for power and autonomy from the heterosexual men who usually tried to control them? That these particular women should be perceived as safe while in the company of gay men stems from the long and special relationship between heterosexual white women and gay men in gay social roles—as hairdressers, designers, artists; a relationship that reinforces sexual and gender norms by putting women under the supervision of non-threatening men during their leisure time, but also covertly gives women adult companionship and esteem from working on projects with men who are not intent on reinforcing their masculine identity by ridiculing women. AIDS might have broken this persistent coupling—already somewhat displaced by feminist and gay liberationist critiques of gender roles. Instead, these two stereotypes were rejoined in a brilliant bid for consolidation of class and male power that diminished women's ability to perceive HIV risks within their homes or construct solidarity with other women about the need to reassess sexual practices.

The new altruism diffuses the political power of community organizing by recasting as "good works" the middle class's effort to help and defend itself in the face of federal funding cuts in social programs. It ends any society-wide commitment to redistributing wealth, instead allocating resources according to who makes an appealing "victim," rather than according to who has been "victimized" by society.[30] It even rationalizes funding cuts by constituting the middle-class volunteer as a role model: "See what the gays have done for themselves with no government money? The Black community can do the same."

1.7 The Price of Organizational Amnesia

Why was there such a need to rewrite community organizing as non-profit altruism? Many gay communities, and to a lesser extent IV drug subculture, were already successful in changing their group patterns to reduce the risk of HIV transmission. These changes were accomplished through a self-empowerment model within highly articulated sexual and drug cultures: they were accomplished by building rather than dismantling communities. Safe sex and safe drug use campaigns consolidated these communities, highlighting the ways in which the organization of sex and drug use were influenced by the anti-sex, anti-drug, anti-pleasure ideology of U.S. culture. This community organizing effort made it clear that AIDS was a product of the medical neglect and legal oppression of gay men and of drug users, especially users who were poor and people of color. The experience inside these communities of coping with AIDS was highly politicizing in the early years—and is still highly politicizing to people who refuse to adopt the "expert"/"volunteer"/"victim" categories.

A growing number of white AIDS activists and AIDS workers from the communities of color view the major AIDS service organizations as generally indistinguishable from government agencies, or from non-profit agencies directed toward less controversial diseases. AIDS groups are now largely dominated by white, middle-class values and staffed by gay male and straight female volunteers.[31] The apparent decrease in middle-class homophobia was an important step in making AIDS an acceptable topic for conversation and education; however, between 1985 and well into 1989, education was directed toward those most likely to accept the middle-class view of AIDS as a tragic disease which medicine would eventually conquer. Although ASOs have been highly flexible and evolved quickly in many areas, their sheer size now produces inertia: mistakes are costly and it seems better to fit different types of people to the existing model, rather than changing the model to accomodate new needs. Those who cannot fit into institutional patterns, or who reject the efforts of these AIDS groups as culturally insensitive or even irrelevant are seen as intransigent, not as potential allies in a coalition seeking self-determination and the just apportioning of medical care and social services. The new altruism of Reaganism divides those in need into the deserving and undeserving; the ASOs divide their clients into the grateful or the ungrateful, ignoring how past and current experience at the hands of medicine and social service agencies may have made some communities cautious. In the end, the voice of those most affected by AIDS has no purchase against the paradigms of the "expert"—and the "volunteers" become speechless participants in the narrow range of programs conceivable to this new industry.

2

Media, Testing, and
Safe Sex Education:
Controlling the Landscape of
AIDS Information

Between 1981–1985, efforts to care for the sick and educate those most immediately at risk happened at a distance from the public view. The epidemic gained its social meaning in relation to deep prejudices about race, class, gender, sexuality, and "addiction;" public ignorance about AIDS and community response to the epidemic fueled discrimination and thwarted education about risk. However, the onslaught of "lifestyle" stories about the epidemic following Rock Hudson's death in 1985 created new problems by *publicly* reinforcing a range of stereotypes which were also at the core of the emerging AIDS service industry. The persistent depictions of people living with AIDS as isolated and the erasure of the social realities which shaped the epidemic within communities of color paralleled both groups' growing alienation from the ASOs.

Aimed at a compassionate society (and *not* aimed at people living with AIDS or anyone "at risk"), lifestyle journalism constructed the person living with AIDS as a figure with a unique vantage point on both death and on the post-modern era. The questions put to the person living with AIDS became so much a part of the psychic unconscious that they were answered even when they were not directly asked. Lifestyle journalists were (with important exceptions) concerned not with the experience of this illness, but with reproducing the calculus of conservative morality in a deeply puritanical culture. Reporters interrogated gay men living with AIDS about their lives; the unspoken clauses rendered the answers ambiguous enough to erase anything positive an individual might try to say. "How do you feel now (read: that your "lifestyle" has betrayed you)?" "Was it (sex) worth it (death)?" In human interest journalism, aimed at a "general public" that wanted to feel compassionate but safe, the person living with AIDS stands in for Anglo-American culture which, at the edge of the twenty-first century, is still unable to separate its fear of sexuality from the vicissitudes of a little understood virus. And of course, the virus itself becomes a character—the little hunk of protein that refuses to give up its secrets. "Perhaps the virus is trying to tell us something," both new right doomsday prophets and scientists have said. The virus is itself overlayed with communications language—messenger RNA, codes, evasion, changing its surface, transcription, long terminal repeats.

Newspapers and magazines usually depicted volunteers as earnest gay men, perky white women, or grandmothers. Scientists and physicians were frequently represented as serious white men, who sometimes appeared to be gay if they were from hard-hit cities like San Francisco, New York, or Houston. Drug use was represented as the cause of AIDS in prostitutes and in the African American and Latin communities. These media efforts to "put a face on AIDS" converged with and created new expectations for the AIDS service organizations. As "gay" organizations, the groups had largely been political outsiders: after about 1985, the media began to suggest AIDS work as a form of middle-class volunteerism, an image that fit nicely with the attempts of many ASOs to mainstream in order to gain power and broader funding.

2.1 Rewriting Myths

Between 1985 and 1989 control of AIDS information was simultaneously professionalized and democratized through a series of inter-related processes, including the appearance of media AIDS experts and the institution of alternative HIV antibody test sites (ATS). While the AIDS service organizations were shaped by their roots in the gay community, and by four years of experience coping with the HIV epidemic, the information institutions were relative latecomers who imposed their own techniques of analyzing problems. Establishing control of AIDS information was accomplished through organizing and absorbing the disjunct issues of the HIV epidemic into pre-existing academic and professional disciplines.

Systematic scientific coverage of the epidemic, dating from about the First International AIDS Conference in Atlanta in 1985, quickly informed people that AIDS existed; however, the emergence of a core of media experts increased the gap between producers and consumers of scientific knowledge. In their efforts to translate science, reporters fell prey to elisions and simplifications. Terms like "the AIDS test,"[1] "promiscuity," "AIDS carrier," and "inevitably fatal" distorted the scientific "facts" and their social implications.[2] Media science frequently articulated pre-existing stereotypes in a new, objective-sounding language. Science reporters often accused gay activists and right-wing commentators of "politicizing" AIDS, but did not acknowledge the cultural politics underlying the popular and scientific media's descriptions of the epidemic.

Media reports on the vast new research industry devoted almost entirely to Human Immunodeficiency Virus (HIV) narrativized the "progress" being made in the "fight against AIDS."[3] Media accounts of the breakthroughs and "forward march" of research are largely an uncritical reproduction of science's own self-narrative; other than identification of a probable virus in 1983[4], progress has been incremental and tentative, at least from the perspective of people hoping for treatments. The scientific gains with practical results of saving or improving lives have come not from experimental new drugs but from perfecting already known drugs for use in treating secondary infections associated with AIDS. While the media have been instrumental in raising social and medical awareness about AIDS, the reportage has consistently misrepresented the basic concepts of HIV, sensationalized faulty research, and selectively reported on conflicting data. Despite coverage of particular events by many excellent journalists (especially those who have covered AIDS for years in spite of the alternating cache and stigma of the "AIDS beat"), the media have comprised a bleak and complex backdrop of AIDS (dis)information.[5]

The consistent confusion of a positive antibody test with an AIDS diagnosis and the failure to distinguish anti-viral treatments from treatments for opportunistic infections create an unnecessarily pessimistic interpretation of the idea that there is "no cure for AIDS." Coupled with images of PLWAs in extreme pain or as romantically sick figures, the media obscure the reality that many PLWAs continue to lead full, "normal" lives.[6] Anecdotal reports in the U.S. and studies in Europe suggest that there is a increased rate of suicide among people learning they are HIV-Ab+, especially among injecting drug users and homosexually active men not connected with supportive, informed communities.[7]

2.2 Gay Visibility and AIDS Epidemiology

In one sense, AIDS constitutes a revolution in concepts of diagnosis and disease, since the symptoms of AIDS are in fact other diseases. AIDS is historically specific, arising (presumably) at the moment when advanced technology could relate a primary causative agent to a set of extremely diverse symptoms. Had AIDS occurred fifty years ago, it would probably have been considered inexplicably untreatable forms of a dozen different diseases rather than as symptoms of an underlying immune disorder. From a sociopolitical viewpoint, AIDS was recognized by epidemiologists because gay men, by the late 1970s, were a visible community. In order to perceive a possible epidemic in the apparently unrelated deaths from *Pneumocistis carinii* pneumonia (PCP) in 1980–81, doctors had first to recognize that the men shared a demographic trait in common. But their homosexuality was not sufficient: it now appears that injecting drug users had already experienced an epidemic of HIV-related pneumonia deaths in the late 1970s.[8] The epidemic, noted at the time as "junky pneumonia," did not trigger public health investigators' interest because it was not considered remarkable that injecting drug users should get sick and die from any number of illnesses as users were considered intrinsically unhealthy. The emerging syndrome was defined as immune malfunction in "previously healthy" people; the rapid and unexplained decline in health which set the Centers for Disease Control into motion was noticeable only because the gay men affected had previously been considered "healthy." That gay men were seen as "healthy" despite having a variety of treatable sexually transmitted diseases attested to the acceptance and positive valuation of gay men and their sexuality in the urban settings where these early cases were under study. Had these cases appeared fifty years ago, and had the homosexuality of the patients been recognized, doctors would probably have viewed homosexuals *per se* as constitutionally weaker and explained their immune system breakdown on this fact alone.

2.3   Media Events and Life in the HIV Landscape

The sheer volume of AIDS research and the real need to share as much data as possible resulted in a loosening up of peer-review standards for publishing new studies.[9] With a flood of preliminary and often conflicting studies, mainstream reporters with more desire for a breaking story than knowledge of AIDS research reported on whatever data caught their fancy. For example, in 1987–88, the mainstream press was filled with particularly sensational—and erroneous—reports that HIV-Ab+ people might develop neurological and cognitive symptoms long before seeing any of the classic diagnostic symptoms of ARC or AIDS. These reports rationalized screening certain "sensitive" employees; SAS, the Swedish airline, seemed to have been influenced by these reports when they initiated HIV antibody screening of pilots in early 1988.[10]

Naturally, gay men around the world panicked; already distressed by lurid reporting on shattered lives and untimely death, gay men were now told they might go quietly mad before they even realized they were ill. More complete reports showed that this early data was wrong: a controlled study of 1543 HIV-Ab+ gay and bisexual men did not even find a trend toward early development of cognitive problems.[11] Researchers tried to dispel the myth of early cognitive symptoms, but the damage had already been done. The idea of "AIDS madness" provided the popular imagination with a pseudoscientific basis for the longstanding fears of the psychologically impaired homosexual or the crazed junky.

2.4 Testing: The Data is in, but Policy Makers Plan on

Mandatory HIV antibody testing (originally developed and based on standards for screening blood donations) for insurance, jobs, immigration, and as a focus of risk reduction education has been criticized by activists, lawyers, and even by the World Health Organization. Nevertheless, testing continues to be used widely in Europe and in the U.S., which requires proof of HIV-Ab- status for immigration and increasingly centers risk reduction education on the testing event.

Many health educators, including people from the gay groups and injecting drug serving agencies, have asserted that knowledge of HIV antibody status is important in promoting behavior change. The apparent self-evidence of a relationship between behavior and knowledge of antibody status rests on the assumption that drug use and sexuality are most importantly individual behaviors, ignoring the social norms and symbolic meanings that determine *how* sex is practiced or drugs are used. In fact, widespread testing only creates sexual apartheid and a two-tiered medical care system. Sweden, often praised as having the world's most progressive AIDS prevention policy, instituted a complicated set of laws to encourage "voluntary" testing and prevent people of unlike antibody status from engaging in sex with each other, regardless of whether "safe sex" were practiced. Under Swedish policy, HIV infection is categorized as a venereal disease, requiring anyone who believes they have been exposed to report for testing.[12] Although it is impossible to enforce this law widely, it has been used to coerce people who have been named as sexual partners of HIV-Ab+ people. Several prostitutes were "medically detained" in a special HIV facility just days before the beginning of the International AIDS Conference in Stockholm in 1988.

There is now general scientific consensus that there is no predictable relationship between knowledge of HIV anti-body status and subsequent behavior change, although policy makers continue to place testing programs at the center of their education and prevention campaigns. The large studies of testing and behavior conducted by the U.S. Multi-center AIDS Cohort Studies (MACS), funded largely by the National Institutes of Health and the Centers for Disease Control, showed no predictable relationship between knowledge of test result and subsequent behavior, attitudes, or psychological stress in year three of the prospective study.[13] Despite its own data, the CDC continues to fund primarily educational projects that focus on test taking. The insistence that there is a relationship between test result knowledge and behavior change means millions of dollars are spent on testing individuals (and studying them after they are tested) instead of spending the money on educational campaigns located within and designed by communities.[14]

The media *have* reported on small, poorly designed studies which showed correlations between test result knowledge and sexual behavior change as proof that widespread testing in itself will result in behavior change.[15] Popular views of the test as a motivator of sexual behavior change, and the conflation of HIV-Ab+ and AIDS, combined with the potential of incorrect self-diagnosis (i.e., deciding one "actually" has AIDS upon receiving test results), have turned a test of limited diagnostic use into an appealing but dangerous quick-information stop. This unthoughtful faith in testing legitimates things like HIV home test kits. Even if they were user-proof, analogous kits would never be released for similarly complex illnesses like cancer, multiple sclerosis, or arthritis because professional interpretation and sensitive counselling would be considered essential.

Reporters largely ignored studies of community-based educational projects in gay communities in the U.S. The CDC-funded Community Demonstration Projects indicate that the greatest changes toward safer sex practices occured in cities where gay men perceive their community to be changing toward the new "safer sex" norm. A dozen-city comparative study analyzed factors like pre-existing gay community institutions, gay media, and the role of specific community education projects. Cities with strong gay communities and positive images of gay men showed greater trends toward safer sex behavior. According to Community Demonstration Projects director Kevin O'Reilly, the "perception of the community's attitude and a belief that men in your community can and are making changes were the strongest factors in individual men's changing." O'Reilly said projects "aimed at individual beliefs are not as effective as programs aimed at community beliefs and norms."[16]

These studies suggest the importance of the women's, Black, and gay health movements' focus on empowering groups to take a role in advocating for their own health.

2.5 Media and the Interpretive Process

Media must do more than present information which seems accurate, clear, and accessible because popular understandings of information are constantly in flux. Media consumers' interpretive processes are complex and even the most straightforward media effort can result in many unanticipated interpretations. Clear-cut relationships between media consumption and individual or social attitudes or behaviors are difficult to quantify because media use and interpretation are embedded in complex social networks. Thus it is critical to understand the individual and group interpretive practices of the people to whom media "information" is directed. No media message is interpretation-proof because consumers already have ritualized ways of using media, which serve as interpretation contexts. Media criticism must evaluate "factual" accounting and assess the reception of information campaigns, as well as examine the historical uses of media by people in interpretive subgroups. A range of evolving practices and expectations (on individual, social, and national levels) may influence interpretation.

The perceived relevance of new information about HIV/AIDS will be affected by whether HIV/AIDS is initially viewed as of concern to individuals, communities, nations, or a mix of these. For example, a risk reduction campaign in the U.S. might be viewed as appropriately directed toward individuals, whereas in Zambia, where AIDS among young men would seriously affect the mining industry, risk reduction would be considered a national economic concern. A nationally oriented safer sex campaign like "Have safe sex and keep America strong," would seem absurd, while a campaign of that variety might be quite meaningful in Zambia.

Consumers also have expectations of what *type* of media is likely to supply particular types of information about HIV/AIDS. If HIV is perceived as an personal behavioral concern, individuals may be more likely to trust a local or oppositional media source for advice or sympathetic portrayals of PLWAs. On the other hand, the same individuals might look to national news media for scientific information. Gay men in the U.S. may view local gay papers as ideal sources of information about social support but seek information on scientific breakthroughs from national or scientific journals.

The form of messages—advertisements, public service announcements, news items, human interest features, editorials—each has different meanings to the media user. In capitalist media, advertising campaigns may be quite effective precisely because readers know that they "cost." Alternatively, editorials in community papers may be more effective because they signal leadership and unity.

Established patterns of group and individual media use and secondary discussions may be the strongest context of interpretation. If people regularly talk in groups about what they read/hear in the media, interpretations are more likely to be thoughtful, uniform, and relevant to local concerns. If media are publicly used, as might be the case with television or radio in poor rural communities, sensitive topics may become legitimated for conversation. The act of passing on print media may be a source of small group discussions; in Western gay communities, gay-produced newspapers are widely passed around providing word-of-mouth reinforcement and reinterpretation of important developments in AIDS research or treatment. However, differing patterns of media circulation may reinforce or contradict particular ideas; for example, small communities in West African countries often first heard about AIDS in sensationalist Francophone or Anglophone radio broadcasts from Europe. These were variously dismissed as a European plot and a catalyst for concern that the government was not taking appropriate steps. For some countries, international broadcasting contains a set of ideas that contradict more carefully created local or national media campaigns. Likewise, conflicts in local and national media, with their differing political investments, shape the interpretive practices of individuals and groups.

The complexity of how, why, and what is communicated about AIDS suggests why apparently neutral information is subject to radically different interpretations. Understanding the field of AIDS information and interpretation as highly contingent on social practices, rather than on individuals' intransigence or ignorance, requires designers of information campaigns to coordinate media on many levels and include participants from communities and micro-groups in order to reflect their interpretive practices.

2.6 The Epistemology of ELISA

Group and individual understandings of antibody testing are also contingent on interpretive practices and on the structure and purpose of testing programs. Testing is used in a range of settings: research, diagnosis, education, counselling, job screening, insurance screening, blood screening. Far from constituting objective meanings, test results take on a range of contradictory individual and collective meanings. Historically specific forms of medical practice, changing sexual and affectional norms, and, especially in the U.S., how antibody status is incorporated into identity politics—all these pull the simple test result into larger discursive and institutional formations.

Most people seem to believe that, barring occasional testing errors, medical testing in general produces infallible evidence. Outside the highly AIDS-informed core of the gay community, the HIV antibody test is misunderstood as diagnostic for AIDS. Many people interpret the test result as a guideline about whether to practice safe sex. Most media coverage and many popular advice books about AIDS and antibody testing promote the idea that a negative test gives you a "clean bill of health" and means you do not need to practice safe sex. Some people understand the negative test as a signal of immunity, others simply do not think about the possibilities of future exposure to HIV.

The mainstream media and many doctors use the term "the AIDS test." They argue that this term is accurate enough for popular consumption, that it was hard enough to raise awareness about AIDS, and thus introducing the term HIV would merely confuse. The test is however more properly called the "HIV antibody test"; this is the term used by most AIDS educators and involved clinicians. But even this term rests on a model of medical knowledge that creates confusion. The test doesn't actually look for the "antibody" to HIV but detects—reacts with—certain proteins which, in sero-epidemiological studies of North Americans and Northern Europeans, appear in the blood of people who have mounted an immunologic reponse to HIV. The two procedures commonly used to detect these proteins are called ELISA and Western Blot. ELISA and Western blot are not tests in the popular sense of absolute diagnostic value, but rather are chemical reactions that indicate that a particular biochemical process has occurred in the blood of the subject. This reaction of blood chemistry is not specific to HIV (the proteins which are considered representative of HIV antibody are *also* characteristic of antibody to malaria), and even in the presence of HIV, it varies in strength. This is nothing new to scientists; all assays are statistically-based procedures which take the presence of a particular compound to be indicative of the presence of a whole substance. This is how the biochemical disciplines work: they rarely "see" what they are studying, but experiment with purified elements.[17] Thus, laboratory scientists must interpret the strength of reaction in order to decide whether a particular blotter strip is to be considered reactive or non-reactive. ELISA interpretation is now done by computer, but Western Blot is still generally done visually—it requires considerable skill and practice to interpret "correctly" a reactive versus a non-reactive strip.

What is important to understand, then, is not that the test may be "wrong," but that it is not one hundred percent *specific*. However statistically insignificant these cross-reactions (with malaria antibody and other unknown factors) are, they mean that there is a margin of error in every individual test. There is an important difference here between scientific and popular understandings of the test: the laboratory scientist simply establishes whether, in a situation which meets the required laboratory standards (though these may vary somewhat—there are also errors caused by poor lab controls) the assay performed reacts or does not react, or produces a partial reaction that is inconclusive. It is in the counselling process that the categories "positive" or "negative" are assigned to the test, supposedly after the counselor has determined whether the person tested has any traits (exposure to malaria, recent pregnancy) that could potentially cause test reactivity in the absence of HIV. In practice, such assessment is usually omitted, except when people who deny any exposure possibilities actually return reactive tests. In this case, CDC guidelines direct the counselor to advise the person that the test may be inaccurate and to suggest that she/he retest at a later time.[18]

Although there are several forms of antibody testing now in use, I prefer to call the reaction by its proper name, ELISA or Western Blot, to highlight the procedural nature of "testing." The "test" is a series of events, not a moment of transcendentally assessing truth; there are important differences between a reactive ELISA/Western Blot (what happens in the lab) and a positive test (the interpretation made in the counselling setting and modified in the subsequent social interactions of the person who has tested). Numerous studies attempt to link behavior change directly to knowledge of test results, or examine these same links as they are made in the sequence of counselling, testing, and ongoing therapy. What such studies fail to understand is the interplay between specific interpretations of ELISA; the ongoing social production of meanings about "the test" in the media and in daily conversations; and the disciplinary effects of using ELISA in marriage licensing, job or insurance screening. This does not mean the ELISA and associated counselling are never useful; some people clearly construct those experiences in a way that helps them start or maintain behavioral changes and renegotiate the meaning of their lives in the context of this epidemic.[19] But this is never a simple effect of either serostatus knowledge or counselling. Individual changes only occur *and take on meaning* in the context of complex interaction among shifting community demographics, changing relationship patterns, individual interactions between sexual partners, friends, and counsellors, and as a result of the haphazard assimilation of information gleaned from a variety of news and educational sources. A mixture of community and individual changes have continually shifted the context of test-taking—for example, the heavily debated change from testing to enhance sexual behavior change to testing as a route to early treatment. It is impossible to separate the effect of debates about the value of test taking from any direct effect of either serostatus knowledge or counselling; ELISA literally means substantially different things at different times and within different interpretive communities. The issues raised by testing are located, then, not so much at the level of possible inaccuracies or legal problems, but at the level of the organization, disruption, or reinforcement of the processes of meaning production which take place as individuals and groups make sense of their relationship to the AIDS epidemic.

2.7 Instituting Widespread Testing

In 1984, the U.S. announced the development of a test for the antibody to the then recently identified HTLV-III (now called HIV)—the putative

AIDS agent. Testing, with its counselling component and apparent objectivity and simplicity, appeared to democratize AIDS education in the face of impenetrable facts about exotic viruses and an ever-changing cast of amazing new drugs. CDC and NIH (National Institutes of Health) officials early advocated widespread testing, even before the test was through its clinical trials, and despite the fact that it had less diagnostic value than research value. It did not show who would get AIDS or ARC and who would not, who was infectious and who was not. The test had been designed to accept a high false positive rate as a trade-off for decreasing the number of false negatives, as is typical in calibrating tests for screening blood products. Early estimates of the test placed the false positive rate at as much as 10 to 30 percent. However, false positivity rates in actual use are a statistical function contingent on the probable seroprevalence within a particular group. Thus, statistically speaking, in groups of heterosexual non-injecting drug users, the false positive rate would be higher because the likelihood of infection would be quite low.[20] On the other hand, in a group of highly sexually active gay men in a large urban area, again statistically speaking, the rates of false positivity would be relatively low. Counselling protocols are based on these statistical functions, so that positive results among people reporting risk behaviors go unquestioned, even though a number of gay men and injecting drug users are among the false positives.[21]

Subsequent testing protocols began to remedy the problem of false positives in the commonly used ELISA by adding follow-up testing with Western Blot, a technique which had a somewhat higher false negative rate and was thus unacceptable for blood banking purposes. Additional research over the past four years has refined test technology and created a range of testing procedures which assess different aspects of antibody response. But whatever the accuracy of testing now, it is important to recall that the early calls for mass and mandatory testing were made at a time when the test had inordinately high false positive rates, at a time when no one knew the incubation period of the virus (from infection to symptoms—indeed the assessment of symptoms and thus of diagnostic criteria for AIDS was still in considerable flux), and when no one knew the length of time between infection and production of antibodies. Initial calls for mass testing, and the administrative system that developed around testing, were expanding in a context of considerable ambiguity over test accuracy, counselling procedures, and over the relationship between knowledge of test results and behavior or attitudes. There were no prophylactic treatments and no civil rights guarantees specifically for people with HIV or AIDS. Though in retrospect these fears seem paranoid, in 1985, the calls for mass testing seemed to point in the direction of quarantine and detention.

Certainly, the wish to prevent any infected blood from entering the blood supply prompted quick government and drug company action—a reasonably good test was available within a year of identifying the virus. Research and technological development to improve the test moved *much* more quickly than research on pentamadine, which early proved highly successful in combatting *Pneumocystis carinii* pneumonia (PCP) even in highly immune-compromised patients. However, intravenously administered pentamadine caused severe side effects in many people. It was immediately clear that another means of administering the lifesaving drug was needed, but it was nearly two years before a simple aerosolizer was developed and released. In other words, the research trend was toward improving the surveillance capacity of the test rather than providing a prophylactic treatment for the number one killer of people living with HIV.

It is important to remember that, in 1985, when testing became feasible, CDC and NIH officials widely believed that transfusion and blood products were the chief route of transmission from the gay and injecting drug user populations into the general population. The idea hardly crossed their minds that there might be significant numbers of non-gay-identified men who had sex with other men, or that there might be substantial recreational drug injection occurring among "nice" suburbanites. In addition, when the tests first went into use, little was known about the epidemiology of HIV, especially outside the original, hardest hit communities. Indeed, some scientists still believed that HIV might be endemic in certain populations, perhaps in society at large, and that gay men and injecting drug users were experiencing a newly fatal version of a formerly benign virus.[22]

2.8 Gay Community Reactions to Testing

AIDS activists and gay leaders in the mid-1980s moved quickly to discredit the testing programs. In advising public health officials before the testing programs were established, gay leaders expressed concern that widespread, non-anonymous testing might drive underground those who would most benefit from this knowledge. If testing demanded an admission of homosexual sex or drug use, then individuals who were not already comfortable with their sexuality or who feared legal consequences for revealing drug use would simply avoid testing. Public health officials agreed that a poorly designed testing and counselling program would only make things worse. At the same time, the gay press launched an effective campaign to educate the core of the gay community about AIDS and about cautions on testing. The gay community had been coping with AIDS for three years before testing became available as a mechanism for making social and personal adjustments to AIDS, and in the absence of treatment, testing was initially of mixed benefit. Sharing concerns about testing did however create informed gay consumers, though this broader debate about testing did not extend to people outside the gay community.

Activists did not only criticize the test on grounds of potential inaccuracy, or of the psychological impact on those tested; they also argued that those testing positive would be at risk of losing jobs, housing, insurance (insurers had already tried to claim AIDS was a pre-existing condition, and in some cases, an "elective" illness). Some feared that positive test lists would leak from agencies and might be used to round up people for quarantine, to legitimate the harassment of sex workers, or as a pretext for accusing those seeking the test of being gays or drug users, statuses not protected under most civil rights laws.

The government countered these concerns by offering to fund anonymous sites, called, in true government doublespeak, "alternative test sites."[23] This was made to seem like a concession to gay activists, but in fact, the use of the traditional STD clinic as a model for the new test sites, coupled with financial stringency on the basis of government cost/benefit analysis, severly curtailed the counselling activites of ATS. It would only take another year before demand for testing was so high that a substantial number of people would be tested by private doctors who were not trained in counselling and often knew very little about AIDS and HIV infection. These demands for testing legitimized testing over counselling, education, or community awareness—though all of these had been proven to influence the meaning and consequences of test taking.

Between 1984 through 1985, most gay-based AIDS groups—the overwhelming majority of non-profit and volunteer groups—advised gay community members against test taking. At best, they saw alternative test sites as a means of getting the government to pay for counselling gay men about AIDS. Groups in Chicago and New York produced material for wide public distribution that admonished "don't take the test," and emphasized the importance of practicing safe sex regardless of serostatus. But by the spring of 1985, gay activists in San Francisco had begun to argue that test taking would promote behavior change. They accused East Coast gay communities of paranoia, saying that properly designed record systems could assure the confidentiality of those taking the test— even though there were already four documented cases of government agencies accidently releasing test lists. Some went as far as to accuse antitest activists of irresponsibility for counselling against taking the test. There are some important epidemiological features which may account for some of this difference in attitude toward testing: in San Francisco, and to a lesser extent in Los Angeles, the overwhelming majority of people living with AIDS and HIV were gay. In Chicago, Boston, Philadelphia, Atlanta, Washington D.C., and Miami, a large number of PLWAs and HIV-Ab+ people were non-gay IV drug users, women and children, and the epidemic was increasing in the Black and Latin communities. The politically powerful San Francisco gay community was able to control the image of and responses to the epidemic in a more uniform way than could gay communities in other cities who were grappling with the different effects of and responses to AIDS in other communities. It is also important to remember that there was in San Francisco a cohort of some 8,000 men who were already socialized to be study subjects, having participated since 1978 in hepatitis B vaccine trials. Confidentiality structures, perceptions of trust and control, and willingness to frame experience in terms of scientific tests thus seem likely to have been already well established in San Francisco's gay community. In addition, some sexual behavior change may have already begun in response to education about protecting men from hepatitis B, a sometimes fatal illness and a debilitating epidemic in some gay communities.

The debate about testing eventually coalesced into the consensus that the pros and cons of testing be listed, and the decision left up to the individual. Lost was the recognition that people sought testing based on erroneous information gleaned from media accounts, and on the expectation of learning things which the test could not tell them. Nationally, AIDS hotlines still spend a huge amount of time answering test-related questions.[24]

2.9 Expanded Testing: Gay People and Heterosexual AIDS

Until there was wide discussion of AIDS among heterosexuals, gay and AIDS activists held the line against widespread testing. There were dissenters, including those who believed that knowledge of test results facilitated behavior change, a position that is now disputed. From about 1985 until late 1986, gay activists, civil libertarians, and AIDS activists were quite successful in controlling how and when the test was used. But social concern about the "innocent victims" of AIDS increased and began to focus on pregnant women, and women who unknowingly married an HIV-infected person. In the critical two years after testing began, but before it came to dominate AIDS policy, feminists failed to take up AIDS or HIV testing as an issue, while gay men failed to recognize that arguments for testing women would become pivotal in a process that dragged testing down the slippery slope toward isolating those infected with HIV. Social stereotypes about women—especially African American women—and sensational reporting about sick babies made policy-makers irrational and contradictory in formulating AIDS policy. Their notions about individual responsibility in sexual behavior, and about women's capacity (or supposed lack of it) to make reasonable decisions about childrearing, were based on social stereotypes rather than on careful analysis of the decision-making options, life priorities, and information available to women at risk. Educational strategies, therefore, were based on stereotypical notions of risk perception and behavioral ethics among those thought to be at highest risk.

In 1985, Army researchers at the Walter Reed Hospital in Maryland announced that they had men with AIDS whose only risk contact had been with female sex workers in other countries. Women, especially sex workers, immediately came to be viewed as the "vector" moving HIV from the sex and drug underworld to heterosexual men, who then passed it to their wives, the "vessels" of procreation. Only privately did anyone challenge the Army data, suggesting that claiming to have visited an out-of-country (and therefore untraceable) sex worker was more acceptable than admitting to homosexual sex or drug use. Thus, while for both good reasons (the resistance to testing programs among gay activists) and bad reasons (the perception that gay men infected only each other) gay men were largely left to decide for themselves whether to be tested. Women who were potential mothers were pressured to be tested. The mandatory or aggressive "volunteer" testing programs for pregnant women and marriage applicants were established in several states in the spring of 1987; unwillingness to be tested became a sign of moral dereliction. Calls for mandatory testing of certain groups (usually prisoners, hospital admittees, and pregnant women) gathered momentum; the Army soon began testing all recruits, and in 1988, the U.S. began requiring antibody tests of all immigrants.

The expansion of testing has taken two forms: forced testing of those who might infect "the innocent," however that is socially defined, and voluntary programs for those under pressure to identify themselves as and organize their life around the idea of being a "positive" or a "negative." Few heterosexuals agonize about test taking, though the test may at some point strike them as a mechanism for displacing or relieving anxiety. For gay men by contrast, at least in cities with identifiable gay communities, life now requires them to take a stand on testing; serostatus has become part of the identity of gay men involved in urban gay communities.

Complicating the meaning and role of HIV testing is the persistent confusion over "heterosexual AIDS." Testing and counselling centers report great upsurges in appointments from heterosexuals in the wake of any extensive news coverage of heterosexual AIDS. To further complicate the issue, in the mid-1980s policy seemed to change monthly on whether all heterosexuals or heterosexuals *per se* or only heterosexual partners of IV drug users and bisexuals were at risk and should be tested. There is indeed still ongoing discussion about the cost efficiency of testing people with no probable exposure in order to catch the minute number who fail to recognize that they may have been exposed. While gay men who do not know the serostatus of all past partners simply assume there is a good chance they have been exposed to HIV, heterosexuals have difficulty accurately assessing their potential risk. Counselors are told to discuss the test taker's past behavior, making the counselling strategy and decision to test contingent on the counselors' skill at eliciting sex histories, on their perception of the probability of the individual's exposure to HIV, and on their willingness to take responsibility for influencing the decision of the person seeking the test.

2.10 Socializing Individuals to the AIDS Reality

The alternative test sites have emerged as the center for socializing individuals (as opposed to communities) to the new reality of HIV. The media and the government-funded AIDS education programs, promote HIV antibody testing as the centerpiece of their efforts to stop AIDS. The belief of many policy makers that it is widespread testing and not community organizing that has slowed the spread of HIV among gay men makes plausible legislation like the Helms Amendment in the U.S. (1987) and Section 28 of the Local Government Act (1988) in Britain. The Helms Amendment forbids AIDS funding to projects which "promote homosexuality," which has been construed to include any gay-positive material. In Great Britain, local governments have been prohibited since 1988 from funding any activity (exclusive of AIDS education) which promotes homosexuality or "pretended family relationship." The passage of these ultra-homophobic laws stems directly from denying the role played in risk assessment and reduction by positive gay identity, or by measures to decrease prejudice against homosexual behavior for those not "gay-identified." The public health debate in the U.S. pretends that "neutral" testing can solve the problem, although nearly every other country in the world rejects widespread testing programs as expensive, ineffective, and misleading as an educational strategy.[25]

Non-diagnostic uses of the HIV antibody test promote the construction of sexual identities based on perceived risk and test result. Although it is often argued that testtaking reinforces or stimulates behavior change, identifying as a "high-risk person" is not in fact synonymous with thinking through the exact practices which create risk and non-risk in their social locations of sex and drug use. In the early years of the epidemic, we fought to get people to talk about "risk behavior" rather than "risk groups," the latter category being defined at the time by social identity labels such as homosexual, IV drug user, prostitute, or partner of any of the above. Testing simply revises the categories to "positive" and "negative"—with no regard for significant mislabelling as a result of testing error—while pretending to ignore race, class, and sexual bias. The implicit association between positivity and high risk behaviors, negativity and purity serves further to reinforce the stigma and patterns of discrimination already insinuated into AIDS risk logic: the "risky behaviors" for which testing is essentially a confirmatory exercise are already connected in the public mind with gay men, prostitutes, drug users, and people of color.

2.11 Professional Safe Sex

Finally, the introduction in around 1985 of health education professionals to a pre-existing HIV and safe sex education framework brought a further shift in attitudes toward reducing the incidence of AIDS. Traditional health educators demanded empirical proof that particular strategies worked; their behaviorist orientation blinded them to the symbolic meanings and social organization of both sex and IV drug use. They failed to recognize that the people they sought to educate pursued their pleasures in communities and subcultures that operated by rules different from those of mainstream society (which itself, of course, fails to adhere to the rules it has itself asserted). Health education professionals trained in the "scared straight" style of education manipulated existing fears, making it difficult to separate false, pedagogically inspired panic from justifiable alarm. Overly individualistic in their approach, the traditional professionals never realized that gay men and IV drug users had coped with the fear and reality of AIDS long before the traditional professionals began *en masse* to confront this "new" phenomenon of AIDS. Both subcultures—though in different ways and to different degrees—had already begun to adapt to new group mores promoting safer practices and to mount a defense against the new repression accompanying the AIDS epidemic. Especially for IV drug users, safer practices brought increased social attack: getting one's own needles meant risking arrest for carrying. For gay men, promoting condom use meant publicly highlighting the practice of anal sex, a great social taboo in the U.S. Nevertheless, major sexual risk reduction among gay men had occurred by 1985, well before professional educators exerted influence in the burgeoning AIDS industry. These shifts in mores—enough to reduce sero-conversion in San Francisco to less than 2% per year in 1987[26]— were the result of efforts by activists who had little knowledge of traditional health education theory or strategy.

2.12 Safe Sex: Why Do Men Do it?

Safe sex organizing efforts before about 1985 grew out of the gay community's understanding of the social organization of sexuality and from extrapolations of information hidden in poorly constructed epidemiological studies. Reliant on a self-help model indebted to the women's health movement critique of health care and to the gay liberation discussion of sexuality, safe sex was viewed by early AIDS activists, not as a practice to be imposed on the reluctant, but as a form of political resistance and community building that achieves both sexual liberation and sexual health. It is this liberatory subtext that seems to have most raised the ire of the far right, and it was the first premise of safe sex organizing lost when professionals unveiled their plans for safe sex education.

The first safe sex advice was put into circulation by gay men, and was constructed in opposition to the insulting dictates of doctors. By 1983 enough safe sex information was available for a group of gay men, including men with AIDS, to write a forty page booklet called "How to Have Sex in An Epidemic." It still stands as the single most comprehensive guide to safe sex, including explanations of theories of transmission, sexual techniques, and the psycho/social problems of coping with the change to safe sex and with the fear of AIDS. It is important to realize that this booklet was written before a retrovirus was associated with AIDS: men understood and made major, effective changes without the benefit of HIV antibody testing. The lines which divide safety from unsafety have not changed since the first safe sex guidelines; yet the professionalization of safe sex education in 1985–86 led people to believe they could not come up with a personal safe sex plan based on a few facts and a lot of common sense. Professionalized health education displaced authority for understanding and enforcing safe sex standards from the people who engage in sex, and placed that authority instead in the hands of medical experts.

Despite the existence of several community organizing projects promoting risk reduction, and despite the active role of local gay organizations and the local gay press in safe sex education, professionalized health education—especially testing—was credited with the dramatic community-wide shifts in mores represented by the San Francisco seroconversion statistics. The national news played a key role in promoting the idea that professionalized education and testing were responsible for this success, although to a lesser extent, "San Francisco" is held up as a model gay community against other cities where behavior change seems less dramatic. As indicated above, however, San Francisco is hardly the best case study from which to draw conclusions about risk reduction nationally. The opinions about testing, studies of the role of testing in behavior change, and fears about abuse of testing are quite different in San Francisco from elsewhere in the U.S. While small scale studies from the densely gay areas of San Francisco indicate that test knowledge seems to reinforce behavior change, virtually identical studies conducted among gay men in Baltimore and Chicago, and differently structured studies in New York City among gay men and IV drug users, do not show a correlation between test knowledge and shifts toward safer sex techniques.[27] As noted above, in San Francisco about 95% of cases are among gay men, whereas the other cities have sizable clusters of cases around IV drug use, within communities of color, and within linguistic subgroups. The conflicting social concerns of those groups fragment those engaging in high risk activities into multiple communities, making targeted education more complex and normative shifts difficult to identify.

There are, in sum, serious questions to be raised about the effect of differing demographics on the use of testing programs to promote behavior change. It may well be that the apparent correlation between test knowledge and behavior change in the San Francisco studies is an effect of the community's general agreement that such a correlation might exist—an assertion widely publicized even before studies were conducted. San Francisco has a longstanding and highly articulated sexual culture with extensive political clout, a culture that was easily formed into an extensive social support structure for people living with AIDS or testing HIV-Ab+ (at least, for white gay men, the largest subject group in the behavioral studies). It may indeed not be test knowledge *per se* that promotes safe sex, but subsequently being referred to tailored support groups which function as places to meet partners who will carry out safe sex commitments. Anecdotally, counselors and psychotherapists who run safe sex rap/education groups remark that for some men, groups have replaced bars as a place to find sexual partners who can be assumed to be willing to practice safe sex.

Professionalized education programs ignored or let atrophy the more innovative grassroots programs because they did not fit traditional models and because they could not be evaluated by traditional pencil and paper tests or statistical methods. Gone were programs that trained bartenders as educators, or community involvement projects where leather-clad hunks raided bars to pass out condoms and AIDS literature.[28] Although the late 1980s saw more innovative programming, especially for "hard-to-reach populations" (the rationale being that you might as well try anything), traditional evaluation measures are poorly equipped to show the rich changes occurring as a result of such programming. Under increasing pressure for standardized, clonable, and statistically evaluable short-range projects, even gay health educators became reluctant to take social risks in order to promote sexual safety.

This traditional pedagogy also sets up a system of categories which make those who do not "hear the message" subject to special emergency measures and laws. Professionalized AIDS education tends to direct programs at good learners, not at the people who most need concrete, non-judgmental information and support for making changes in their lives and social groups. Professionalized education which emphasizes clonable programs loses sight of the needs of local groups and overlooks the long-term value of participatory projects in which groups generate their own strategies. Even among gay educators, homosexual subcultures outside the urban gay male community are viewed as aberrant variations on groups targetted in tried and true urban projects. Evaluation techniques like pre- and post-testing of fact-based information and charting sero-conversion levels within communities do not adequately reflect the forms and degree of long-term change in groups that are subject to the pressures of poverty and policing, or which have differing conceptions of risk, safety, and the value of the community. The Centers for Disease Control (CDC) require a testing component in most educational programs they fund, not only because they believe testing reinforces behavior change, but because it enables them to monitor seroprevalence in communities where consent for testing would otherwise be difficult to obtain.

There are, despite all this, some very exciting projects underway in communities disenfranchised by the white middle-class AIDS industry—in communities of color, among IV drug users, among sex workers, in communities in post-colonial and post-revolutionary nations. These projects rely on community involvement, are open-ended, and view the *process* of AIDS education as important in determining how AIDS will be perceived and how well behavior changes will succeed. But these programs are under funded and in danger of the absorption which homogenized the early projects by and for the gay male community.

2.13   The Return of Unnatural Acts: Notes for a Genealogy of Safe Sex

It is now commonly believed—among gay men as much as in society at large—that gay male sexual culture before AIDS was chaotic, amoral, and thoughtless. Randy Shilts' epic *And the Band Played On* has been particularly influential in confirming just this view. Shilts argues that gay men used doublespeak to avoid the "truth" of the epidemic, which in Shilts' view is that the community's sexual heyday was over once the epidemic set in, and that it was time to adopt relationships like those of the heterosexual mainstream. Describing the ethos of gay culture of June 1983, Shilts says:

"The linguistic roots of AIDSpeak sprouted not so much from the truth as from what was politically facile and psychologically reassuring . . . The new vernacular allowed virtually everyone to avoid challenging the encroaching epidemic in medical terms."

In marked contrast are the many gay periodicals and gay-produced advice pamphlets. The May 1983 News from the Front publication, *How to Have Sex in an Epidemic,* advises:

". . . limit what sex acts you choose to perform to ones which interrupt disease transmission. The advantage of this approach is that if you avoid taking in your partner(s)' body fluids, you will better protect yourself not only from most serious diseases but also from many of the merely inconvenient ones. The key to this approach is modifying what you do—not how often you do it nor with how many different partners . . . As you read on, we hope we make at least one point clear: Sex doesn't make you sick—diseases do... Once you understand how diseases are transmitted, you can begin to explore medically safe sex.
Our challenge is to figure out how we can have gay, life-affirming sex, satisfy our emotional needs, and stay alive!"

AIDS words—the linguistic constructs used to talk about AIDS—are never simply "facts" or "truths" but take on particular meanings at particular times, and are understood differently by different people.[29] The challenge to AIDS organizers is to understand how much information and how much disinformation is conveyed by each term at any given point. For example, "body fluids" is a useful term—it highlights the importance of biological transportation, the *active* movement of infected fluid from one body to another. While it is less specific than "semen and blood," its use avoids the difficulties of dealing with the heavy moral baggage carried by both semen and blood in this culture—both are already constructed as venal, fatal fluids. Juxtaposing "body fluids" and "blood and semen" in a single safe sex pamphlet conveys two sets of ideas, each of which has particular symbolic resonances, but which together may convey a more useful understanding about the biology of safe sex.

Even "safe sex" has had different meanings. The term emerged in about 1983 and rang as a radical slogan within the urban gay male community. In its originating moments, it suggested that sex could indeed be safe. As the slogan made its way through scientific meetings, the media, and into heterosexual parlance, it took on new meanings and became fixed as if it were an absolute practice which had only one interpretation. Reconstructing the history of the shifts in the context for understanding safe sex provides some guidelines for devising a "medically safe sex" that is also powerfully liberatory.

2.14   The Pre-History of Safe Sex

In the highly articulated urban gay male culture of the late 1970s and early 1980s, there were intersecting discourses about sex. There was sexual identity, which meant "gay" for most of these men, though other identities were included, such as leather man, clone, or disco queen. This rich plethora of sexual possibilities was included within the category "gay." There was also sexual practice (the acts men engaged in) and sexual location (the places where men engaged in such acts—sex bars and clubs, bathhouses, outdoor cruising areas, at home). Oral sex, for example, might mean something different and be conducted according to different rules in a bar or in the bushes, when done by/with a leather man or when done by/with a disco queen. There were also affective constructs around sexuality: monogamy, open relationships, casual relationships, anonymous sex. Each of these carried varying meanings and rules depending on practice and location. For example, an open relationship might include anal sex at home, and jerking off with anonymous partners at a cinema. This was the fantastic world of possibilities open to urban gay men, the economy of pleasures and representations in which their sex was negotiated.

These gay men knew a lot about sex. One of the most interesting products of this culture was the hanky code, the expanding semiotic use of bandanas of different colors indicating the specific preferences of individual men. While this has been viewed as a commodification of sex, it was also the embodiment of a sexual ethic. On a practical level, use of the code avoided the problem of getting home with a person of non-compatible practices. But even more, the hanky code rested on the assumption that sex was to be negotiated between rough equals. Choosing a hanky or hankies drew identity and practice together in an articulation of who one was sexually and how one expected to enact sex. In Foucaultian terms, the hanky code was a discourse about the care of the self. By contrast, heterosexuals in the late 1970s had little sense of themselves as "heterosexual" and functioned under an implied ethical code in which vaginal intercourse was the paradigmatic practice and in which women negotiated from a position of lesser power. Given these different sexual ethics, it is no surprise that it is heterosexuals—the amorphous general public—who have such profound difficulty accepting safe sex.

This was the sexual symbolic terrain onto which the first information about safe sex entered. In the days before "The Test," the urban gay male ethic derived its principles from the possibility that anyone could be infected, and thus required everyone to protect others and themselves from further infection, or infection with possible co-factors. The first safe sex pamphlets—*How to Have Sex In An Epidemic* and others—tried to reinforce the broad range of practices traditional to urban gay male culture, while at the same time getting men to make specific, transmission-interrupting modifications in those practices. In symbolic terms, the strategy was to keep the hanky code and the negotiation structure it represented, but make some changes in the conduct of particular practices (largely in the navy blue hanky of anal intercourse) to prevent transmission of the postulated virus.

In 1984, the safe sex hanky was invented by a group in Texas. This reversed the previous understanding of the relationship between safety and a multiplicity of practices. The black and white checked hanky constructed safe sex as a single practice or set of practices, under which might fall variations. This formed a new logical structure for thinking safe sex. Now, safe sex was a category unto itself—there was safe sex and all other sex, rather than a broad range of existing practices which might require modification to make them safer. The safe sex hanky did however, make safe sex a positive choice rather than a limitation, and laid the groundwork for constructing a notion of self—an identity—around safe sex: "I demand (am) safe sex."

At about the same time doctors began equating safe sex with reduction in the number of partners. "Number of partners" had not existed before as a preferential category, although doing often and with many people the various sexual acts one enjoyed was celebrated as part of this open sexual economy. Promiscuity was always a loose concept among gay men—often as much a symbolic badge of belonging as it was a numerical reality. The advice to reduce partners was based on a probability model and erased the notion that some *practices* were risky, others safe. What was actually achieved by the shift to an emphasis on reducing the number of partners was not so much behavior change, as a change in the mythology of promiscuity. Men in long-term relationships who had always had multiple partners, and who had formerly projected an image of themselves as promiscuous, now talked more publicly of their long-term relationship, while often retaining the same number of actual partners.

Then in late 1984 came the Heterosexual AIDS Panic, Phase One. The appearance of a half dozen or so "heterosexual" cases (these were heterosexuals who did not fit the previous categories of gay, IV drug user, prostitute, hemophiliac, or partners of the above) recast the notion of safe sex in two ways: first, it strongly promoted the idea that there are safe people (true heterosexuals) and dangerous people (closeted gay men, bisexuals, IV drug users, prostitutes); and second, since among heterosexuals, or at least in the public culture of heterosexual men, penile-vaginal intercourse is the hegemonic and identity-creating act, the meaning of safe sex shifted toward abstinence, monogamy, or the use of condoms. On the rare occasions when non-penetrative means to heterosexual orgasm were discussed, they were posed as alternatives to the real thing, in much the same way that teenagers learn that petting is their alternative to intercourse. Adults who develop their sexual practice around non-penetrative activities are thought to be either kinky, or doing it for some medical reason.

This insistence that intercourse is the real sex soon spilled over into gay safe sex literature. Condom advertisement controversies in 1986/87 created the first, if limited, public discourse about safe sex that actually made reference to genital sex rather than number of partners or body fluids. Yet they also contributed to a situation in which safe sex discussions inevitably began with a discussion of the importance of condoms, and only then discussed the range of other possibilities for a fulfilling sex life.

When the so-called "AIDS test" arrived on the scene in 1985, it was widely interpreted to be a means of determining whether one needed to practice safe sex. The widespread implementation of sexual counselling around ELISA and ATS further reinforced this new understanding of safe sex. Implicit in the testing process and explicit in some health advice and nearly all media accounts was the idea that any act between ELISA negative people was safe, and any sexual contact with ELISA positive people was unsafe. From now on, people rather than acts defined what was safe sex. This totally disrupted the negotiation logic of organized gay male sexual cultures. Under the regime of ELISA, paradoxically, any discussion of safe sex carries with it a presumption of danger—if you demand safe sex practices, you must either believe yourself to be infected, or you must fear your partner is infected.

The discourse of safe sex has become involved in constructing identities around infection or presumption of infection, instead of focusing—as in the early years—on the biology of transmission, and on the technology and practice of safe sex. For those confronted with the possibility of testing, safe sex becomes a symbol of danger, with ELISA as an indicator of safe versus dangerous persons. Safe sex ceases to be a practice of sexual pleasure, and becomes an avoidance of sexual danger. Thus, for example, Masters and Johnson's 1988 *Crisis: Heterosexual Behavior in the Age of AIDS* articulates a bizarre idea of safe versus "natural" sex. The authors are particularly disgusted by the implications of using latex accoutrements, and never seriously consider non-intercourse practices. Their attitude projects a deep-seated fear of the cultural danger of safe sex:

> "sex partners of uncertain [HIV antibody] testing status [could] . . .
> wear disposable plastic gloves during all intimate moments. These
> gloves, after all, aren't too different from condoms. Yet we are unwilling

to seriously entertain such an outlandish notion—right now, it seems so unnatural and artificial as to violate the essential dignity of humanity."

Masters and Johnson willfully ignore the difference between creating "intimate moments" and the practical realities of transmission; the point is not to wrap oneself in a latex barrier at the moment of sexual transcendence, but to don appropriate protection before a potentially transmission-enabling moment. They assume a seamless, natural sexual narrative with a beginning, middle, and end, and the premeditated disruption of this story with techniques of safe sex is not seen to restore health to sex, but rather to dehumanize it. The old hanky code, and the wide range of identities, sites, and practices of sex it implied constructed sex as perverse and fragmented, a montage of inchoate desires, objects charged with symbolism, and unexpected orderings of the sexual drama. Masters and Johnson imply that safe sex is unnatural, and that "natural sex," which in their view is intercourse between ELISA negatives, is safe. Lost is any notion that acts, not people or transcendence, create the condition that allows HIV to move from point A to point B. This safe sex discourse neatly reinscribes normal and abnormal sexuality along the lines of heterosexual intercourse without condoms, versus all forms of safe sex; "safe people" (as determined by ELISA) can have sex naturally, while everyone else—those who "fail" or simply refuse to take the test—is punished with unnatural, dehumanized (that is, "safe") sex.

3

What 'Science' Knows about AIDS: Formations of AIDS Knowledges

The several institutions that arose to produce and control information about AIDS were each grounded in implicit theories about the role of knowledge in daily life and in the work of experts like scientists. Thus, simultaneous with the emergence of institutions to deliver AIDS services was the formation of a set of "AIDS knowledges," systems of thought that often overlapped with, but were sometimes at odds with the commitments both of the industry and of groups of people living with HIV and AIDS. The emerging social roles within the industry were each believed to possess unique forms of knowledge—the "experts" knew about the virus and treatment, the "person living with AIDS" knew about suffering and death, the "volunteer" knew about the courage of the human spirit. In fact, the social role categories which defined how to be an expert, or volunteer, or person living with HIV/AIDS rarely corresponded with the lived, multiple experiences of the epidemic; AIDS knowledge formations tended to silence people speaking out of character. These silencing effects are grounded in the political commitments which cordon off the knowledge of science into an unbreachable, unquestionable domain; people living with AIDS are not supposed to become actively involved in treatment concerns and are considered highly biased. However, activists gained medical competence and became involved in self-help by pirating experimental treatments and conducting trials based on the methods of clinical science, but grounded in an ethics of community survival, rather than in future-oriented altruism. This incursion into the protected domain of medical science resulted in two unique but related developments within twentieth century medicine: first, the rise of research subjects able to speak about their conditions rather than simply serving as agar plates; and second, the disruption of some peculiarly North American, post-war notions about the conduct of medical experiments.

By the late 1980s, it had become clear that virtually the only Western medical treatments available to people with HIV would come through clinical trials, which would be fast-tracked under a new Federal Drug

Administration category called "Treatment Investigation of New Drug," and through compassionate release trials. The mere existence of "compassionate release" trials and the emergence of an underground market for experimental HIV-related drugs quietly undermined some of the basic premises of medical ethics, especially the assumptions necessary to conduct placebo-controlled trials. In theory, placebo-controlled trial participants should enter research freely and altruistically with a full understanding that the trial drug is not known to be "better" than the placebo ("no treatment"), so that their primary motive for participation may be construed as contributing to an increase in scientific knowledge for the betterment of future generations.[1] Even though there are still calls to "volunteer" for trials on these grounds,[2] most people living with HIV would laugh at the idea that they are doing anything other than being extremely smart shoppers in a new market with unknown products. "Choice" rhetoric has replaced informed consent rhetoric within the ranks of treatment activists and spilled into both clinical and ethical discourse. It is the medical knowledge of the person living with HIV/AIDS, not altruistic detachment, which has become today's ticket to experimental treatments.[3]

The production of epidemiological data about sexuality resulted in another challenge to the established modes of constructing scientific knowledge. The HIV antibody positive gay man or sex worker became something like the voice of the virus, speaking the inchoate desires believed to drive them to the risky behaviors which "cause AIDS." Thus, whatever the person living with HIV has to say is pressed into the service of science and converted into scientific knowledge through behavioral studies that are understood by science to be adequate summary representations of the experience of sexuality for those living under the sign of HIV.

3.1 Circulating Knowledges

In private conversations, in public health campaigns,[4] and in the scientific and para-scientific literature,[5] "knowledge" is promoted as the essential ingredient in the effort to slow the transmission of HIV. To the fearful citizen, knowledge means information which proves that she/he will not develop AIDS. HIV antibody testing has been widely misunderstood as the route to this knowledge. To the far right, "knowledge" means information that promotes homosexuality and promiscuity—it is carnal knowledge, and thus dangerous. Far right rhetoric often speaks of "real facts" about AIDS which counter "cover-ups" and "plots" by militant homosexuals.[6] Health officials and concerned activists seem to view knowledge as based in a system of neutral information with the magic power to change attitudes and behaviors by "empowering" people to make what seem to be self-evidently wise "choices."

Despite the obvious differences in the meaning of the term knowledge, all of these usages attempt to shore up the idea that there is some centrally effective knowledge with a privileged access to reality, a knowledge which at the most needs sensitive translation in order to be applied in everyday life. In the media, most health education campaigns, and ordinary conversation, "what science knows" is viewed as the arbitrator of disputes and the court of appeal for variant interpretations of safer sex guidelines or concerns about casual contact. Only in extreme conditions—in the context for example of angry disputes over children with HIV attending school—is the belief in the ability of science to *decide* questioned. [7] In this and other emotionally charged debates, scientists equivocate and refuse to provide the certainties sought by interlocutors who want emotional safety as much as mathematical proof. Scientists analyze contingent causalities and statistical outlyers; parents want assurance that their child won't be the one in a million infected by HIV, and demand levels of protection that far exceed those they might demand for more routine dangers over which they feel they have some control.

Even more rarely do we question the ability of science to *know*. For the most part, science serves as the master discourse that administers all other discourses about AIDS. Although science is often not specifically referenced, the common assumption underlying debates on public policy or the voicing of personal views about safer sex, is that science can, ultimately, answer any troubling questions. Knowledge is perceived to arise from science and filter out into the social and imaginary world. The knowledges that come from the social and imaginary world—knowledge about surviving with a chronic illness, about reinventing sexual pleasure in a disaster zone, about finding the courage to transcend the narrowly defined roles of the AIDS service industry—these knowledges are either pushed to the margins of scientific knowledge or are rewritten as scientific data about odds of survival or aggregate behavior change. The knowledges of the epidemic arise and compete (most visibly in the policy arena) but it is the logic of *science* that anchors the power relations which determine *whose* knowledge counts as "real," as "objective." Scientists rarely even need to testify in policy debate because scientific thought modalities have long been popularized and already underpin the structure of thinking in the social and political sphere. We approach the end of the twentieth century, not so much as "technological man," robbed of emotionality and cultural depth, but as cyborgs for whom science is our culture, our mode of constructing identity. It hardly seems possible that it could be otherwise—but how did science reestablish itself through AIDS after a decade or two of declining public confidence? And whose interests does the prominence of science now serve?

One measure of the apparent success of AIDS science is the proliferating production of public forms of AIDS knowledge. From workshops to pamphlets to HIV antibody tests to public service announcements, there has been an apparently unstoppable growth in AIDS knowledge, and in the numbers of people knowledgeable about AIDS. And indeed, the level of common knowledge about the complexities of HIV and AIDS *is* astonishingly high.[8] Several studies and polls suggest that nearly everyone with access to the media (and given the degree of radio broadcasting and informal oral reporting of media information, few people, even in very remote areas, have no access to reportage) has *heard* of AIDS, and that the majority have the basics facts "right." Especially within the Euroamerican gay communities, terms such as "antibodies," "P24 counts," "AZT," and "CD–4 receptors" are common lingo; the gay press reads like a medical journal, and gay readers may perceive themselves as largely able to grasp the technical aspects of HIV. Activists in such groups as ACT UP New York and Project Inform in San Francisco are autodidactic medical experts. Individual gay men are in large numbers taking their treatment plans into their own hands, supplementing information and drugs they are able to obtain through medical channels with information and drugs or alternative therapies obtained through the activist networks. It doesn't seem at all unusual to most gay men that their hairdresser or a man picked up in a bar knows as much about AIDS medicine as many doctors.

However, the impression that what we know is most importantly based in science forecloses the exchange of crucial forms of information about transmission interruption both within and between communities. Promoting science-logic over complex folk-logics steeped in the rich metaphors and mores of a community makes people dependent on the medical bureaucracy instead of pursuing their own strategies for social change, and leads to the idea that information *by itself* is capable of producing behavior changes. Once science becomes the foundation of AIDS knowledges, ethical and normative shifts are shortcircuited—knowledge is applied *in relation to* the logics of science, which are largely behavioristic. Science logic remedicalizes sexuality and recolonizes bodies once partially wrested free from the medical empire.[9] We now "know more" about (or have a totalized language for) HIV and our immune systems than we "know" (or can say) about the sexual practices and community norm formations which might constitute a basis for resisting the ideological power of "unsafe" sex. Science proposes an objectivizing methodology for the study of the virus and the immune system. Perhaps this will ultimately produce useful treatment modalities (I want to challenge here the basis of the cultural acceptance of science's claims, not the results of its work).[10] But it also produces the particular disciplinary formation within which HIV and AIDS are most commonly framed. In AIDS medical science, the body becomes a screen or agar plate on which disease is in play. The complex of symptoms, diseases in themselves, produces repetitions[11]—bouts of PCP, for example (although it is only the first bout which marks the boundary between AIDS and not AIDS). Diagnostic medicine abstracts the symptoms from the body to produce a totalizing explanation with a single or primary cause, a pathology. Because the immune system, understood metaphorically, transcends the place of the body, the abstraction "AIDS" folds back to correspond exactly to the *space* of the body. The virus is lost and, metaphorically speaking, the homosexual/prostitute/African/injecting-drug-user/hemophiliac body *becomes* AIDS.

The paradigmatic representation/embodiment of the "AIDS virus" is the gay man. Thus gay men are in the uncomfortable position of being constantly spoken *about,* though there is virtually no context in which men can speak of their sexuality and community processes without being rendered a "case study" or subject of confession. The world of AIDS knowledge mobilizes a dispersed panopticism which directs everyone's eyes to the sex lives of gay men. Like the architectural panopticon Foucault describes as arising in prison, school, and factory construction in the late seventeenth century, expert keepers of AIDS knowledge possess a *discursive* centrality from which to observe their charges without themselves being observed. For Foucault, the space of the observer is foregrounded in architectural style: it is obvious that this tower, this corridor, this window is the place from which scrutiny comes, though it is not possible to tell when and whether the keeper is actually there looking. Likewise, where gay men were once hidden (metaphorically, in closets from which they could observe but not be observed), epidemiology, public health police power, and the social voyeurism of lifestyle journalism now serve as central points from which to observe the sex lives of gay men. The love that dare not speak its name is now asked endlessly to repeat that name in public in order to inscribe and reinscribe the ineluctable sexual difference that reassures a shifting "general public" that it is not subject to AIDS.

It is the assertion of the correctness of science over community that has made it possible, via such legislation as the Helms Amendment in the U.S. and Section 28 of the 1988 Local Government Act in Britain, to criminalize messages in dissident vernaculars[12]—or at least, to render them unfundable. Federal funding for U.S. AIDS education was circumscribed from the outset; the first monies for "innovative projects" (i.e., funding to community-based groups) came in 1985 and represented less than $500,000.[13] This initial funding came with a provision that federally funded education must have an HIV antibody testing component and that printed materials should be acceptable according to "community standards," a phrase clearly taken from obscenity law. There was considerable protest in 1985–86 about both provisions, especially since there was no evidence that test result knowledge was of any particular value in risk reduction education. The documents describing what would be required of grant recipients defined the type of language to be used in educational materials and presupposed the existence of a distinct infected subculture and an unaffected general public. Guidelines for AIDS education for young people combined the idea of a sexual subculture with prudish notions about teenage sexuality to position youth *only* in the general public. Youth AIDS education materials were designed to quell fears about casual contact ("you can't get HIV from doorknobs and toilet seats") but neglected to mention that you also can't get HIV if you practice safe sex and needle hygiene. By government mandate, the language of print or video material was to be accessible to "a broad spectrum of educated adults in society"; it "should be able to communicate to a specific group like gay men, and should be judged unoffensive (sic) to most educated adults beyond that group." In addition, visuals were to "communicate risk reduction methods by inference rather than through any display of the anogenital area or overt depiction of the performance of safe sex or unsafe sex." *Gay Community News* reporter Kim Westheimer, in a January 18, 1986 article on the controversies surrounding the guidelines, quotes CDC official Dr. Michael Lane: "Censorship means you can't do it. What we're saying is if you use taxpayers' funds you have to make it acceptable. We're specifically doing what the Supreme Court dictates in issues of censorship related to pornography."

In debates on every subsequent federal AIDS research and education funding bill, conservative North Carolina Senator Jesse Helms succeeded in attaching riders prohibiting federal funding of any form of education that "promotes homosexuality." In 1988, the federal government finally passed a standing law which set the formula for AIDS funding, so that instead of passing a new AIDS funding bill each year, only the dollar amount needs to be set. Helms was successful in having his "no homo" rider attached to the enabling law, which prohibits funding projects which "promote homosexuality or promiscuity."

Following the federal lead, several states have attempted to pass similar laws to extend this prohibition to state funding. Oddly enough, federal agencies—the Centers for Disease Control (CDC) and Public Health Service (PHS), for example—continue to ask for proposals for projects aimed at educating homosexual men (or "men having sex with men").

Where such proposals are accepted, agencies are required to ensure that this program corresponds to "all other relevant federal guidelines."

Similarly, the provisions of Section 28 prevent British localities from spending government funds on anything "promoting homosexuality as a pretended family relationship" (the wording is designed to prevent claims to political rights based on family, as opposed to minority status). Although the law contains a provision that this funding restriction is not to affect "AIDS education," it makes it impossible to educate about risk reduction and certainly rules out projects aimed at supporting the emotional and community norm negotiations which most educators view as essential to maintaining lifelong change. This is the first British law that in any way limits the spending prerogatives of localities.

AIDS science privileges the domain of the objectively researchable (viruses, Western biochemical treatments, sex data as compiled in epidemiological study) over communicative and symbolic community processes. The dominance of science as *the* logical paradigm rationalizes systems of social control which predate the HIV epidemic, especially systems which silence or distort the speech and culture of "minority communities" by constructing them as lacking in the forms of discourse which enable people to "make sense."[14]

3.2 Promoting Science

The rise in credibility of scientific explanation is ironic. Despite highly publicized stories alleging that research scientist Bob Gallo stole the virus from his French counterpart Luc Montagne;[15] despite revelations that Burroughs-Wellcome lost track of over a thousand (nearly 1/4th) of its compassionate-release AZT trial subjects;[16] despite the inability of international research after nearly a decade to produce an anti-viral agent or immune booster that effectively and predictably halts HIV;[17] despite the apparent failure of tens of thousands of scientists to make significant headway against HIV infection; despite all of these highly publicized assaults on the progress of research, *science* as an ideal has increased its stature and successfully claimed itself to be above politics. We seem to believe in science more in 1989 than we did in 1980—or at least, popular science has become a hot media commodity.

The reification of science and the increasing invocation of its logic to work out conflicts in other domains stem not from its successes, but from its ability to "see" what ordinary people cannot. Science visualizes the microscopic through imaging technologies and the macroscopic through statistical modelling and the rapid handling of large epidemiological data sets which are taken to represent the global or national experience of AIDS. Like the media, science communicates that which we cannot experience in everyday life, privileging the details of micro-experience and the extraordinariness of macro-experience over the daily experience of human life as it is lived in the medium range.

3.3 Virology and Immunology: Cultural Tropes/Scientific Pursuits

Modern health concepts vacillate between two models—one locating health in internal dynamics and the other conceptualizing health as a state of normalcy which external pathologies might diminish. Although we commonly characterize modern medicine as a move away from mystifications about the body, from notions of humors and spirits, and toward such ideas as viruses and antibodies, both science and popular culture retain the logic of older symbolic systems. From the standpoint of popular culture, virology and immunology can be viewed as new articulations of more longstanding basic models. Although scientifically, immunology and virology are inextricably related in AIDS research, each discipline's own stories of its rise and triumphs virtually ignores those of the other.[18] Although science operates as if these two ways of medical thinking are compatible, each in fact carries incompatible cultural meanings and political metaphors.

The rise of virologic and immunologic thinking about AIDS demonstrates how cultural metaphors converge with scientific thinking. Both subdisciplines emerged after "germ theory" was accepted at the end of the nineteenth century and both developed in spurts as technological breakthroughs enabled the verification or falsification of theories. Both were constituted as independent disciplines only in the post-World War II era, and only in relation to specific discoveries that "proved" the existence of their fundamental unit of study. The protein structure of antibodies and the genetic composition of viruses provided immunology and virology with distinct domains based on unique basic units of study. The two disciplines operate autonomously (although many laboratories have both types of scientists working on common problems); thus until a virus was discovered which was causally related to immune failure, the fact that virology and immunology proposed fundamentally different concepts of health was deemed unproblematic. Suddenly however, the two disciplines could no longer conduct research without accounting for the principles of the other—immunology cannot progress without accounting for the specific trigger that sets in motion the immune reaction and its subsequent malfunction, and virology cannot study the life of HIV unless it can be observed in relation to host cells. And yet, going back and forth between sessions on virology and immunology at any major AIDS conference leaves even the sophisticated lay person with the impression that two totally different phenomena are being studied in these two fields.

In 1981, when the first cases of what we now know as AIDS were identified, both immunology and virology were experiencing major breakthroughs as scientific disciplines. However, immunology was deemed to have broader explanatory power at both the scientific and cultural levels. Immunology got the first crack at the new disease because the first cases were characterized as unexplained immunological break-down in a handful of gay men. The syndrome was first called gay-related immune deficiency (GRID)—a name considered blatantly prejudicial by gay activists.[19] But the term was entirely logical within the premises of immunology, and the legacy of immunological thinking was retained in the subsequent name, Acquired Immune Deficiency Syndrome (AIDS). Virologists and others have argued by contrast that the syndrome should be designated "HIV *disease*," which would "begin" upon infection with the virus. The two names—AIDS and HIV disease[20]—represent in relief the differences in thinking between the two subdisciplines, differences duplicated in education strategies, treatment trials, and public policy. In the various arenas where we "think AIDS," multiple and contradictory logics modelled variously on virology and immunology are in play.

Changes in science reflect a process of evolution in technology and in the forms of interrogation of discrete problems, but that process cannot explain why particular forms of scientific inquiry gain control of the metaphors that provide larger cultural explanations of a range of phenomena metaphorized onto the body. Why, for example, did immunology provide such an appealing narrative between the late 1960s and the early 1980s? A few answers suggest themselves.

Immunology came to public attention in the 1960s,[21] at a time when holistic models of health were re-emerging in the U.S. The idea of a delicately balanced internal ecology nicely mirrored the growing perception of the human being precariously perched in a world ecology. Immunology met the cultural needs of an "America" fascinated by a return to homeopathic ideas, but unwilling to abandon the miracles of modern medical technology. Moreover, immunology had radical implications for popular understandings of the body. The bacteriological body had been static before and after the assault by germs; the endocrinological body ran hot and cold, oily and dry, not coincidentally (in the first anxious post-war years when endocrinology briefly had its heyday) mapping the gendered tropes of emotionality. The immunological body was more gracefully fluid and fragile, like a dancer in a delicately balanced environment in which it was placed almost without boundaries.

Inside and outside broke down as imaging technologies produced new views of "natural" parasites—images which rivalled the 1950s and 1960s

B-movie monsters.[22] It was revealed that there were "good" bacteria, which produced our favorite cheeses and which made our digestive systems work, and "bad" bacteria which made us sick. Some diseases resulted from getting good bacteria in the wrong places. According to both holistic and immunological accounts, it was our own bodies and not outside invaders that were the problem; our bodies were increasingly inscribed within a futuristic scenario of massive environmental stress. The chief evil was a modern society that wore our bodies down—we were breaking ourselves down from within. The very structure of modern life became the locus for negotiating health logics. Health in the immunological body was sustained by careful management; indeed by the late 1970s, management science and terminology had themselves adopted these same metaphors of self-care and self-empowerment.

Immunology provided the grammar for shifting dominant metaphors of disease from offense to civil defense. Increasing concern with domestic unrest and lingering Cold War paranoia demanded that our immune systems should conform to a policing and confessional ideology which suggested, *not* that the Commies had got through the door, but rather that there was a more general weakness within the body politic. Immunology was based on the fundamental principle that the body could make fine distinctions between self and non-self, even if the Other was only minutely different. Autoimmunity—a condition in which the body "attacks" itself—created a theoretical problem, but the anxious sixties culture had a ready answer. In a society racked by the shift from a melting pot/assimilationist ideology toward defiant minority group pluralism, immunology could coopt and justify the idea that the maintenance of selfhood required self-scrutiny and regulation. Suppressor cells were there to stop killer cells when the "enemy" had been vanquished, avoiding revolt (cancer) by renegade "self" cells. Immunology was not so much about the Other as about the marginally different that had already been admitted to close proximity. Pathology was no longer conceived in terms of assault by an overwhelming enemy, but as a slow degeneration that occurred after the tolerant host had diminished its controls or surveillance.

Rapidly improving imaging technologies coincided with an era described as one of unprecedented world peace. People could now visualize their bodies as filled with tiny defending armies whose mission was to return the "self" to the precarious balance of health. Immunology tacitly made the individual responsible for the success of these little wars on pathology: if you failed to defend yourself against germs, it was because you did not personally succeed in managing your army.[23] The metaphoric slippage between self-management and military management echoed the anxieties about "losing" in Vietnam because officers lost control over their troops. Perhaps more agonizing, though unconscious, the generation of men first hit by AIDS was roughly that of Vietnam veterans (there were of course many Vietnam veterans among early diagnosed cases of AIDS); thus both AIDS and the war are cast as masculine experiences in highly eroticized male-only zones.

3.4 AIDS Science

The various branches of AIDS science account for early research successes with stories that contradict each other, but demonstrate the workings of each subspecialty's logic. In the early 1980s, immunological interpretations of AIDS emphasized the relationship between environmental management and internal bodily breakdown. Early epidemiological studies were cited as evidence of gay men's failure to thrive in the high-stress "gay" lifestyle. Immunological explanations of AIDS emphasized immune overload due to drugs, "fast" living, an excessive exposure to semen (this was alleged for gay men, but not for female sex workers; too much semen was bizarrely believed to cause a rejection of "self" in men), or simply too much sex. The early recognition of AIDS cases in Haiti and Africa posed no threat to this insistent identification of AIDS with gay culture. Cross-metaphorization of the homosexual body and the "Third World" provided a new set of metaphors which both "explained" social problems in post-colonial countries, and equated the attempts of the gay communities to make claims about their historical status in U.S. with nationalism. Gay men were said to have made of their bodies something of the order of the sewerage system of a Third World city, while "third world" inhabitants were said to engage in anal sex, an activity coded as "homosexual" within U.S. culture. This metaphoric slippage had stabilized by 1988 to become the World Health Organization's concepts of Pattern One AIDS (homosexual) and Pattern Two (*African*) AIDS, the latter of which was claimed to explain AIDS among heterosexuals (African Americans) and injecting drug users (who were living in the social equivalent of purportedly "African" urban social disequilibrium). By 1989, epidemiologists were describing the demography of AIDS in various cities in the U.S. as "Pattern Two," or even as "like" African AIDS.

In 1981, virology was evidencing some important technological breakthroughs, yet it was still considered a highly specialized science, incapable of generating wide-ranging explanations for disease processes. By the end of the 1980s, however, several broadly defined ailments—arthritis, multiple sclerosis, and the elusive chronic fatigue syndrome—had been broken into etiological subcategories, with some forms being hypothetically defined as viral or retroviral diseases. In 1988, scientific controversy broke out over the discovery of a "virus-like particle" (VLP) correlated with clinical AIDS.[24] Thus virology, retrovirology, and now "virus-like"-ology vie with each other to gain recognition as the most precise explainers of disease.

When virologists analyzed the same AIDS epidemiological studies which immunologists saw as evidence for a social or environmental cause of AIDS, they saw instead evidence of a sexually transmissible pathogen. Until this point the immune system and etiological agents belonged to different if interacting domains of study. Never before had a pathogenic disease of the immune system been conceptualized. Some cancers and multiple sclerosis, had been hypothesized as "autoimmune" disorders where the body unaccountably understands itself as "enemy"; other cancers were understood as phenomena of excess in which the body overproduced an ordinary form of cell which then "took over." But in AIDS, a compromise occurred between competing systems of explanation; etiological agent and immune system breakdown theories were brought into line via the discovery of an agent which "attacked," or more accurately, disarmed the immune system. (The idea fit perfectly with the notion of strategic arms which could foul major Soviet defense systems in order to allow attack by conventional weaponry.)

The research compromise did not constitute a new "paradigm" between the incommensurate scientific schemes of immunology and virology, but only in part because of their logical and procedural differences. The greater technological and financial commitments (and potential rewards) of virology linked data and dollar to become the dominant way of thinking about AIDS. AIDS research ended, for now, a struggle between the two subdisciplines.

An important difference between the subdisciplines can be seen in their concepts of "side-effects." For virology, an anti-viral agent that demonstrably extends the life of a patient, even with serious harms, is a relative success. Immunology counts its success in the balanced well-being of the person as measured by the body's ability to function better. In the immunological framework, something like a chronic, manageable disorder would be dealt with by enhancing the person's ability to cope with opportunistic infections. In the virological framework, only the halting of the progression of viremia would constitute a "cure" to a "fatal disease."

The conflicts between virology and immunology and the greater financial and scientific power of virology are easily observed in the modelling of clinical trials. Early treatments for people diagnosed with AIDS included immune boosters, notably interferons, and megadoses of known drugs specific to the particular opportunistic infection for which an individual had come to the physician. High mortality rates were considered evidence that "known treatments" did not work; however, the toxic mega-dose regimes (based on attempts to compensate for lost immune power, but often succeeding only in overloading other parts of the body) may well have killed as many patients at they helped.

Once HTLV-III, later renamed HIV, was identified in 1984, immune system support therapy researches took a back seat or were abandoned to non-Western therapies.[25] Biomedical research was oriented toward a virologic model, seeking a "magic bullet" along the lines of AZT. Research on combination therapies—an anti-viral coupled with immune system supports—could not be pursued extensively within the virological frame since it was impossible to evaluate the effects of an anti-viral if another agent of unknown efficacy was simultaneously boosting immune function. Some combination trials began in late 1987, though the majority either did not get underway until late 1988, or are still under protocol development. Most are conceived of as "diminishing side-effects," a conceptual sleight of hand which re-understands immune boosters within the virological model.

In a particularly odd twist of biomedical logic, a Chinese herb known as Compound Q was licensed in 1989 as a research "drug" for investigation in human trials. Herbs and holistic therapies based in totally different conceptual frameworks are now researchable under Western-type protocols; yet taking "real drugs" still counts as an exclusion criterion under drug company protocols. One cannot be on AZT if one wants to get into the ddI trial (an analogue of AZT, under investigation to see if it is as effective and whether its side effects are fewer), yet one may meditate, take herbs (other than Compound Q), or engage in any number of other "treatments" which claim a range of immunomodulatory effects.

Virology's assumption that a virus can simply be eliminated or blocked has mis-directed research efforts for nearly three years, denying thousands of people potential therapies which could have prolonged or improved the quality of their lives. It is at the same time difficult to assess the clinical experience of the immunomodulators in the early 80s, because PCP prophylaxis had not yet come into use. One early AZT study ultimately bases its claim to the drug's efficacy on the number of extra months lived by AZT-taking subjects; its conclusions are problematic, however, since PCP prophylaxis also increases lifespan. This is, again, a conflict between the virologic model which measures success of drugs which attack virus itself, versus an immunologic model, which sees "success" in support of the whole system (i.e., supplementing the body's attempt to fight the diseases which are symptoms of AIDS). Newer AZT data suggests that AZT works best in people with relatively intact immune systems, though PCP prophylaxis also works well at this point. The perceived slow pace of research has led to the emergence of black market research into both virus blockers and immune-boosting agents, research that challenges not only foot-dragging on the part of the research empire, but also cultural notions of the patient, research, and science, and the assumptions that underpin post-War medical ethics.

3.5 Metaphor and Public Policy

The dominance of virologic thinking has had several effects on evolving risk reduction strategies in the U.S. First, virology promotes the idea that there can be a "cure" and a "vaccine" for HIV infection. "Magic bullet" fantasies combine with the behaviorist notion that unsafe sexual practices stem from pathologies in the individual, to produce the idea that behavioral changes are simply stop-gap measures, only necessary until science "puts things right." This obviously sells out those who are currently infected or those who will become infected before virology accomplishes its feat. This logic implicitly makes individuals morally culpable (both self-destructive and homocidal) for engaging in activities which might result in HIV infections in the absence of a "cure" or "vaccine." The very same activities and potential ensuing infections will be considered "chance" or "slipping" once a cure or vaccine are available. AIDS now is understood as the fate of the deviant; some acts, but not others, engaged in by some classes of people, but not others are the "cause" of "AIDS." Once a "vaccine" or "cure" for AIDS is available (and these possibilities are disputable), HIV antibody testing will no longer be useful as an objective tool for reproducing class, racial, and sexual discrimination.

Identifying a cure or a vaccine depends on locating a single agent with highly predictable effects. HIV, however, apparently requires some set of co-factors to produce its various chronic or fatal *sequelae*. Although it may be "a matter of time" before a very high percentage of those infected develop symptoms, that "time" may well be ten or fifteen years. This suggests both that HIV is better understood as a chronic and manageable disorder, and that high priority should be given to research on what differentiates people who progress more slowly from those who progress more rapidly through the HIV spectrum. Until about 1988, that difference was sought in variations in the virus. New research is exploring immunological (and genetic) differences. Maintaining the immune systems of those who hang on for a long time may enable them to benefit from treatments developed later. But attempts to lengthen the lives of infected persons are encountering resistance. The August 1989 editorial of the magazine *Nature* said that an increased lifespan among HIV-infected persons might "ironically" result in their infecting others. The same society that denied and continues to deny accurate and accessible risk reduction education seems willing to deny life-prolonging treatment as well. The cultural/symbolic difference between a disease conceived as "inevitably fatal" and a disease course which may run twenty years from infection to death, is significant, and parallels the symbolic differences between immunological and virological thinking.

3.6 "What Science Knows about AIDS"

The October 1988 issue of *Scientific American* has a rather astonishing cover: burned in white type over a elegant reproduction of a budding virus are the words, "What Science Knows About AIDS." Not, "The Progress of Science Toward a Vaccine or Cure," or, "What Scientists Have Learned About AIDS." Two elements in the title give the game away: *science,* as opposed to non-science or commonsense; and *knows,* rather than posits, imagines, or thinks. The issue is filled with micrographs and diagrams of HIV, and advertisements from the companies who make imaging systems. Science, it seems, can actually *see* the virus; ordinary people can enter this world by looking at pictures.

In the same issue, we are presented with romantic, tragic photographs of "real people" with AIDS—a white, North American family. We are told that the father is a hemophiliac who "infected" his wife before he knew he was himself infected, and she in turn gave birth to an infected son. The Burkes encode the story of the tragic innocence of those who lack knowledge, pitted against those who have it (the gay man or drug user who is said to infect knowingly or recklessly). The photograph, inexplicably included in a section entitled "HIV Infection: The clinical picture" (an unconscious recognition that Mr. Burke's infection was iatrogenic—a disease caused by medical treatment for something else?), privatizes this family, which was one of the few families to speak publicly about its experience of AIDS. They are portrayed as stricken *as a family,* they are *a family with AIDS.* There is nothing here which explains the history of discrimination against hemophiliacs, nothing to indicate that this family is embedded in two communities: first, the white general public, which will reject them because AIDS is a marker of difference; and second, the national and very protective network of blood product consumers who are connected through hemophilia clinics and newsletters, people who will be driven deeper into hiding by the Burkes' very openness. The Burkes are part of a besieged subculture, but in *Scientific American,* and in the media generally, they are silenced as members of the community of blood product consumers and held ransom as the nice family, the innocent victims destroyed by AIDS.[26]

"The Epidemiology of AIDS in the U.S." section is accompanied by a full-page black and white closeup photograph of a "drug user" sticking a needle into his arm. This photograph is the only one in the issue with a caveat: the Centers for Disease Control officials who contributed this article "note that the photographs accompanying this article were not provided by the CDC." The photograph is an attempt to "show" transmission—the caption reads: "Intravenous (IV) drug abusers [sic] share hypodermic needles and other paraphernalia that can be contaminated with blood infected with HIV." The caption cites "IV drug abuse" as "responsible" for "most of the HIV infections in the U.S. among heterosexual men and women as well as among infants." The photograph, especially in relation to the other photos in the issue, neatly reproduces all the stereotypes of "who gets AIDS." Heterosexual AIDS in the U.S. is related to drug use, while "African AIDS" will be related to (African) heterosexual practices. The drug user picture makes sense at all because "homosexual AIDS" is already stabilized and can serve as an unpresented reference, the real or "original" AIDS, against which other demographic groups (especially heterosexuals) must articulate their difference. On one hand, the photograph disrupts the conscious expectation of seeing a man coded "homosexual" as exemplary of AIDS. On the unconscious level, the photograph serves as a displacement of that *other* image, the fear and fantasy of witnessing "transmission" under the guise of sodomy. This photograph was eliminated when the special issue was republished as a book.[27]

In another picture, illustrating "The International Epidemiology of AIDS" (meaning outside the U.S.), we again see people said to be affected as a group: a crowd of barefoot black people in shorts, meant to stand in for a continent awaiting destruction by the slowly ticking bomb of HIV. Walking down a dirt road through a low forest, they are apparently part of a funeral procession; the caption tells us that in the town of Kyotera, Uganda, funerals for "AIDS victims" are "a daily occurrence." The caption cites seroprevalence rates for "certain segments of the adult urban population" (is Kyotera *urban*? the photograph is of forest, not city . . .) at fifteen to twenty percent. The caption does not tell us that this figure is much lower than the rates for "certain segments of the adult urban population" in cities like New York, Newark, or San Francisco, where funerals for people who have died of AIDS-related illnesses are also "a daily occurrence."

And finally, we learn about the "social dimensions" of AIDS, here accompanied by photographs of a gay pride march and of "boarder babies" (the name given to children with HIV/AIDS abandoned in hospitals) barely discernible in their machine-cribs. By the time we get to this back-of-the-book piece, we understand that social here must be opposed to private, the latter being nice white people who have sex at home. Social must mean those people banished from privacy, people whose lives we can now examine in voyeuristic detail. Social means socially deviant—queers and black junky mothers who become separated from their babies. The "social dimensions" article discusses issues that might plague the conscience of those who will be part of the "future": "AIDS exposes the hidden weaknesses in human society; how the epidemic is dealt with will have a profound effect on society's future. A crucial issue is protection from discrimination." Clearly discrimination is a critical concern, but so is access to treatment, and acknowledgement of the reality of daily lives under AIDS. The "profound effect" will occur when society learns how it has fared after the epidemic, that is, after all of those affected are dead.

These pictures represent only a handful of the many representations of the virus which create our popular image of the terrain of AIDS and science. We learn to "read the virus" by learning to read the faces of AIDS. Educational campaigns hammer readers with the point that "you can't tell by looking if someone has AIDS"; but at the same time, we are bombarded with images of what it looks like "to have AIDS."

The process of "putting a face on AIDS" was a major thrust of media and public education interventions between 1985 and 1988; here, the illness was concretized, but also romanticized.[28] The health and vulnerability of certain groups of people have been valorized by demonizing the lives of others. It is in the encodings of the "real people" images, as much as in the cool logic of policy debate, that it becomes increasingly possible to view wholesale discrimination as uncomfortable, but in the public interest, and to see such things as the placebo trials for vaccines planned for African nations as noble, not genocidal.

3.7 Locating Science

Like images of the virus, popular knowledge of science is always mediated, enlarged, colorized, stylized. But scientific knowledge itself is also mediated, produced through and around particular cultural symbols. The ideas of science derive as much from the popular imagination as from the great minds of scientists.

Historians and philosophers of science have devoted their considerable energies in the twentieth century to reassessing the meaning and role of modern science in society. From a cultural standpoint, the crisis of faith in science came about in part because of the theory of relativity (how can something as "fixed" as the physical world be "relative"?) and in part as a reflection on both nuclear bombing and on the excesses of Nazi science, which was not so very different in logic and principles from that practiced in the U.S. Historians tried to explain why and how scientific ideas arise and are modified, why a particular scientific theory seems so essentially explanatory for a period of time, and then, after some set of historical or technological changes, is deemed quaint and unscientific. Until the popularization of Thomas Kuhn's now classic (if beleaguered) 1962 *Structure of Scientific Revolutions,* the common view of modern science was that it progressively solved objective problems, which added incrementally to a store of knowledge. Methodological improvements were seem simply as refinements to a basic objective science. Pre-scientific ways of approaching the physical world were simply wrong, or part of older religious or mystical worldviews. Once the "scientific method" was discovered, science was on a path to totalized knowledge in a single and ultimately systematic theoretical structure.[29]

Kuhn argues that "paradigms" of scientific thought and method compete until such time as one emerges which seems best to explain the range of phenomena that constitute the field of objects. The settled paradigm produces the feeling that science is operating "normally": a paradigm acts as a foundation (albeit incomplete) for the science-work completed under its aegis. Some truly brilliant people make "discoveries" outside the paradigm, but for the most part extra-paradigmatic work is viewed by normal science practicioners as heretical or foolish. Kuhn identifies various points in history during which "paradigm shifts" (changes in foundational assumptions) cause science to operate without an agreed paradigm, a situation he describes as "revolutionary." Revolution is a powerful and significant choice of metaphor, suggesting that science is a competitive field in which ideas do battle, a metaphor compatible with both evolutionism ("survival of the fittest idea") and the anxious pluralism of the mid-twentieth century with its stagnated evolutionism and lost ability to use racial and gender markers as signifiers of evolutionary differences. Kuhnian paradigm theory both legitimates particular scientific ideas as the best their times could produce *and* validates a social idea of distinct and incommensurate moral "paradigms" which must be tolerated as they vie for their niche in history.

While philosphers of science have lodged numerous critiques of Kuhnian paradigm theory (its questionable evolutionism, its lack of attention to how participants throughout history have viewed the interplay between "paradigms" with their "normal" and "revolutionary" periods, its failure to account for the cultural sources of paradigm change, its reliance on a notion of "incommensurability" which is insufficiently complex to explain how work is accomplished across incommensurate paradigms), the theory clearly describes the popular understanding of science and conforms to—or rather, has inspired—the format of contemporary science reporting both by journalists and by scientists themselves when they describe their work for lay audiences.

Clearly, new retroviral research, the recent and unanticipated association of retroviruses with some long puzzling medical syndromes (multiple sclerosis? arthritis?), and particularly the discovery that viruses evolve in response to host response (something previously believed to occur largely with more complex organisms like bacteria) suggest that we ought to be in the middle of a paradigm shift, in Kuhnian terms. The competition between explanatory schemes for AIDS also fits the Kuhnian narrative, and the current dominance of HIV-etiology theory suggests that we have arrived at a "new paradigm," despite scientists' claims that the old paradigm is still valid.[30]

Yet the Kuhnian understanding of the progress of science obscures the extent to which AIDS research in epidemiology, virology, and immunology relies on cultural stereotypes. Further, the separation between science and society proposed in pop-Kuhnianism offers no way of understanding or adjudicating the conflicting moral claims of the people most directly affected by science. In HIV research, we now have a subject population with strong views about the conduct of research making demands about the construction of research protocols. By ignoring the power of metaphoric analogues between science and society, we reproduce notions of scientific advance without understanding how shifts in research ethics affect research methods, and how research frames affect the concepts of the body and person on which scientific and ethical theory rest. Kuhn's work continues to be enormously influential on a popular level. Anyone who has taken a high school or college science course since the seventies will have imbibed some part of his paradigm theory. At the same time the pre-Kuhnian idea of the progressive "march of science" remains influential. Yet the appearance of something as "new" as AIDS has suggested that there are surprise questions which require new frames of thinking. When AIDS appeared, there was both scientific and social debate over whether this was a "new" disease phenomenon for which science would have to reorient its paradigms, or whether anything that appeared "new" should simply be regarded as something older and forgotten reemerging.

The idea of a new disease was reinforced by the apparent high fatality seen in AIDS. This was upsetting to Westerners, who had for several decades believed that the major epidemic illnesses had been controlled by modern medicine, and that finding a "cure" for cancer was only a matter of time. The blatant racism undergirding the search for a "source" of AIDS in Africa stems from the wish to discover that AIDS is an "old" disease which was confined somewhere else until technological change created contact with "isolated" peoples. Constructing AIDS as "old" (if not primordial) and situating the virus in "Africa" naturalized the disease, reinforcing the view that science solves the problems thrown up by nature and society, and is therefore separate from both. The various pop epidemiology books cast strange medical phenomena as objects for "detective" work, a metaphor which suggests that the answer is there, you just have to find the right clues. The Legionnaire's disease epidemics were presented to the public in just this light. The first two years of AIDS investigation were also represented in similar terms; the search for the "source" of AIDS in Haiti and Africa, and the continuing press coverage of claims that AIDS was originally something "simple" like syphilis now gone out of control, are examples of the kind of episodes that make sense in the disease detective narrative.

The search for an historical as well as geographical origin was accompanied by theories that saw AIDS as the product of medical engineering gone out of control—AIDS as a bad sequel to the Andromeda strain. In this version of the AIDS story, scientists themselves were seen to be tampering with "nature" and creating hunks of protein which took on unanticipated lives of their own.

Despite differences in popular conceptions of science, there is a fundamental belief that scientific facts can be deployed to enlighten decision-making in the public sphere. Science is above and outside the polis; the knowledge of science is "theoretical" in nature and thus unbiased. How the special knowledge of science moves into the popular realm is rarely interrogated, and yet, it is in this movement that the social effects of science's privileged status make themselves felt. The objective knowledge of science, supposedly separate from the inherently self-interested play of social life, must nevertheless be rendered usable for society. Thus, theoretical knowledge is weeded out and a watered-down version of practical information is presented for lay application. Typically in medicine, health educators and clinicians are viewed as the conduits for this knowledge transferral, receiving scientific knowledge at one step removed and then paring it down to pass on to the "audience" or "client." Evaluation of whether knowledge has been correctly conveyed proceeds by objectively testing the recipient and by obtaining measures of the educator's ability to remain neutral, consistent, and credible in the eyes of the recipient. This system of information conveyance is thought to work best when the intermediaries add as little as possible, while at the same time convincing the audience that they "know what they are talking about." The clinician/health educator engages in a performance of scientific legitimation; the success of that performance depends on the extent of her/his theatrical competence.

3.8 The Discourse of Science and the Practice of Education

The conception of knowledge as an inverted pyramid bounded by a single logical construction which transforms knowledge from pure science to popular understandings has become standard social mythology. It is a popular hybrid of Kuhn's work, which sees science as coherent only within a given framework or paradigm, and as truly a description of reality produced by specialists and special technologies. Hard science is considered the leading edge in the formation of popular knowledges and forms the model logic for lay thinking. The metaphors used in lay thinking are seen as the tools of the common mind, mere analogues to the "pure" signs and semantics of science. This view of science not only obscures the power relations between science and public policy; it is fatal to people in danger of HIV infection and catastrophic for the communities and nations in the developing world which are currently and inextricably the objects of scientific research on AIDS. It masks the way in which medical research reconstructs colonial relationships under the dual guise of scientific objectivity and efforts for the "good of mankind." It obscures the ways in which pressure to adopt the organizational schema of science as representative of lived experience reinscribes hierarchies of social difference. And finally, it reads as progress the destruction of vernaculars and the adoption of scientific language.

Yet it is this model of knowledge that informs the behaviorist-oriented traditional model of health education. In crude terms, the model locates "unhealthy" behaviors in the individual, and implicitly relates them to an inability to overcome an essential drive for pleasures or self-destruction. The cause of this problem may be ignorance of the dangers of certain behaviors, or it may be a more fundamental attitudinal or group (social) deprivation which thwarts the natural process of maintaining one's health. The solution in this model is chiefly information-giving along with some form of counselling. Social deprivations are generally dealt with in the short run by instilling the missing virtues. It was this notion which undergirded sociological theories that attempted to locate "class" and "ethnic" differences in the failures of subcultural groups to acquire the moral and conceptual skills supposedly found in the "mainstream." The same argument has been revived in AIDS education aimed at "the hard to reach." The model assumes that information-giving will "correct" behavior in some cases, and that attitude change will take care of the recalcitrant. There may still remain a group which does not respond, and is thus deemed "deficient," "compulsive," or, if the impediment to change is perceived to be social, "hard to reach." In all cases, "behavior" is constructed in terms of acts that arise from the unconscious and are modified by self-objectivizing knowledge ("facts"), self-reflection ("attitude"), or social factors ("cultural deprivation" or "peer pressure"). Peer pressure here is understood as a collective will which enhances or suppresses natural instincts. The term "peer" is understood in conventional health education more narrowly than in empowerment projects, which view peers as the collective reservoir of a rich symbolic and moral language from which the meaning and social reality of behaviors are constructed.

In this traditional and still dominant model, the lay person is not thought capable of understanding the "science" which has studied and quantified the effects of bad behaviors. Health educators, as para-scientists, must therefore act as translators, taking their best understanding of science and putting it into "everyday" terms. The ordinary person is believed to need metaphors from daily life in order to understand scientific concepts, which are viewed as non-metaphoric and *real*. If the correct, culturally sensitive metaphors are found, the information given to the lay person is roughly equivalent in its practical effects to that produced by science.

Alternatively, a social constructionist understanding of the role and rise of knowledge about HIV and AIDS would suggest that the "metaphors" in vernaculars are already part of, and even direct, science. A useful starting point here is Ludwig Fleck's analysis of the differences between the actual steps in the development of the Wasserman test for syphilis and the final account of the discovery produced by Wasserman's lab. Most importantly, Fleck traces the way in which two very different theories of the cause of the disease, which entailed different definitions of what counted as syphilis, were reconciled when a reliable test was finally developed. Fleck suggests that much of the work on the test was accidental, since the test was developed to prove a different theory of syphilis from the one that would ultimately be verified by it. What Fleck could not perceive, writing as he did on the eve of Nazi accession, was the extent to which the Nazi social ideology of syphilis defined the framework of German scientists' quest for a test for the "disease," which the Nazis viewed as a degenerative blood disorder at the root of all evils, from mental retardation to homosexuality and the pathology of Jews. (Indeed, Nazi rhetoric is full of syphilis imagery, and Nazi eugenics uses the social conceptions of syphilis as medical proof of the necessity of its methods.)

Fleck suggests that we examine science in terms of two types of "thought communities": esoteric communities, which involve closed ranks of members socialized to a specialized format of inquiry; and exoteric communities, which consist of members with popular knowledges, frequently or easily communicated knowledges, or who lie outside the guarded circles of particular inquiries. Esoteric circles require special training to understand the meaning of the knowledges and problems they address. Exoteric circles have some understanding of the work of esoteric circles, but are not fully initiated to the "thought style," or way of making sense of that group. Fleck argues that the exclusivity of esoteric communities varies according to social and political factors that set the requirements of membership. He also suggests that individuals participate in a range of exoteric and esoteric positionings in relation to different domains of knowledge, and therefore have a range of available thought styles. Thus, changes within esoteric realms sometimes occur because one member brings in other thought styles which become reworked in the esoteric domain. This transportation and transformation of thought styles through both social interaction *and* as a result of the inherent fuzziness of the boundaries of a thought community are precisely what paradigm theory tries to explain away. Rather than revolutionary changes in ways of addressing problems, Fleck's theory suggests that there are constant small negotiations among members of exoteric and esoteric circles, no matter how tightly guarded their borders. Indeed, Fleck suggests that the "social" does *not* pollute pure science by making practical demands, but that scientists themselves unconsciously bring to their work concerns that derive from their participation in exoteric domains.

In his study of the Wasserman lab, he suggests that the drive to find a "blood test" for a disease which many clinicians treated as a dermatologic (that is, surface) disorder comes more from the social obsession with blood ideology than with reasoned scientific processes designed to determine which theory of syphilis was accurate. We might read Fleck as arguing that the Wasserman test did not "prove" the truth of the theory of syphilis, but rather that syphilis was reconstructed to match the technical requirements of the Wasserman test. In practical terms then, "science" houses an inconsistent set of theories related to cultural meanings and values which can be partially described and questioned. Those meanings and values predate scientific discoveries, but are often lent rational legitimation by them.[31] The problem then shifts from one of translation from realm to realm, to one of exploring the power relations between realms, the relative status of people who are "native" to several realms, and the methods by which some realms are able to assert the superiority of their thought style. Activist health educators and the scientists and people with HIV involved in community research initiatives must be understood as people with commitments in different esoteric circles, but who interactively affect the meaning construction of science.

Exposing the shaky moorings of science creates great anxiety—it removes the apparently clear-cut reference points for adjudicating conflicting thought styles and their products. It also means letting go of the idea that there is a "perfect" educational format, which needs only a little tinkering for different target groups. It means that is is not possible to know in advance how science-knowledges will be reworked and made meaningful in exoteric circles and to what extent specialized esoteric knowledge will conform to stereotypes already existing in exoteric circles.

3.9 Esoteric and Exoteric Knowledge: the Power of Exchange

A better understanding of the movement of information from science to people and the influence of culture on science can be attained with a model that views interaction between realms not as translation, but as the co-evolution or negotiation of a new knowledge; if interactions are prolonged and power relations reordered, this knowledge produces a new "thought style" which is the possession of a new community. The health educator, the lay person, and the scientist are each conceptualized in this model as coming from linguistic and symbolic systems rich in personal and social meaning. Some esoteric meanings will be shared or easily grasped by all because they inflect broader cultural metaphors. Some meanings will seem alien because of their specialized development in a tight esoteric sphere. None has a privileged access to a fixed or pre-given reality. Each arena contains its own specialized knowledge and has its own set of logics for incorporting new information or new ways of thinking, for accepting and recognizing as "new" ideas coming from another realm or appearing as a result of revelation, research, or reframing. Different thought styles will have different understandings of the rise of new knowledge—as suggested above, there are several competing cultural logics for determining the status of apparently new events. Each arena has its esoteric knowledge base (a sort of epistemic fragment related to the larger cultural episteme) and its own way of speaking (its vernacular).

In this model, any group is understood as communicating from one realm to another. This enables us to analyze the motivation (or intention, in the sense of movement relative to another) to "communicate." There will be a large number of conscious or unconscious assumptions in the interrelation of two groups around any given communication event. Unlike the translation model which does not call into question the power relations articulated in these assumptions, a negotiation model suggests that in the process of moving across the perimeter of a thought community, a great deal of violence may be done. This violence does not simply take the form of distortion (a term which assumes that metaphor can, at least in principle, approach a state of one-to-one correspondence with reality), but is embedded in the very power relations created or imposed through the hierarchical valuation of forms of knowledge. This form of power may be highly coercive if a group urgently needs information from a tightly guarded esoteric group. In the traditional expert model, people with HIV or AIDS were viewed as complicit with unethical medical practices as a result of their acquiring black market trial drugs in a context where "experts" were supposed to control access to research protocols. A negotiation model which takes each realm as possessing unique forms of "expertise" better describes how activists, researchers, and ethicists exchanged forms of knowledge which resulted in community research initiatives, and thus dramatically changed key ethical assumptions about the conduct of clinical trials.

Health educators also have a range of motives—helping others, self-improvement, a desire to become a scientist, social role conformity, etc.—which provide the context for their involvement in the reconstruction and mediation of AIDS knowledges. For example, health educators working in the context of AIDS who wish to bring about specific behavior changes may be schooled in certain general assumptions about the origin of behaviors. These health educators combine the available scientific literature on HIV with whichever techniques from their field are considered appropriate to this type of "problem": the educators' project thus combines prefigurative logic from both health education and from the scientific studies which framed the definition of the problem.[32] The prefigurative logics and the immediate motives of the health educator in relation to *particular* individuals may thereafter obscure the power relations in the interactions described as "education," from the production of leaflets to the conduct of workshops. The educator may fail to recognize that the behaviorist assumptions on which the problem definition was initially based create a system of meanings about sexuality which are coherent with the prefigurative logics of science. Even if the educator consciously disagrees with some of the assumptions of science, or even with behaviorism, the knowledge formations to which she/he refers remain based in these logics. This makes it very difficult for oppositional educators to engage the information available in the sphere of science, even though that data may be of value. Critical educators may point out the links between what science produces and what lay people demand, and thus help individuals and communities better define the forms of information and styles of learning most useful to them.

4

Inventing "African AIDS"

Western science today is slowly consolidating around a particular construction of "African AIDS," which elaborates on the colonialist mystifications of the past century.[1] Debates about the conduct of vaccine trials in Africa constitute an especially dangerous form of neo-colonial ideology masquerading as benevolent medical science and as culturally sensitive medical ethics. The illusion of an Africa little changed since *The Heart of Darkness* preempts African ethicists' and philosophers' participation in these debates. Debates about ethics in particular occur in a middle ground between two cultures, but the "second voice" (the "African perspective") is carried by Western ethicists and researchers who speak of an "African culture" based largely in their fantasies. In this middle ground of pretended cultural sensitivity, virtually the only audible speech is that which occurs within, or is translated into, the conceptual categories of the modern Western *episteme*.[2]

In this chapter, I want to investigate how Western representations of the national and sexual cultures of post-colonial Africa direct the international AIDS research and policy agenda. Working from AIDS conference presentations and media reports on AIDS in Africa, I will link some of the apparently silly or innocuous assumptions made about Africans within the agenda of Western science. In particular, I will investigate how Western inventions of Africa as poverty-stricken and as heterosexual set medical science on a genocidal course which masquerades as Western altruism toward the client-state "Other."

A note on the terms employed here: in Western discourse, Africa, a continent of roughly 11½ million square miles and 53 countries, is treated as a homogenous socio-political block. Yet this supposedly "unknown" continent—unknown, that is, to its pale neighbors to the north—is in fact, vastly more culturally, linguistically, religiously, and socially diverse than North America or Europe. Much political and social violence is accomplished by collapsing the many cultures of the African continent into the invention, "Africa." In order to problematize this Western construction, "Africa," I will employ the equivalent constructions "North America" and "Euro-America" to indicate the collection of relatively homogeneous Northern administrative states as we appear to our southern neighbors. North Americans should take note of their discomfort at having their cultural space discursively reduced in this way.

The following are compressed versions of statements widely and frequently offered at scientific conferences on AIDS, and implicit or rendered almost verbatim in both the popular press *and* scientific literature on AIDS in Africa. I have chosen these particular statements as "texts" because they are commonly used as if they "go without saying," requiring none of the usual kinds of justification (e.g., supportive data, argumentation) and receiving little challenge. The three texts use different rhetorical maneuvers, but the procedures for producing "truth" reveal the workings of their discursive formations.[3] "Text One" hinges on an implicit comparison to an unstated norm; the norm is taken to be *us*, but a closer examination suggests that *two* norms must be in force, since there appears to be little real difference between *us* and *them* within the parameters suggested. "Text Two" argues on the basis of a plausible description, but uses that description to argue that "AIDS" is a thing-in-itself and defines the ability to detect AIDS as a measure of scientific advancement. "Text Three" exemplifies the mystification which lies at the heart of both classic Marxist and classic liberal economics: the confusion of biology (here, a viral infection) with historical specificities (here, colonialist underdevelopment) in an attempt to describe not only a material, but more importantly, a cultural difference between pre- and post-industrial societies.

4.1 Inscribing Difference

Text One: "Africans won't use condoms." As if North American heterosexuals have taken up condom use in any significant numbers.

Text Two: "Africans have such poor medical care that they can't properly diagnose AIDS." Not only does this insult the many fine researchers and clinicians working in teaching hospitals as well as village clinics throughout Africa, but the claim of poor diagnosis is used as a rationale for inflating statistics on the incidence of AIDS in Africa. This issue is extremely complex, blurring the line between contemporary AIDS science and long-held cultural beliefs about race legitimated by earlier *colonialist* science.

From the standpoint of current science, the problematic of "African AIDS" lies in the unreliability of epidemiology and diagnosis in Africa. But this is not a problem of Africa, this is a problem of Western ethnocentrism: the epidemiology of HIV in Africa relies on tests and clinical definitions developed in the West, which assume a Northern hemispheric distribution of pathogens (i.e., which assume that common cold and flu viruses are endemic, ordinary, and "clean" pathogens, but polio or malaria viruses are rare, exotic, and "filthy"). The epidemiology produced in the first five years of the epidemic was thus doubly flawed; clinical AIDS was haphazardly diagnosed in some regions of Africa because diagnosis relies on the identification of a "difference."[4] But the diagnostic "differences" of AIDS were premised on health expectation and disease patterns in the North. The vaguer symptoms of AIDS (nightsweats, weight loss, malaise, even thrush, diarrhea, respiratory problems) are characteristic of any number of ailments common in equatorial areas (and in Western innercities, one might add). It isn't so much that the medical facilities in Africa are flawed—although, much like U.S. public health clinics serving the uninsured, they can barely meet the basic preventative needs of people in their seriously underfunded systems—but that the definition of AIDS is itself problematic. African clinicians had diagnosed an epidemic of "slim disease," characterized by rapid and fatal wasting, but Western scientists viewed this diagnosis as quaint and prescientific. Thus, their attempts to be "culturally sensitive" in the clinical practice of AIDS diagnosis itself reinscribed colonialism. The problem Western scientists set for themselves in Africa was to map slim disease against AIDS, a procedure which served their own epidemiological purposes, but did little for local clinical practice. In the insistent colonial discourse, the very concept of slim disease (whatever its usefulness and problems in medical research practice) has been outlawed in favor of the imposed category "AIDS," a category which of course carries with it a whole range of political connotations.

The mainstream Western media meanwhile remain obsessed with the quaintness of slim disease; reporters working in villages use the term duplicitously and condescendingly, as if slim disease were a vague popular notion which must however be used if one is to be culturally sensitive. This denial of the specificity and cultural meaning of local terms ultimately raises important ethical questions for "AIDS" research conducted in Africa. If the abstracted terms of Western medicine ("AIDS") and local empirical terms ("slim disease") are socially constructed in relation to alternate sets of "facts," then translating across the two discursive fields (which can never perfectly correspond) renders the behavior and consent of the "research subject" uninterpretable. This was one of the problems in the Tuskegee studies, where researchers adopted the term "bad blood" to refer to syphilis in their dealings with the research subjects. While the term was derived from local usage, the relationship between tertiary stage syphilis and the disorder's initial sexual or perinatal modes of transmission was obscured. Thus, while research subjects may have understood that syphilis was sexually transmitted, the persistence of the term "bad blood" led subjects to believe they were being treated for something else. The use of the vernacular term "bad blood" in a context of evolving ideas about a disease "syphilis" prevented the participants from recognizing the benefits of sexual precautions or electing to take emerging forms of anti-bacterial treatment, and thus, the entire "experiment" was both unethical and "unscientific." To the extent that some subjects indeed did seek other treatments for syphilis, misunderstanding the researchers' intention to maintain them as a natural history study, the use of the term had pragmatic disadvantages—the results of the research were themselves flawed.[5] Similarly, it has been virtually impossible to produce "true AIDS" outside the major African teaching hospitals, not only because confirmatory HIV tests were only calibrated for and made financially feasible in Africa in the last two years, but equally because many people do not believe in the cultural and medical assumptions through which AIDS (as opposed to HIV) is constructed. This has surely affected epidemiological reports relating behavior and serostatus in Africa, since individuals' perceptions of how to catch and avoid diseases shapes their responses to questions about "risk behaviors."

The HIV antibody test used in early epidemiology cross-reacts consistently with the antibodies to malarial plasmodium, which is endemic in equatorial Africa, resulting in huge numbers of false positive results. To make matters worse, there has been little medical investment in Africa (with notable exceptions where former colonial powers had an interest in solving problems in tropical medicine that were troubling to Westerners) and certainly little basic research. Blood samples stored in Kinshasa, for example, which have become the anchor for claims that AIDS began in Africa, have no patient history attached to them—this might as easily be the blood of Europeans, or of their sexual or injecting drug partners.[6] To assert that the stored samples are "African blood" relies on the Western belief in (and desire for) an Africa intrinsically and perpetually isolated from Euro-American contact.

Text three: "In Africa, AIDS is a disease of poverty." As if a *lack* of Western-style industrialization, rather than a virus, were the cause of AIDS in Africa. Since evolutionism reared its ugly head, there has been persistent confusion between economic-evolutionist and biologistic-evolutionist argumentation, yet the two are united in their mapping of racial difference.

Take, for example, the contribution of genetics to recent discussions of the racial parameters of the AIDS epidemic. There has always been ambivalence among biologists about the significance of the genetic variation which produces pigmentation difference. Well into the twentieth century, skin "color" in itself was considered exactly correlated with moral and mental capacity. Increased scientific sophistication now requires that "genetic" arguments submerge their confirmatory racism by statistically linking "black" *genes* with evolutionary unviability. But genetic-logic is no less racist in its newer, more technologized, versions; we think that the ability to "see" genes in the electron micrograph makes genetic differences *signify*. Far from becoming more "scientific," the improved ability of geneticists to visualize and quantify fine distinctions reflexively continues to *explain* pre-existing cultural beliefs and to justify their administrative effects.

The latest contribution of genetic logic to AIDS science is, typically enough, by psychologists, not geneticists; a symptom of the historical problem of genetics is its easy cooption by social scientists in need of biological backup for arguments that would not otherwise hold water in the indigenous logic of their own discipline. J. Philippe Rushton and Anthony F. Bogaert's "Genetic Variations in Susceptibility to AIDS"[7] applies sociobiology (the most dispersed contemporary form of genetic logic) to argue that race *per se* (as a marker of intelligence level, degree of sexual control, and social organization) ought to be considered a risk factor in the transmission of HIV. Having "established" the genetically linked lower intelligence of "negroids" and accepted as agreed that "within the constraints allowed by the total spectrum of cultural alternatives, people create norms and environments maximally compatible with their genotypes," Rushton and Bogaert argue that:

> Lowered levels of intelligence must also be considered a risk factor. Observation of contingent danger may be less, both in terms of acquiring the disease, and in transmitting it to others. There are many problems in Africa in educating people to avoid intercourse with prostitutes, or other at-risk behaviors such as scarification, tattooing, ear piercing, male or female circumcision, blood-brotherhood ceremonies, etc. In the U.S. it is becoming clear that drug addicts who actively seek out heroin with street "brand names" such as "death wish" and "suicide" are not likely to readily modify their at-risk behavior. It is conservatively estimated that there are 100,000 addicts in New York alone who carry the AIDS virus, and in some samples, seroprevalence among Afro-Americans has soared to African proportions.

The problems only begin with Rushton and Bogaert's obvious unfamiliarity with even the most basic AIDS terminology (there is no such thing as an "AIDS virus"; rather, the Human Immunodeficiency Virus (HIV) is the putative agent leading, for unclear reasons, to immune suppression which sometimes renders the infected person susceptible to the unchecked ordinary infections which diagnostically count as "AIDS"; one cannot, therefore, either "acquire" AIDS or "transmit" it). Further, their reference to "African proportions" suggests that seroprevalence in Africa is higher than the U.S.; this relies on a thoroughly misleading comparison between high incidence cities in Africa with the U.S. as a whole. (Seroprevalence in any locale worldwide is a general function of the time of introduction of HIV to an area, the time of instigation of education, and to a lesser extent, variations in patterns of sexual practice, blood screening, and needle sharing.) Finally, Rushton and Bogaert rely on disputable claims about "intelligence" and "sexual promiscuity" and ignore the success of risk reduction programs in dozens of African countries, not to mention the success of both drug-related and safe sex programs in African American communities in the U.S.

Linking disease and poverty in a simple way leaves the way open to the unconscious reflex of Westerners to relate *poverty* as well as disease to some transcendent racial/ethnic difference rather than situating both in larger and historically specific patterns of colonialism, capitalist statism, and a global economy increasingly controlled by supranational corporations. The fundamental "difference" between Africans (and "blacks" among the urban poor in the West) and Euro-Americans is maintained in a complex set of constructions: the race(black)/class(lower) construction of Africa is paired with a race(white)/sexuality(perversion) construction that identifies AIDS in North America and Europe as a disease of sexuality, unmediated by the effects of class and gender status on health care, information, and access to services.

The insidious, unifying theme reiterated in texts one through three is that disease and the interruption of disease in Africa are of a different type altogether from disease in North America and Europe, and that science, a logical system requiring Western "intelligence," can never be conducted by Africans.[8] Disease in Africa is considered natural, conjured out of the primordial nought or caught from animals imagined to live side by side with Africans. In fact, the average laboratory technician in the U.S. lives in closer proximity with suspect AIDS-monkeys than does anyone in an African town, much less anyone in the bustling urban areas where HIV seroprevalence is highest. The genocidal Western fantasy of the essential economic/genetic and moral unviability of Africa combined with the idea of disease as natural selection enables the former colonial administrators to forget their complicity in the underdevelopment and exploitation that created the particular patterns of poverty that mark Africa today. The disease-as-nature trope is doubled by an evolutionary view of geopolitics: conflict between the nuclear super-nations is depicted as grave, but rational and negotiable; civil and intranational conflicts in Africa are portrayed as frivolous, hopeless dramas of uncivilized tribal disputes. Western countries are said to be threatened by environmental pollution and nuclear war, problems created by and purportedly solvable through science and rationality. Africa, by contrast, is described as subject to acts of nature such as tropical disease and famine. In Western eyes, Africa's problems can only be solved through civilizing forces—or in the romantic version, through a withdrawal from civilization and a return to pristine "tribal ways."

4.2   Fantastic Voyages

When the West found itself beset by a deadly little virus of unknown origin, it sought the source elsewhere; nothing of this sort, it was argued, could have arisen in the germ-free West. So the best research minds of the Western world set off on a fantastic voyage in search of the source of AIDS. They went to Haiti and Zaire because the first non-Euro-American cases were diagnosed in people from these countries. No "cause" had been established for AIDS and no timeframe had been established for disease progression. Thus, there was no scientific reason to believe that these Haitian and Zairean nationals had "acquired" this theoretical virus in their native countries rather than in the countries (U.S. and Belgium) where they were currently residing. Indeed, it was only the fact that AIDS was already well-documented among white Europeans and U.S. citizens that enabled the unusual illnesses of the black Haitian and Zairean nationals to be classified as AIDS.[9]

The data collected by Western researchers on prevalence in selected Central and East African countries proved equivocal; it turned out that the HIV antibody test developed in the U.S. could not distinguish between antibodies to HIV and antibodies to malaria, which is endemic in rural, equatorial Africa. Nevertheless, Western media reports on data published in 1985 claimed universally that AIDS was devastating Africa. The image of wasting "African AIDS bodies" fit neatly into the pre-existing Western image of a wasting *continent* peopled by victim-bodies of illness, poverty, famine. African nations *have* experienced uneven economic development and problems wrought by environmental anomalies, civil war, and fiascos, in their post-colonial or post-revolutionary periods. However, the U.S. mainstream media do not present successful developments, but instead portray Africa as a romantic tragedy in which poverty is so total, so basic, that there is nothing to be done to save the continent. Proposals to run HIV vaccine trials in Africa which would never pass ethical muster in the West are justified by invoking precisely this image of a dark continent perpetually on the brink of natural disaster. The typical Western images of Africa present African lives as cheap, and thus there is seen to be a numerical surplus of African research subjects (objects). In this curious calculus, the risk/benefit ratio which medical ethicists require to be demonstrated by researchers is one in which the risk to members of this vast, undifferentiated mass of people is falsely presented as minimal, and is further legitimated by pointing to the great benefits of vaccine trials to the unique, individuated peoples of the Western world. Western researchers argue that African trials are not only economically but also morally efficient. The reality is that Africans won't benefit from most medical advances, since on the one hand there is no profit in the African market for Western drug companies, and on the other hand, at least under current HIV medicine practice, drugs are calibrated for diagnostic and treatment conditions in the North. African research subjects are thus constructed simultaneously as noble savages, helping science improve the lot of humanity, and as a sort of postmodern Agar plate, a halfway house between humans and the animals conventionally used in drug testing. Far from representing an advance in biomedical ethics, and despite the claims to cultural sensitivity and the rescue of Africa, scientific AIDS research relies today on marking some people less than human and silencing them through a cacophony of soul-searching discourse.

4.3 Culturally Sensitive Ethics?

The Fifth International AIDS Conference in Montreal[10] saw the first public debate about the ethics of conducting vaccine trials on African citizens. During a major panel on ethics and AIDS human subject research, Nicholas A. Christakis (a recent graduate of Harvard's joint MD-M.P.H. program) took great pains to define the problems of cross-cultural research programs, especially in cultures like "Africa" where concepts of "personhood" and the relationship between the individual and society are different from those proposed by Western, post-Nazi biomedical ethics. While he raised important ethical issues, and his analysis is certainly at the cutting edge of cross-cultural concerns, his argument does not go far enough. I want to be clear on the importance of Christakis' intervention: there has been very little debate concerning the ethics of research in Africa at all. Nevertheless, the cultural sensitivity argument which he put forward is still within the domain of post-colonial discourse. I critique his position here in an attempt to open up ethical debate to a form of discourse that is controlled by and couched in the terms of the ethics of researchers from the African countries in which research is to occur.

Christakis argues, correctly, that "where the notions of persons as individuals is not dominant, the consent process may shift from the individual to the family or to the community."[11] He notes, in line with past experience with treatment trials in Africa, that obtaining informed consent in this context may often involve working with community leaders, whose own interests in cooperating with researchers might be complex.[12] But it is a mystification to situate these problems solely in supposedly fixed "cultural differences" between Africa and the West, for this ignores the reality that Africa has for centuries been negotiating the logic of Western ethics; thus for example, almost half of all Africans (that is to say, about 200 million people) profess some version of Christianity.[13] Further, to mystify differences in social ethics by setting them on the slippery slope of moral evolutionism (however unconsciously that slippage may occur in Western ethical discourse) shortcircuits the obvious need to consult not only local political leaders, but the actual peers of Western ethicists—African professors and theorists of *African* social ethics and theology, who can be easily located in their offices at the many major universities in Nairobi, Dar-es-Salaam, Lukasa, Kinshasa, Brazzaville, Harare, etc. Not a single one of these African theologians or ethicists was invited to speak at the Fifth International AIDS Conference in Montreal to discuss the conduct of current or future biomedical research into AIDS and HIV infection; this huge silence was covered over by the pretense that African research subjects could be approached only through Western "cultural sensitivity."

The romantic ideal of cultural sensitivity embraced by researchers such as Christakis has to be seen, then, as the product of a specifically Western discourse; at its very best, this discourse can only deal with local custom by interpolating it into a social ethics which can then be translated into the "proper" Western categories of informed consent, risk/benefit, etc. Anthropologists have long known what Western medical ethicists have yet to realize; namely that subalterns frequently use one discourse with Westerners (to defend, deflect, appease), but articulate quite different concerns within their own nation/locality/culture. This should hardly be new or startling. Neither the dual discourse competency of the dominated, nor the local variations in social ethics and their relation to local systems of political power in Africa are any different in structure from the situation in the West where, as feminist and African American theorists and activists have long argued, dominated communities are called upon to possess equal competence in the language of the white, patriarchal mainstream and in their own protective cultural vernaculars. (So, for instance, U.S. human subject research requires that individuals from the "community" sit on biomedical ethics review boards.)[14] Western ethicists retain control over research subjects to the extent that they can deny that research subjects may dissimulate ("lie strategically"). Once the altruism and "truth" of the subjects' statements are in doubt, ethicists can no longer stand as the sole interpreters of the subjects' intention and consent. Western ethics loses control at precisely the moment African subjects articulate their own social and ethical categories; Western discourse cannot speak its own language and that of the "Other" without giving up its claim to be the totalizing, metaethical discourse. Truly "cross-cultural"/"cross-ethical" debate on vaccine trials also destroys Western scientists' claims to objectivity since they must now admit that they cannot "know" what their subjects are saying.

Though current medical ethics may constitute an advance over those of Nazi science (though the U.S. conducted, until the early 1970s the similarly unethical, if less spectacularly bizarre, researches on Southern blacks), it is only so in situations where research subjects are *perceived* to be "like us." "Cutural sensitivity" arguments are designed to interpolate the "Other" into "us" long enough to allow "us" to feel good about "their" informed consent. The risk/benefit assessment demanded by Western science, in which the risk to the individual or her/his class must be less than the anticipated benefit to one or both, is said to exist in an analytically neutral space; yet it always rests on assumptions about the social value of the class in question, and on the evaluation and meaning of the cause of its exposure to the etiologic agent. Classes deemed particularly "prone" to an ailment such as AIDS or to a "risk behavior" are seen to benefit more from a possible treatment or vaccine, but if those classes are in general terms socially devalued ("Africans"), the harm of their ailment is considered less than the harm of that ailment in more valued people ("the general population"). Scientists who conduct trials among socially devalued classes are thus seen to be taking less risk for more individual and social benefit.

The disavowal of the social and political economy of scientific research ignores the broader ethical obligations existing among nations in a world community. Developing nations have no option but to refuse or allow research, and no opportunity to affect the theoretical framework of Western science nor plead for a better place in the economic plan in which that science operates.[15] A vaccine, and especially a vaccine for a disease easily avoided by the continuation of good educational programs, the availability of cheap condoms, and the additional investment in clinical sterilization techniques and universal blood screening, may simply be too costly. Even after the problems created by the trials are over (i.e., increased transmission among the placebo group, potentially disrupted educational programs resulting in decreased concern about safe sex among those outside the trial), an HIV/AIDS vaccine only leaves Africans where they were before the epidemic. By contrast, investment in education, clinics, and health awareness has benefits that increase the general well-being of Africans; condoms mean lower sexually transmitted disease (STD) rates in general, improved clinical procedures reduce a variety of iatrogenic illnesses, and health awareness programs create baseline knowledge and interest that other health-related programming can build on. Yet given international economic imbalances, the West believes it has more to gain by throwing its weight behind African vaccine trials—drug companies' expected profits, the future benefits of the knowledge gained (i.e., the possibility of using the HIV vaccine as a model for other retroviral vaccines), and the political power that will surely accrue to those who control the administration of the vaccine for such a controversial disease.

4.4 Black Bodies/White Trials

The vaccine trials set for Africa differ in significant ways from those slated for Britain and those already underway in the U.S., where in some cases noble researchers try the vaccine on themselves. The trials in England and in the bodies of the researchers are Phase One and Two trials, designed to determine whether the person taking the vaccine experiences any side-effects (Phase One) and what the exact dose and administration schedule should be (Phase Two). It is improbable that these vaccines will produce HIV-related immune suppression, though there is a possibility that anyone who has been erroneously tested as free of HIV infection could become sick as a result of the response of the body to the vaccine.[16] Because of the risk that the varying doses of vaccine administered in Phase One and Two might not be effective, and indeed that they might make it impossible for subjects to respond to a future, more effective vaccine, the small number of subjects in these trials is chosen from among people least likely to contract HIV in order to insure that they will never subsequently be exposed to HIV. There is, however, concern expressed that these noble, low-risk people might be falsely branded as "carriers" should their blood be tested and found antibody positive as a result of the vaccine rather than as a result of infection proper. Subjects will thus be issued identification cards stating that their antibodies have come from vaccination.

The trials slated for Africa, by contrast, are Phase Three trials, designed to determine whether the vaccine actually works as a deterrent to HIV infection.[17] In other words, under current plans the trials in England and the U.S. will determine whether the vaccine is harmful to British and American bodies. In Phase Three, African subjects will discover whether they have received enough vaccine to stay uninfected. Clearly, this scheduling of trials in Africa rests on two assumptions which reveal the complicity of science in actually making AIDS in Africa worse:

1) Vaccine trials are based on the assumption that Africans will continue to be exposed to HIV in large numbers—you can't test a vaccine's effectiveness unless people are subsequently exposed to the agent. Barring mass inoculation of trial subjects with HIV, vaccine trials must

assume that "Africans won't use condoms," and that risk reduction campaigns are destined to fail.

The October 1988 *Scientific American* special issue on AIDS contained an ad for Repligen, one of the companies working on a vaccine. The advertisement demonstrates the symbolic leakage between scientific process and lived experience. It read, "To develop an AIDS vaccine, you must choose your partners carefully." "Choice of partners" unconsciously reconstructs the multiple relations of power and the need to gain the cooperation of subjects which constitute AIDS research. Indeed, whatever its pretenses to objectivity, science would not exist without at least some docile object-bodies.[18]

2) The high risk involved in Phase Three vaccine trials[19] is obscured by the colonial unconscious of ethical evaluations. There is a widely promoted image that Africa and Africans are already lost to the HIV epidemic;[20] this is combined with the controversial new ethical concept of catastrophic rights,[21] according to which trials which don't quite pass ethical muster should be allowed as "compassionate." While this concept has been important in opening up the complex political economy of drug trials (chiefly by letting drug companies off the hook for liability for the harms of "compassionately released" drugs), Africa is *already* considered a catastrophe in the context of which Western colonialists are released from liability. If the notion of catastrophic rights is introduced into Africa, it seems likely that it will designate the "right" of Westerners to exploit the catastrophe they helped create, instead of giving those affected by HIV the right to receive a benefit that would otherwise have been withheld.

Even beyond the mental gymnastics required to imagine that "catastrophic rights" would entail "enhanced right to therapeutic self-determination" for anyone in Africa, there are several more basic questions. First, existing epidemiological data certainly does not suggest that HIV is more rampant in any African locale than in, say, San Francisco, Newark, Paris, or Amsterdam. Second, if all of Africa is dying of AIDS, as Western news reports suggest, who is left to serve as trial subjects? Third, if preventive measures *can* be successful,[22] as some African governments claim (and here, ethicists must explain where and why prevention works—if it works in the Sodom of San Francisco, why not the Eden of Dar-es-Salaam?), then who benefits from the risks of the vaccine trials? Fourth, if some important number of the HIV cases in African cities are attributable to poor blood screening resulting from the low efficacy and high cost of the Western-developed tests, are we funding vaccine trials instead of improved screening? Is the moderately high (and unavoidable) risk of receiving an HIV-infected blood transfusion to be another route of exposure for potential vaccine trial subjects?[23] Finally, what provisions ensure that Africans, and African societies as wholes, will actually be first to receive the vaccine, once developed? Here, the precise arguments about the problems in rural clinical practice—"They can't properly diagnose AIDS in Africa"—come into play as alibis for not distributing the vaccine.[24]

The contradictory nature of the racist perceptions which construct the idea of Africa renders them all the more insidious. On one hand, researchers who want to run Phase Three trials in Africa argue that "AIDS" in Africa and "AIDS" in the West are the same. On the other hand, epidemiologists argue that "African AIDS" is something altogether different, with different modes of transmission having to do with dramatic differences in Western and African sexual practices. The desire for a radical and incommensurable racial difference runs rampant here. Miscegenation fears, oddly enough, seem to lead some epidemiologists to argue in support of white homosexuality; Alan Whiteside, a researcher in South Africa who analyzes demographic and economic trends in South African mines, has argued that because male-male relations in the migrant work force are "patron relationships" which, unlike white homosexuality, do not involve "anal intercourse," the Chamber of Mines need only worry about anti-discrimination education.[25] What is in play here is not only the desire that black and white blood should not mix in the issue of heterosexual union, but also that black and white homosexuality be different and not a possible source of sexual congress. Whiteside describes the country's "risk" demographics in terms of "white homosexuals" and "foreigners [meaning migrants from Botswana, Lesotho, Malawi, Mozambique, Swaziland, Zimbabwe, and Zambia] and heterosexuals who are black." "Ironically," he says, "political isolation and apartheid may have slowed the spread of AIDS." In fact, Whiteside is one of the few researchers who acknowledges the existence of male-male practices at all. Although there are no seroprevalence studies of black males by work groups, many commentators claim that truck drivers, not miners, and heterosexual behavior, not male-male relationships, account for the movement of HIV.[26] Infected miners, Whitehead suggests, brought HIV infections from home but did not acquire them in South African mining camps.

The irony, of course, is that there are gay-identified black South Africans, and numerous forms of male-male sexuality in the Southern African cultural traditions, some existing before colonial regimes and continuing in the countryside, and some existing in the townships, reformed or created in resistance to colonialism. Indeed, Moody argues that the degree of male-male, cross-age relationships (with the younger or novice miners taking on the role of "mine wives") helped create the economic base for buying homesteads in countries of origin and for resisting the "proletarianization" which occurred when the miners became involved in town life. He suggests that like the formation of gay communities in Europe and North America accompanying proletarianization, some migrants chose to stay in or move to the townships in order to maintain their "gay life." The forms of wifery in the mines may not have dominantly involved "anal intercourse," as Whiteside suggests; however, the complex social transitions occurring before the 1970s (even the numbers of mine wives have declined since the 1970s due to shifts in the host countries and the general increase in permanent migration to cities) have to some degree sharpened the distinctions between lifelong "gay" relationships and economic/social male-male relationships circumscribed by migrancy and integrated into cross-gender, procreative economic relations. To reduce Southern African male-male sexuality to mine relationships ignores both historical and contemporary shifts in sexual patterns which are directly related to colonialism and apartheid. To locate all "homosexual" HIV transmission in the mines ignores black gay men outside the mines. To overrate the possibilities of HIV transmission among men in the mines results in crackdowns on male-male practices (crackdowns which have occured throughout mine history in the twentieth century, especially under the influence of Christianity), and destroys important social bonds which enable blacks to resist cultural destruction.[27] Ironically then, black male-male relationships are invisible, and "homosexuality" is illegal under laws governing *white* conduct. White male-male relations are unlawful and black male-male relations invisible in the eyes of the South African government. Two entirely different television campaigns (similar in strategy to campaigns in the U.S., though the "white" campaign actually represented "homosexual men") were produced; the white campaign was aimed at reducing homosexual practice, the black campaign promoted monogamy and the closing of family ranks against outsiders, a covert *apologia* suggesting that apartheid and monogamy, both products of white colonialism, might protect blacks from AIDS.

The efforts of Westerners meanwhile are focused on explaining the reasons for the apparent dominance of "heterosexual transmission" in the sub-Saharan continent overall (called Pattern Two by World Health Organization officials, but African AIDS by numerous researchers), versus the apparent homosexual (Pattern One) and injecting drug transmission in Northern Europe and North America. (Southern Europe claims transmission patterns more like those in Africa.) The attribution of transmission routes, of course, depends on self-reports of homosexual behavior, a social construction which varies, not surprisingly, according to these very same geographical clusters.

Ironically, the concern of Western researchers about possible heterosexual transmission among U.S. citizens came from looking at early African data at a time when the available U.S. data was particularly skimpy. The possibility of large-scale heterosexual transmission in the U.S. was initially dismissed (in 1984) because, scientists alleged, anal intercourse was the sole route of sexual spread, and unlike African heterosexuals, Euro-American heterosexuals were not believed to engage in this "primitive form of birth control." No data was ever offered in suppport of this belief and no one mentioned that anal sex might actually be a pleasure indulged in by heterosexuals worldwide. Thus when cases of apparent "heterosexual transmission" were identified in the U.S., the first explanation combined stereotypes about prostitutes with anxieties about anal sex—doctors alleged that men (mostly those under study by the Army's Walter Reed hospital) had been infected with HIV through anal sex with prostitutes. One researcher told me that men had anal sex with prostitutes because their wives "wouldn't do it."

In the early years of the epidemic, then, "black"/"heterosexual" AIDS and "white"/"homosexual" AIDS were banished to an imaginary space, "Africa," and linked together, not through intimations of cross-racial/cross-preferential pairings, but through a metaphoric cross-inscription of bodies. U.S. (white) homosexuals were said to have made of their bodies something of the order of the sewerage system of a third world country—free running waste comprising a prominent Western image of underdevelopment. African (black) heterosexuals were homosexualized through their allegedly greater practice of anal sex—anality being a chief Western symbol of homosexuality.

The attempt here on the part of researchers was clearly to reconcile cultural anxieties and stereotypes with certain curiosities in their own data. Their efforts were directed toward explaining how in the West, and among whites, active homosexuals passed the virus to passive homosexuals, while in Africa and among prostitutes and people of color in the U.S., women engaging in anal intercourse passed the virus to heterosexual men. The collision of homophobia and racism provided the anus with a curious but pivotal gender: the female anus was thought capable of doing what the male anus was not.

HIV prevalence and sexual practice studies in the mid-1980s quickly showed however that rates of anal intercourse among heterosexuals varied little around the world, not so much because Africans engaged in less than expected but because Euro-American heterosexuals engaged in more. (In general, African sex lives were disappointingly ordinary, squashing both the hopes of scientific explanations of epidemiological differences and Western racists' fantasies of exotic sexual otherness.) That theory was put forward in an attempt to explain why in Africa male-to-female seroprevalence ratios ranged from 2:1 to 1:1, while in Northern and Central Europe and North America, the ratios were between 7:1

and 9:1. This was taken to be evidence that in Europe and North America, AIDS is a "gay disease" while in Africa it is "heterosexual." This is a perplexing form of "new math" in the age of sophisticated computer modelling. Paradoxically, of course, the African ratio of 1:1 suggested that Africans were more prone to Victorian heterosexual bonding, while the ratio of 7:1 among Europeans not only suggested promiscuity, but somehow intimated that the female "1" was always the hapless victim of male homosexual forays into heterosexual intercourse. The mediating factor of injection drug paraphernalia-sharing—which was in fact occurring both within homosexual and heterosexual relationship systems, and in groups where both sharing and pairing were not rigorously governed by sexual labels—was politely ignored (especially in African contexts) as was the continuing inability of some African countries to screen blood to Western standards, and to gauge the range of people infected with HIV. Furthermore, African medical practice, in general, frequently transfuses women and children,[28] and the subsequent higher levels of seroprevalence of these two groups is the "evidence" for Western researchers' view of "heterosexual AIDS."

In fact, the research on heterosexual AIDS in Africa was trying to explain away the wrong question; the insistent denial of homosexual routes and erasing of transfusion-related cases only confirmed the long-standing stereotype that prostitutes must be "spreading AIDS." Heterosexual AIDS in Africa (and soon in the U.S.) meant men who claimed to be heterosexual who "caught" HIV from prostitutes. In most African cities there is a wide variety of male-female quasi-commercial relations as well as traditional polygamy and post-colonial modifications of formal polygamy, and it is not unusual for one man to support, in part or whole, several women. They may be wives, periodic partners, or occasional "prostitutes." In addition, most women who Westerners identify as "prostitutes" are entrepreneurs who use "prostitution" to acquire capital. There are certainly some migrant women who strike economic bargains with men, but these men are likely to be locally understood as temporary husbands. (These patterns also hold in the U.S. and worldwide—the construction of the role "prostitute" has much more to do with laws designed to constrain women within narrow sexual contracts than they have to do with the self-identity of women themselves.) Nevertheless, the hyper-heterosexualization of African AIDS aims at tracking the spread of HIV from prostitutes, not the other way around. But this actually flies in the face of both epidemiology and genito-urinary clinical data. Even with the hypothesized greater transmission of HIV from women to men if men have genital ulcers, the probability of transmission cannot, and in the epidemiology does not, become equal. If prostitution were the chief explanation for AIDS in Africa, even if each "prostitute" "infected" several men, each of those men could in turn be expected to infect several other women (his wives and other prostitutes), since the odds of male-to-female[29] (or male-to-male—it is the receptive partner who is at increased risk) infection are still greater. Combined with the increased infection of women due to blood transfusions, we should have *more* women than men, not the same number. Clearly, developing a coherent understanding of male and female cases internationally requires much more extensive analysis of the exact routes via which men versus women are subject to infection.

One thoroughly unethical study among "prostitutes" in Nairobi demonstrates both the real frequency of women becoming infected during intercourse, and the callousness that anti-woman, and especially anti-prostitute, attitudes engender. The abstract for the study, which was presented at the Fifth International AIDS Conference, reads:

EFFICACY OF NONOXYNOL–9 IN PREVENTING
HIV TRANSMISSION

Kreiss, Joan*; Ruminjo, I**; Ngugi, E**; Roberts, P*; Ndinya-Achola, J**; Plummer, F***. *U. of Washington, Seattle, USA, **U. of Nairobi, Kenya, ***U. of Manitoba, Winnipeg, Canada

Objective. To assess the efficacy of N–9 in preventing HIV transmission. [*N–9 is the active ingredient in many commercially available spermicides.*]

Method. A prospective randomized placebo-controlled study was conducted among HIV seronegative prostitutes in Nairobi, Kenya.

Results. Ninety-eight women were enrolled, assigned to the use of N–9 contraceptive sponges [*something like the Today Sponge commercially available in the U.S.*] (51) or placebo vaginal suppositories (47), and followed for a mean of 10 months (range 1–22). N–9 use was associated with a higher incidence of genital ulcers (17 vs 7% of exams, p>.001) and fungal vulvitis (19 vs 10%, p>.001) and a lower incidence of gonorrhea (21 vs 36% p>.001). HIV infection occurred in 20 women in the N–9 group and 15 in the placebo group. Excluding women who were lost to follow-up or who seroconverted within 2 months of enrollment [*and therefore were already infected before the study*], 16 (46%) of 35 N–9 users and 10 (28%) of 35 placebo users developed HIV Abs by ELISA and WB (p=NS). . . .

Conclusion. In this study of Nairobi prostitutes, we have failed to demonstrate efficacy of N–9 use in preventing heterosexual transmission of HIV. N–9 use was associated with an increased frequency of genital ulcers and of genital ulcer-associated seroconversion. Spermicide studies in other high risk populations are needed before recommendations regarding spermicide use can be knowledgeably made. [*Abstract M.A.O.36—this study was orally presented to hundreds of researchers.*]

"High risk" from where, we might ask? Unethical researchers? No one recommends use of N–9 sponges alone, and the only basis on which to study N–9 versus nothing (as opposed to a control group of condom users, a known "improvement" over "nothing") is the assertion that "Africans won't use condoms." In fact, there is a highly successful, prostitute-run condom promotion project in Nairobi, which began in 1986. The executors of the above study knew this, since they are also the researchers evaluating that project, which they reported on the day after presenting the study above.[30] That study showed marked increase in condom use by the women's clients (the most frequent reason for non-use of condoms was customer refusal), and STD rates tracked among males in the surrounding region were reduced during the first year in which the project was run to less than half their 1981 level. Indeed, a report from the U.S. Agency for International Development (the major condom supplier in developing nations) presented in Montreal suggested that supply, not resistance to usage, was the major problem in HIV prevention.[31] The report shows that if all 120 million condoms supplied to developing nations had gone only to Nigeria, less than 6% of the men aged 15 to 49 could have been supplied with condoms for a year. The reality of condom access problems was brought home to me when I was in Youande, Cameroon at an AIDS education conference. A young woman approached me and asked if I was attending the AIDS conference, and when I replied yes, she asked if I could give her condoms. The condoms placed on display at the conference hall were almost immediately taken by the Army guards and civilian cafeteria workers, and soldiers asked conference attendees if we could bring more.

In 1988, scientists quietly dropped the anal sex differential argument in favor of the theory that sexually active Africans are afflicted by genital ulcers which increase the potential for transmission of the virus from women to men. Conference visual aids during the genital ulcers era were never complete without pictures of diseased genitals—projected to 6 or 8 feet high to get over the point that the equipment of men and women in Africa is "different." What remained unspoken here was that those differences occur, not at the level of sexual, but of medical practice—at the level, that is, of differences in the availability of STD health care services (which incidentally vary as much in the U.S. as they do in other countries). The implication of this STD-ulcer research was however once again that STD-infected individuals were somehow able to produce HIV *sui generis*. This continuing attempt to locate gender differentials between the U.S. and Africa in the bodies of self-reported heterosexual Africans rather than in the social processes which create the economy of sexualities once again distorts both the demographics and sociology of HIV in Africa, and thus inhibits properly directed risk reduction campaigns.

The persistent conflation of HIV with secondary factors in Africa,

particularly its linking with poverty and sexuality, has finally led researchers to hunt for differences in heterosexual practices instead of recognizing the existence of male homosexuality in countries and cultures where
male-male sex is practiced under another name. In fact, a number of
African cultures have long-standing, culturally specific structures of
male-male sexual practice; yet there is inconsistent data on the existence
of "homosexuality" in Africa, largely because of the categories and stereotypes of Western researchers who understand homosexuality as a preference or identity in Western terms, rather than as a form of social or
economic bond. Zulu gay activist Alfred Machela has described the male-
male sex structure widespread in his own and in geographically adjacent
cultures.[32] Male-male sex is part of a social/paramilitary bond of serious
dimensions but is not considered "homosexuality," a category which is
taboo and recognized as a Western or Arabic perversion. He suggests
that when Western researchers ask about the incidence of homosexuality
in African nations, the governments' prudish "not here" reply is a self-
protective denial of European concepts of homosexuality rather than a
denial of male-male sex practices, which remain unspoken or ritualized
in social or economic bonds. As Gill Shepard has noted, there were a
wide variety of homosexual roles and relations articulated in pre-colonial
cultures. Many of these were subsequently banned by Christian, colonial
governments, who condemned them as "perversions" or "primitive" se-
ductions. For colonized peoples, denying homosexuality could be seen
therefore as a means of evading the legal and moral sanctions of the
administrative state. In some cases, the strength and values of homosexual relations were totally destroyed during the colonial period. In other
cases, as in Zulu culture, homosexual practices remain, but are doubly
coded, in some contexts as perversions, in others as ritualized forms of
male bonding.

Gay theorists have argued that gay identity and the notion of homosexuality are historically specific concepts in the West whose emergence
coincided with the appearance of psychological explanations of sexuality.
And indeed, current studies of sexual practice, launched worldwide in
attempts to provide an epidemiological basis for HIV education, suggest
boringly little difference in heterosexual and homosexual activities, in
rates of partner change, or in acceptance of the new sexual practices of
"safer sex." It is sexual identity and the relation between identity and
"risk" that vary so dramatically around the world. The social arrangement
and meaning of sexual acts differ from city to city, country to country,
era to era; yet the acts themselves, even when Western definitions are
used for what "counts" as sex, remain more or less the same. Unfortunately of course, the virus follows the routes of particular acts, regardless
of whether they are considered homosexual acts, acts of male dominance,

of sodomy (irrespective of gender), acts of economic exchange, acts of romantic male bonding or of species perpetuation. The virus enters any given locale through an accident of history, and slowing down the transmission of HIV depends on understanding the exact interrelationship between sexual actors of whatever gender or sexuality, whatever national or political formations. The key question, then, is how to understand the interrelation of sexualities internationally, and we should address this question, not as voyeurs or guardians of sexually overdetermined "Others," but as equal participants in an economy of pleasures. We should also understand what is at stake politically in current representations of "Other" sexualities.

Beneath the dramatic media accounts of Africa as a continent devasted by a virus lies the vision of a continent experiencing medical and scientific exploitation. Beyond the post-colonial and post-revolutionary administrations fighting for credibility and political survival on a global, Western-defined stage are people interrelating and seeking pleasures in their bodies. Cultural organizing to fight HIV must work in micro-networks to enable people both to recognize the acts which allow transmission of HIV, and to sustain and re-symbolize those cultural/sexual practices which prevent transmission. We must also understand the political and social difference between the Western closet which circumscribes in order to *occlude deviance* and the traditional cultures which articulate homosexualities into economic and social and religious bonds in order to *sustain difference.*

Internationally, AIDS is constructed through a deadly set of assumptions about cultural and political difference. AIDS is mapped directly onto pre-existing national and cultural formations. But HIV knows no geographical boundaries. HIV traces a geography unrecognized by governments intent on reducing sexualities which subvert economic production, thwart social control, or merely stand as politically embarassing reminders of richly symbolic and less rigidly conformist ways of life, once characteristic of traditional cultures, but now labelled as perverted and as a political liability by Western discourse. HIV follows the lines of transportation created by capital investment and traces a geography of bodily pleasures that defies the medical cops who police every country's border, no matter how many tests they devise. The HIV epidemic poses a unique moral challenge and will re-form both the meaning of sexuality and the meaning of local and international cooperation.

The scientists, policy-makers, and media tycoons have the power to produce masks of otherness which create discrimination against people with HIV and AIDS. They have the power to thwart prevention by allowing people to ignore the necessity of speaking about sexual practices out of a false sense that HIV is somewhere else, in the bodies of others.

Local activists—who slowly find each other through the improbable routes of international scientific conferences, ex-lovers, and FAX machines—will transform the meaning of geographical boundaries. Though many of us will die in this epidemic, the network of survivors will form a new, supranational community of resistance.

5

Teaching About AIDS

The comforting causal-logic knowledge of science, ineffective even on its own terms, has set the standard for mastery of AIDS information, even while the very process of acquiring information has increasingly become the basis of expanding discrimination and surveillance. The effectiveness of science-logic in policing society has both reified science-logic and inured us to science's inability to solve the problems it sets for itself. The categories of science, especially the conjuncture of epidemiology and virology, have placed a barely invisible *cordon sanitaire* around minority communities, "deviant" individuals, and around the entire continent of Africa. We no longer need camps or border passes, although several countries have used them in an effort to prevent the spread of HIV. The ideologies encoded in AIDS research have laid a more sublime foundation for selecting groups of people for detention and destruction. The mechanism for this is, ironically, an education strategy which separates the "general public" from "communities."

The discourses of expertise position recipients of educational messages in a way that disables their ability to actually apply information to their lives, and leaves them liable for failing to have understood that they were to have appropriately responded to the "danger" of AIDS. Even the simple admonition to "reduce risk practices" systematically distorts the meaning of "safe sex" because the cultural presupposition is that only "dangerous people" engage in "dangerous sex (or drug use)." There are two contradictory positions from which to interpret the "danger" of AIDS, and thus, two solutions to "reducing risk."

Most educational efforts so far have been directed either toward a general public thought to be ignorant of the fact that HIV cannot be transmitted via doorknobs (a strange displacement of sexual fantasy), or toward communities in which the so-called risk behaviors are believed to recalcitrantly occur. This division of educational strategy, and the illusory epidemiology on which it is based, constitutes the terrain in which legal and social discriminations occur. The supposed goal of public education is to reduce discrimination by quelling public fears and to promote compassion toward people living with HIV. However, targeting of education, anchored by the mobile metaphor of the HIV antibody test, enables rather than decreases discrimination. The more education that occurs under this ideological division of labor, the more deeply inscribed becomes the system of discrimination against people associated with AIDS. The mere idea of a test—regardless of what it actually detects, and regardless of its reliability and validity—means that individuals *could* know their status, and that a policing public health system *could* find it out. This displaces all responsibility for "safety" onto the putatively or proveably HIV seropositive person and implies that there could be no such thing as consent to unsafe sex with a seropositive person. While we may be concerned about the rationales for such "consent," each individual's perceptions of safety and danger are based in complex structures of identity and in the symbolic values of particular sexual (or drug use) acts: few people will be consciously "consenting" to transmission. By confusing the relationship between safe sex (as a set of acts) and serostatus (as a determinant of the possibility of infection) promoted by test-backed education, many people have difficulty associating transmission promoting acts with the people they love and trust. The symbolic meaning of engaging in intimate acts and the logics in the events leading up to those acts—even if the acts have been declared unsafe by science—may be more powerful than the recognition of risk. An ethnographic study of gay men in Oslo[1] documented a phenomenon anecdotally described by safe sex educators around the world: for gay men (and heterosexual men in different ways) the exchange of semen is a symbolic act indicating intimacy, trust, equality. To introduce condoms or eliminate such acts makes men feel as if they are being callous or unkind toward sexual partners. Ironically, the use of condoms to promote safety on the biological level cancels the feeling of "caring" on the level of human interaction and brotherhood. Heterosexual women also report fears that requesting condoms is insulting to a male partner, and most couples, regardless of sexuality or age, perceive a magic point in a relationship when to stop using condoms represents a deepening of mutual trust and commitment. Outside the core of the gay male communities in the large urban areas, "safe sex" seems to be adopted or rejected based on known or perceived serostatus of the partner or the quality of feelings of trust, rather than on universal adoption of practices which prevent transmission.

5.1 "You Don't Have AIDS"

The consequences of test-backed public health interventions are both an inability to reduce overall *patterns* of transmission (that is, in the long run we need to change the patterns of behavior, not simply eliminate HIV-positive people from those patterns) and an increase in the mechanisms of discrimination. A large poster appeared on the walls of several New York City subway stations in 1988. In stark white letters against a black backdrop were the words, "You don't have AIDS, now prove it," followed by the phone numbers for a hospital sponsored testing service. The AIDS Discrimination Unit of the Human Rights Commission of New York City is suing the hospital.

The original AIDS educational message was straightforward enough:

You cannot get HIV through casual contact, but you can become infected with this virus by getting HIV-infected semen in the anus or vagina, or by injecting HIV-infected blood.[2]

Because gay-positive government-funded education was prohibited from the beginning, the political economy of AIDS education produced a curious bifurcation of this message after the "heterosexual AIDS" scare following Rock Hudson's death in late 1985. The perception of shifting demographics of HIV became a media event, most vividly depicted on a *Life* magazine cover with the simple, stark headline "No One is Safe." Who we were to read as the "no one" and how we were to understand "safety" were already determined by a logic which constructed both "AIDS" and the social-status-defined "risk categories" as absolute phenomena. Far from breaking down the sharp dichotomy between "risk groups" and the "general public," the rhetoric of "no one is safe" produced a policing of identity borders as well as community borders: "no one is safe" because you can't tell who is queer.

Once the "public" could no longer ignore the presence of AIDS, educational projects were split into "public" education and "community" education, with each group getting its own special message. "Public" was no longer those who had managed to keep AIDS at a distance and became instead, those people "not at risk." "Risk group" terminology broke down under protest from the minority communities, who soon discovered that the once-empowering word "community" would now be equated with "risk group." The new messages, "you can't get AIDS (from a doorknob or on a crowded bus)" and "you can get AIDS (from 'risk practices' contained in 'communities')", changed the question for the individual from "how do I avoid this virus?" to "which of these 'you's' am 'I'?" The selection of information now depended on an individual's perception of membership in either the "public" or a "community," a change in nomenclature which retained the confusion between difference and risk. Not only does this rest on inadequate ideas about how identities are constructed, but it increases the persistent denial of homosexuality and drug use outside the the identified "communities." The appearance of infected persons within the "general public" did not result in an erosion of the sharp identity distinctions, but instead created a new meaning for "the closet": drug injectors and non-gay-identified men who had sex with men were only masquerading as members of the general public. Testing shored up the anxious distinction between the "public" and the "communities," and a positive test reassigned the individual from "public" to "community." The government persistently claimed that there was no evidence that "AIDS" would move into the "general public": admission to the general public being by definition a negative ELISA. This reinforced the equation risk=infection=AIDS, and assumed that each person has only one relevent aspect of identity (that associated with "risk"). Splitting identity in this way resulted in paradoxical messages that fatally disabled the interpretive powers of individuals who were trying to make well-informed choices.

Consider a gay male nurse: at work he is told he can't get AIDS, at the bar is told he had better take extraordinary precautions or he will get AIDS. In the context socially constructed as "work," he is assured that saliva cannot trasmit virus, but in the context socially constructed as "dangerous venue of sexual possibility" he is told not to "deep kiss" his lover for fear of contracting the virus.

Or take young people, who, except for the "hard to reach" (by whom? the educator?), are considered fledgling members of the general public. Young people are told that good citizens do not fear people with AIDS. While older youth are allowed to understand that people living with AIDS engaged in unseemly drug or sexual activity (acts which demarcate the public from those infected), they are given virtually no practical information about HIV transmission relevant to the practice of sex or the use of drugs in their own lives. The benevolence they are asked to bestow on people living with AIDS is directly contingent on their understanding of such people as irrevocabley "Other" based on the set of sex practices which encodes deviance, and in the case of white youth, the set of drug practices which in AIDS discourse encodes race. Reciprocally, young people's ability to access meaningful risk reduction information in a restricted economy of facts controlled by adults is contingent on identifying with the "Other," thereby disrupting the logic of self-disengaged altruism.

 The silence surrounding safe sex education for youth (except for the "hard core, hard to reach" street youth who we educate because we fear them) leaves many young people with the idea that only dangerous people need to know about safe sex. My own experience suggests that "dangerous people" to these youth are adults of approximately yuppie lifestyle. Few young people perceive themselves or their friends to be dangerous, and believe they can proceed without any special knowledge or techniques. They are smart enough to realize that something is wrong here, but unfortunately, many are too terrified or simply don't how to get better information on their own. If asking for birth control is an admission of planning for sex, asking for safe sex information must seem like an intention to court death. The silence surrounding applied sexual and drug behavior education for young people is morally bankrupt and lethal,[3] which the new epidemiology from urban areas in the U.S. reveals.[4] Differences in access to information by class, ethnicity, gender, sexuality make HIV pedagogic practices complicit in the punitive public health practice of maintaining stigmatized people in relative ill health.

But the problem does not end here. There is a hidden ethical structure underlying information-giving models of health education which directs different strategies at what are perceived as "high" and "low" risk groups. Even though each group received "facts," the "public" is given information on the assumption that they have a *right to know,* that is a right to "protect" themselves, while "communities" are educated on the assumption that they have an *obligation to know* and protect the "public." (In haunting echoes of racist eugenics, this society still does not care whether large numbers of gay men or African Americans die.) Even if there is some awareness that not everyone in "communities" is infected and that increasing numbers of people in the "general public" are, the two groups are nevertheless defined as audiences with different reasons for needing the "facts about AIDS," and in practice are actually given different facts. This hidden moral loading in the information model, at least as it is currently used, cannot break down the dubious idea that it is risk group susceptibilities rather than how one engages in specific sexual and drug acts that creates the possibility of HIV transmission. Until this simple confusion is cleared up, we will continue to see high rates of transmission as HIV finds its way into groups who believed they were "safe" because no one like them was infected and who did not therefore change their practices. The moral judgment hidden in the mode of address to the general public versus communities means that most people engaging in risk behaviors who are not already self-identified with a subculture in which participants are actively promoting changes in behavioral norms will not be able to apply safer sex information to themselves. They will instead seek the HIV antibody test to discover whether they are "at risk" or whether they need more education. They may instead discover that they are already infected. The outcry among middle-class heterosexuals, especially evident in women's magazines, mainstream newspapers, and recent popular texts about (or against) practicing safer sex[5] hinges on the inherent contradiction between the right-to-know versus the responsibility-to-know underlying information-giving initiatives. Nearly all the information aimed at heterosexuals advises *first* to form a mutually monogamous relationship with an HIV antibody negative person (the reader is always presumed uninfected). To the extent that negative antibody test results are seen to absolve an individual of her/his "responsibility to know" and responsibility to practice safe sex and enables her/him to practice unsafe sex techniques once having exercised the "right to know" (other people's status), the HIV testing process becomes a game of Russian roulette.

Recent U.S. criminal cases in which one person is accused of assault with HIV demonstrate that only the HIV antibody positive person is responsible for ensuring the practice of safe sex. Apparently, there is no such thing as consent to unsafe sex and by extension, one cannot be construed to have consented to transmission-enabling acts with someone who does not reveal (or know) that they are infected with HIV. HIV serostatus changes the legal status of a sexual act from a consenting adult practice to an act of assault or even attempted murder. Like earlier cases where HIV antibody positive prisoners were found guilty of assault for spitting on their keepers and saying, "I'm going to give you AIDS [sic]," fantasies of transmission or of immunity loom larger in case law than the real possibilities of protecting oneself by using a condom. This is a rather odd twist, since it has never previously been possible to charge men with assault with semen in acts of "unprotected" heterosexual intercourse that may have lead to pregnancy. Indeed, it has been difficult to press any claim of sexual assault among adult heterosexuals at all.

The result is that ordinary people in the "general public" are thought of as ignorant if they fail to absorb the fact that you can't get HIV from a doorknob, but they are not held liable for acts of discrimination that stem from that ignorance. Gay men, prostitutes, and drug injectors are believed to be morally derelict for refusing to be tested for HIV antibodies, even if they have been practicing safe sex and needle hygiene. The intransigently stereotyped "high risk" people are increasingly held legally accountable for failing to act on information that they are thought responsible for knowing, or for failing to find out their antibody status when they knew or should have known they were "at risk."

I have taken great pains to show how AIDS science, represented in the HIV antibody test, shapes the practices of education in order to point out that educators cannot simply "empower people to make good choices." While I agree that increasing individuals' ability to choose wisely is crucial, it is critical to recognize that education does not take place in a neutral environment; even empowerment-based education must contend with the undergirding moral and scientific reasoning of this culture. Not only are prejudice and misinformation rife, but the very educational system in which we operate implicitly loads some information with liabilities, while leaving much ignorance tolerated. Critically, the symbols and logics of science anchor this educational environment, making it virtually impossible to escape certain ideas, like the notion that some people are intrinsically at risk because of who they are.

People have more than a responsibility to know, more than a right to choose. People have the right to understand the ideologies of science and of education: HIV/AIDS education must always be political. HIV/AIDS education either reinscribes the sexual, class, and racial ideologies that are propped up by moralism and science, or disrupts the heirarchical formations of knowledge and opens up space for groups and communities to work out their interrelationships with information *they* have decided is relevant.

5.2 Disciplining AIDS

Education about AIDS occurred first in the gay community, followed by the injecting drug, African American, Latino, and other ethnic/racial communities, and only in the mid-1980s in the "society at large." The virtual media blackout on AIDS issues from 1981 until the death of Rock Hudson not only made it difficult to find information, but suggested that AIDS was a phenomenon of importance only to special groups. Because mass media have become critical gatekeepers to information and common references for popular knowledge, it is not really surprising that the first university courses taught on AIDS were in the areas of media studies: Jan Zita Grover, Simon Watney, and Craig Owens, all media historians and AIDS activists, conducted such courses in the mid-1980s. University courses aimed at social workers, medical, and counselling professionals began to include sections on AIDS, and courses on social and legal policy frequently invited speakers from local AIDS groups. But this disciplining of AIDS rarely gives students an opportunity to think through how HIV and AIDS are affecting their personal lives and private choices. As soon as it was permissible to speak of AIDS in the university, such discussion was circumscribed by traditional curricular ideas: the "health education" aspect of AIDS should be dealt with by health services, and any other discussion would be in the guise of professional training.

The absurdity of trying to contain the discussion of one of the most controversial and fear-inspiring issues of our time produces baffling and unpredictable situations in every classroon. In the course of a freewriting exercise in my Freshman composition course, students were asked to reflect on their choice of the University of Massachusetts. One woman said she had taken her second choice over her preference to attend a Florida university because she was afraid that if she went to Miami she would get AIDS. I couldn't simply send this student off to health services or to a course in the biology department. I could not even change her views of a few basic AIDS facts because as a writing teacher my presentation of "facts" does not bear the authority of a scientist's. What I could do was teach her to question her own thought process, to be sensitive to sources and to power relations among authorities, and to reflect on how the information she incorporated into her belief system affected her life choices. I could, as a cultural critic and teacher of the art of reading well, help her understand how mass media texts, from "AIDS prevention" pamphlets to newspaper articles, construct her experience of HIV/AIDS and how her belief system affects her decisions about sex and drug use practices.

A decade into this epidemic, people working on the complex issues emerging in and through the AIDS epidemic are frustrated by the limits on teaching about HIV/AIDS. From individual risk reduction to helping specialists recognize the ways AIDS and AIDS backlash are changing their work, the problems of the epidemic frequently require interdisciplinary approaches and involvement of people whose vast stores of knowledge are not designated "expert" by traditional standards. What we need to teach about AIDS—and what people want to learn—is seriously constrained by traditional approaches to education and credentialling. And, because AIDS is linked in the public mind to sexuality and drug use, how we teach about AIDS is circumscribed by puritan notions of "good taste" and the appropriateness of introducing "adult" information to young people.

The problem is easily attributable to homophobia, sexism, the hyper-individualism of this generation, the financial cutbacks in educational institutions (both universities and community health programs), the increased conservatism that heightens the fear that being positive about sexuality and non-judgmental about drug use will result in job loss, and the unspeakable pain at not being able to share our experience of the multiplicity of ways in which AIDS has touched, often devastated the lives around us. The people in the best position to explore with students the many personal and social effects of the AIDS epidemic are the most vulnerable to accusations of "being inappropriate" or non-objective. Nevertheless, it is critical to prepare high school and college students for life in a world where old repressive ideologies are gaining new power from their association with particular representations of AIDS. We need to teach history alongside biology because, as one of my students put it, "I have no point of comparison, all I have ever known is Reagan and AIDS—and MTV."

What *we* want to say about AIDS is overdetermined by the rhetoric of emergency at the same time that it is ruled out of bounds by the anxious erotics of Western pedagogy. Discursively, AIDS has multiplied the signifiers of sexual danger, at once terrifying students and promoting an insatiable desire for facts and certainty. Conflicting messages and the impossibility of achieving certainty lead back to reductionist solutions: the belief that their AIDS fears can be resolved by avoiding certain stereotyped people, or perhaps by seeking the commonly-used HIV antibody test.

5.3 AIDS as Emergency

The fact-based approach to AIDS education shores up the idea that public health policy can be objectively debated and politically neutral. Already encoded in public health statutes and procedures is the idea that there are ordinary events and "emergencies." When epidemics, defined by the public health officials as "one more case than expected," become "disasters," defined by civil response agencies as "one more case than can be handled," triage and policing are set in motion. Triage directs attention not to those individuals whose lives are most in danger, but toward those who lives are likely to be saved. Likewise, the broader disaster plan is aimed toward containment, not toward protecting the rights of those immediately affected. Once an emergency is declared (or an epidemic named), medical and public policies shift from coping with the individual problems and rights of particular people, to protecting and aiding people by class, and always along the fault line of whose lives are most valued. Thus, it is important to step back and ask, who declared this an emergency, and for whom, and who benefits from operating under these rules?

Those of us most closely affect by the HIV epidemic are dizzy from trying to divide increasingly precious time between teaching about HIV, fighting political battles, and confronting the medical establishment at the same time as we live through the fears and illnesses of our friends and ourselves. This urgency makes it hard to stand still long enough to reflect about where we are going or how we understand this brave new world. The need to find solid ground, something to hang on to, makes discussions of the symbolic landscape of AIDS seem unimportant and even anxiety-producing.

But we soon experience gaping holes in our sense of reality. At first, AIDS, our dying friends, our own fears of illness and death seem unreal, and we respond by thinking, "If I can just *get through this part*, life will return to normal." As more friends receive various diagnoses, and we live with new fears and new needs to allocate finite time and energy, it begins to dawn on us that *this is our lives now*, and things will never go back to the normal we once knew.

We must begin to question in whose interest it is, a decade into a mishandled epidemic, to promote the idea of AIDS as emergency. Clearly, this designation facilitates the use of archaic and inappropriate public health laws: invoking "emergency" creates the conditions of blame and quarantine, and rationalizes the century-long practice of using the public health system to police, control, and maintain in managed ill health a range of marginalized people. Questioning the logic and power of the trope "emergency" impels us to pursue with our students related discourses of gender and post-colonial social organization; we can propose with our students a deconstruction of "public health" by asking who defines the "public" and who is constituted as having or not having "health." Who administers the systems on which these definitions rest?

But it is also important to realize that the constant sense of emergency becomes a system of control in itself. Keeping the most affected communities in a state of siege is destructive for us individually and as subcultures. With the siege mentality comes a heightened, stark defining of roles: "sick" and "well," "caretakers" and "those needing care," the living and the dead. Representing life as requiring split second decisions with no time to plan or reflect does not leave much space for *living with AIDS,* either as one's own diagnosis or as an aspect of the social world we inhabit. Underlying the practical aspects of life in this war zone is a sense of living in another reality, a sense of alienation from "ordinary life" that obscures the ways in which complex social and cultural attitudes insistently construct the domain of AIDS as unreal in order to contain the fears about sexuality and about death. Demanding that life near AIDS is an inextricably *other* reality denies our ability to recreate a sustaining culture and social structures, *even as we are daily required to devote much time to the details of the AIDS crisis.*

Those who live with AIDS as a constant feature of daily life feel a sharp sense of *living in a different reality* when confronted with people "visiting" our AIDS-world from the other side of the planet. These people seem ignorant and oblivious to "what's really happening." They seem to be suffering from denial or false consciousness, and we direct education *at* them to correct the misinformation that so negatively affects our lives. But more is required: teaching the films, plays, and stories that have emerged from the affected communities can help bridge the gap between the reality of the war zone and the reality outside it. The goal is not to teach "compassion," because this still positions "the public" outside the reality of the AIDS episteme, positions them as a class with the privilege of being kind toward an "Other," positions them as health imperialists nostalgically charting the story of continents wasting with disease. Rather, we want them to understand their complicity in the systems of AIDS discrimination and their position relative to the highly fluid boundaries of the so-called risk groups, a complicity typically assuaged by altruistic "Othering" in our culture. But altruism becomes genocide where risk reduction education is suppressed in "the affected"—"the communities"—by discriminatory laws like the Helms Amendment (which prohibits government funding to sex-positive education).

5.4 The Danger of Pedagogy

AIDS radically calls into question the pleasures and dangers of teaching. Pedagogy outside the sciences is, at its best, not the teaching of a body of knowledge, but induction into a fellowship of inquirers: we do not convey knowledge so much as we seduce into discourse. The post-Socratic pedagogues' anxious status as structural, if not *actual* homosexuals, often silences those who cannot speak from the objective posture of science. Without the crutch of scientific objectivity (the implicit heterosexual subject position?), everything that we need to teach, and everything our students need to learn has acquired a valence of silence and death.

One solution might be to provide a better and more sophisticated version of "the basic facts" or "AIDS 101." This impulse to provide more and more facts rests on a futile hope that some objective truth will constitute education about AIDS. Perhaps it reflects a wish to avoid actually talking about the "deviances" around which both terror and passion circulate. The traditional way of organizing such an educational effort would be to continually test knowledge of AIDS facts and remediate or supplement existing knowledge. But this route is deeply problematic because the very language used to explain AIDS, like the language used to explain everything about sex and about disease, is polysemic: words like "safe" and "sex" are open to almost limitless interpretation. Likewise, "disease" and "death" perform a syncopated dance with "health" and "life," producing unstable metaphors for concrete experiences and their scientific abstractions. We only relieve our own guilt as conspirators in fatal practices of knowledge if we believe we have helped anyone by scoring answers on questions that require more interpretation than comprehension. At best, these tests will tell us how creatively and with what frameworks individuals assemble and apply the statements which are called "AIDS facts."

The problem is that these—or any—facts have little rational or predictable connection with behavior; rather, underlying and often contradictory health logics are what translate fact-language knowledge to richly meaningful acts. In fact, in most parts of the country, high-school and college students demonstrate fairly extensive knowledge about AIDS, most of which has come from the media, yet few practice safe sex. Several studies suggest that teenagers and young adults believe that other people acquire HIV infection or develop AIDS through a specific and known set of acts, while they perceive their *own* susceptibility to HIV or AIDS to be a matter of chance.[6] Anecdotal evidence suggests that the very same students who score high on AIDS facts tests typically abstain from sex until they get drunk enough to overcome their terror, at which point they engage in unsafe sex which they later interpret with a mix of guilt, fatalism, and a euphoric belief in their own good luck. In the ever-proliferating discourse of "AIDS information"—which has the effect of making it appear that one must master a tremendous and growing body of facts—it is crucial that we foreground the one critical "fact:" that HIV moves from person to person when infected semen is transported into the anus or vagina, or when infected blood is injected. From this single "fact" begins the interpretion that it is the performance of specific sexual or drug use acts which enable HIV transmission, and not an association with the stigmatized subcultures. Teaching about HIV/AIDS, then, means teaching *how* to understand, how to *read* and *interpret* both the facts that bombard us and the context of our own lives.[7]

5.5   AIDS Education/Homophobia Education: Conflicting Strategies, Conflicting Messages

Homophobia continues to dramatically shape the evolving concepts about AIDS, structuring AIDS as a "gay disease" within public debate about and medical research on the HIV epidemic. Reflexively, the public discussion of AIDS since 1985 has given homophobia new expression. While discussions of homosexuality and of AIDS are now always unconsciously linked, the anti-homophobia and AIDS organizing have developed quite differently in the 1980s. In Chapter Two, I discussed safe sex education in the gay community, and in the first part of this chapter, problematized the distinction between "community" and "public/general" education. I want to draw out some troubles of anti-homophobia and AIDS education for the "general public," especially in those settings in which the educator takes on the full burden of "being out" and does not expect anyone to stand up and identify as lesbian or gay or as a person directly coping with HIV/AIDS. The educator may be *aware* that lesbians or gay men or people affected directly by HIV are in the audience, but is addressing the group as if they are outside the commmunities most directly experiencing homophobic attack or HIV-related problems. It is difficult to address an audience as anything other than presumptively gay/lesbian/intimately affected by HIV/AIDS or as "general audience," although shifting use of first, second, and third person can problematize the audience's unconscious constructions of "other." It is impossible to be neutral or fully inclusive because social concepts of both homosexuality and of HIV/AIDS already inscribe difference in a way that makes audiences and ourselves assume an interpretive position in relation to any information and educational experience. How audiences and educators receive one another as "same" or "other" strongly influences educational endeavors. Most importantly, ideas of same/other are fluid and multi-faceted: there may be racial, gender, class, or ethnic solidarities which are transformed into "otherness" when sexuality or drug use or political perspectives are introduced. Good educators navigate these hazardous waters of indentity constructions and use identification and difference strategically to confront audiences with their preconceptions and the conflicts in their values which result from marking people as "other." Most educators accomplish this by intuition and experience, but a more careful examination of paradigms of health education and concepts of homosexuality from gay studies provides a framework for choosing or changing strategies on the spot.

The discourse of AIDS is perceived to be a more technical and medical than that of homosexuality, requiring the authority of traditional, neutral experts. Because discussions of AIDS are so medicalized and have a veil of objectivity, it has become more comfortable for many people to talk about AIDS than to discuss homosexuality directly. Liberals are for the most part willing to talk about AIDS and HIV infection and view these as everyone's problem, and possibly even as something anyone "might get." On the other hand, homophobia is still something that few progressive people will put on their agenda, and is rarely perceived as something they "might have." At best, homophobia merits a one shot consciousness-raising event, or is added to the end of a long list of oppressions or demands for civil rights. While liberals are discovering they have gay/lesbian friends and colleagues, few non-gay/lesbian people have much exposure to the diverse cultural and social life of the lesbian and gay community. Outside *avant-garde* cultural circles and some corners of the Rainbow Coalition, it seems much easier to talk about the health care, research, and anti-discrimination needs of lesbian and gay people who are affected by HIV or AIDS-related backlash than it is to talk about the institutionalized or individual homophobia that prevent gay and lesbian people from leading full lives whether we have AIDS or not. The non-gay/lesbian world collapses all of the gay/lesbian community's experience into that embodied by people living with AIDS. While the plight of people living with AIDS is very real, so are the effects of homophobia which work both in tandem with AIDS-related discrimination and independently. AIDS-related discrimination furthermore operates in tandem with sexism and racism, which were accepted as valid social concerns before AIDS, while gay/lesbian concerns have only been marginally legitimated, and only in relation to AIDS. Demands for the civil rights and cultural autonomy of lesbians and gay men are seen as "politicizing" AIDS or as manipulating AIDS policy for an unrelated gay rights agenda. Embracing AIDS-related civil rights while denying the related rights and autonomy of the communities under assault in AIDS backlash maintains homophobia in another form, and enables racism and sexism to reemerge as drug and reproductive health policies which covertly aim at controlling people of color.

Some have imagined that AIDS education, because it encodes homophobia and racism in scientific sounding terms, has overcome homophobia or dislinked homophobia and AIDS. The degaying of AIDS came about partly through the success of campaigns which said "AIDS doesn't discriminate, anyone can get AIDS." But in the context of massive government and media pressure to take the HIV antibody test, homophobia has slipped quietly underground, hidden in attitudes toward the meaning of the test. In a 1989 study, physicians said they would follow different guidelines about informing partners of HIV-antibody positive people depending on the race, gender, and sexual orientation of the infected person.[8] Everything from popular media to the CDC's own counselling guidelines promotes different reasons for testing based on the prior identification of categories of risk. If you're convincingly heterosexual and you don't shoot up, you're told, "Take the test, your results will probably be negative and you won't have to worry any more."[9] The implicit message that accompanies information on testing is that only the queers and junkies need to fear taking the test: fear of taking the test is both proof of risk status and tantamount to an admission of refusal to "take responsibility" for "AIDS."[10] Although there are new reasons for testing in order to make decisions about early intervention for HIV antibody positive people, the reality that most people outside the gay male community associate testing with sexual decision-making continues to cloud the meaning and usefulness of widespread testing.

Although medical and psychological explanations of homosexuality had to some important extent lost their grip by the time AIDS emerged as a social phenomenon, the logic of AIDS as "having a discernible cause" has tended to remedicalize homosexuality. U.S. culture finds scientific logic (while not every scientific fact) unassailable; in the ideological tension between AIDS as viral ("real") and homosexuality as chosen ("role"), science easily wins. The battles in the 1970s to have homosexuality removed as a diagnostic category in psychiatry were accomplished through posing scientifically-based counter-evidence to the claim that homosexuality was pathological. We removed homosexual people from the grips of diagnosis, but that *we never extricated homosexuality from the logic of science.* The right wing is fond of using AIDS as proof that there is indeed something physically wrong about homosexuality. Even if gay people and some scientists and psychologists rejected the idea that sexuality is based in hormonal responses which could be controlled, the public still holds fast to this very powerful pop science idea: homosexuality can't simply *be,* it must have a cause.

The strong belief in superficial markers for deeply hidden traits which characterizes contemporary Western notions of personhood works out in strange ways in AIDS discourse: the unconscious wish for a physical marker or test for homosexuality collapses in the insistent linkage between homosexuality and AIDS to construct the HIV antibody test as a mechanism for revealing hidden homosexuality. Similarly, through the reverse logic, sociobiologists have argued that race already stands as a marker for genetic propensity to behaviors which are related to HIV transmission ("promiscuity," less controlling social structures, failure to perceive "contingent risk").[11] No matter how often people state that HIV is the (probable) cause of AIDS, entrenched popular ideas about hormonal and genetic explanations of human difference formthe popular basis for deducing the "odds" of contracting HIV; stereotyped views of gay and ghetto life or homosexuality and race *per se* rather than opportunities to have unprotected sex or share unsterilized needles are popularly imagined to be the way to "get AIDS." Warwick, Aggleton and Homans confirm this pattern of avoidance of applying risk assessment to oneself by attributing risk behaviors to the lifestyle or traits of others in their open-ended interviews with teenagers. The British teens described contradictory logics about their own versus other people's health, differentially incorporated new facts about AIDS to continue to place risk elsewhere, and, because they attributed risk and ability to control risk to others, and viewed their own "odds" of contracting HIV as a matter of chance, few undertook changes in their own behavior, despite extensive knowledge about HIV transmission and avoidance.[12]

5.6 Health Education Theory/Gay Theory

There are two general pedagogies used in homophobia and AIDS education: those aimed at providing information and those aimed at attitude change. Attitude-change projects target both individual and social attitudes. In the U.S., we have tended to focus on individual attitudes in homophobia education programs, and worked on social attitudes in projects aimed at discrimination, political access, and promoting positive images of gay and lesbian people through our engagement with and in the mass media.

Perceptions about the status of information and the choice of educational style dramatically affect the outcome of educational efforts. AIDS education directed at the general public is generally viewed as a matter of conveying facts (or appealing to values about compassion), while homophobia education is seen as a matter of challenging attitudes (and, unlike the homophile education projects of three decades ago, which sought something like compassion for those afflicted with homosexuality, current anti-homophobia education demands civil rights, not compassion, since gay/lesbian people have an equal "right to exist.")[13] Though this is obviously an oversimplification (groups on sexuality or safe sex often use participatory and attitude-change models) it is largely true that entrenched, prejudiced fears are seen as the source of homophobia while ignorance of facts is viewed as the cause of AIDS hysteria. This emphasis on the efficacy of facts in AIDS education will slowly change as data accumulates showing that acquisition of facts is largely ineffective in countering prejudices about people living with AIDS or people perceived to be "HIV carriers" because they are associated in the public mind with "risk groups."

Even if there is growing awareness that facts alone don't change attitudes about AIDS, it will be difficult to move away from strict information-giving models; AIDS is usually discussed in terms of "facts" or "the truth" about AIDS because audiences demand answers to questions framed in these terms. There is a common belief that AIDS information-giving is politically neutral, but both the progressive AIDS activists and the right wing mean different things when they assert the same facts. Fact-based language is used both by the right, which views mainstream AIDS education as a gay plot, and by liberals who want to depoliticize AIDS. But we can't simply depoliticize AIDS by using neutral sounding terms. In fact, in the current landscape, we cannot depoliticize AIDS at all. AIDS education requires holding in tension the idea that HIV does not discriminate between people and the idea that AIDS has been, from the very beginning, constructed as a gay disease, and secondarily as a disease of addiction. The research models, the educational tactics, the public health measures debated—all rely on seeing AIDS as a sexually transmitted disease existing among men who can't be expected to act responsibly. The homophobia—and racism and sexism, since men of color and any sex workers (though "prostitute" often serves as a code word for many women of color who do not strike traditional, bourgeois marital bargains) are considered sexually dangerous, too—are often so subtle that they act only as a force field that makes certain objects of study or certain research results seem self-evident.

The information model, as long as it defines two different reasons for learning AIDS facts, cuts a wide and discriminatory swath between those already perceived as responsible for "spreading AIDS" and those believed responsible only for their own ignorance. The information model, therefore, forms the foundation for the public health model that intends from the outset to find and punish certain groups of people. If we assigned moral responsibility for AIDS information based on an attitude-change model, we would be locking up a very different group of "dangerous" people. Obviously, everyone needs accurate basic information, but attitudes toward health and sexuality and drug use play a decisive role in how that information is assimilated by the individual and how society decides when we are educated and presumed reponsible for personal and collective behavior.

There are also two different concepts of the nature of homosexuality, which gay and lesbian theorists call constructionist and essentialist, or what we popularly think of as a chosen versus fixed sexuality. In practice, educational projects combine essentialist and constructionist ideas and use both information-giving and attitude-change formats. My purpose here is to use these models to create conceptual categories that might help explain some of the contradictions in educational work. While these contradictions can't simply be overcome by designing educational projects that conform to pure categories, our use of these educational models could be more flexible and strategic.

Essentialists argue that individuals are born or early socialized to be homosexuals, due to biological, familial, or environmental factors over which the individual has no control. This is not simply a rehash of the nature-nurture controversy, nor do essentialists simply propose that biology is destiny. The underlying similarity in the various forms of essentialism is the arguement that homosexuality is "real" and can be compared across time and cultures. Differences in the way homosexuality is practiced and understood are variations on an essential trait of homosexuality.

Constructionists argue that individuals construct and are constructed within categories formed from material, social, and ideological conditions. Individuals have the ability to reform and alter social, cultural, and community formations in ways that alter social and self-perception. Constructionists recognize that an individual may or may not feel they can make changes in their sexuality and that gay people "feel" like they are different. Nevertheless, constructionists argue, same-sex relations are viewed through and arise from the existing or evolving social/symbolic categories. It simply does not "feel" the same to be a lesbian in San Francisco in 1985 and be a female husband in Nigeria in 1950. Participants in social structures of same-sex relations may not view their identity or social role as at all related to their same-sex sexual relations. It is only in the post-Victoria Euro-American culture that sexuality becomes the source of identity, and even in Euro-American culture, there are significant differences in how people understand their sexuality. In the U.S., gay liberationists view themselves as members of a minority; however, Scandanavian, Dutch, and British "gay liberationists" understand their "community" as an extended family, as a national interest group, or as a class, respectively.

Essentialist arguments see homosexuality as something which is real and based in some determinable factor. Constructionist arguments see gay and lesbian people as filling social categories that may feel natural, but are products of historical factors.

These different ideas about homosexuality create a lack of coherence in social attitudes about homosexuality, both in our audiences and among lesbians and gay men ourselves. Although there are predictable audience differences, there remain competing notions of health, homosexuality, and AIDS. Thus, while it is to our credit that most people now know AIDS is "caused" by a virus and cannot be acquired casually, the varieties of health and sexuality beliefs held by the persons possessing these "AIDS facts" render the effect of this knowledge quite unpredictable: they can logically deduce that the CIA invented HIV, that risk populations should be quarantined for the good of all, or that everyone should use condoms. For the purpose here of unravelling the conflicts in our own strategies, I will suggest that homophobia education generally emphasizes constructionist arguments: that we choose to be gay or lesbian, or at any rate, choose to come out, and we recognize ourselves through social and community processes, not through biological imprinting. Though we may say that our sexuality "feels different" or that we knew at a young age that "we were gay," we also emphasize the variety of lesbian and gay experience in a way that aims to de-essentialize homosexuality. We often deflect questions about "causes" of homosexuality by challenging the audience to explain what "causes" heterosexuality or by asking them to reflect on why it is important to them to identity such causes.

This difference in styles—homophobia education tending toward the constructionist, and AIDS education tending toward the essentialist— might not create a problem if homophobia and AIDS education never overlapped. But they do, especially as activists and public health officials—for different reasons—tried to break the association between homosexuality and AIDS.

5.7 Degaying AIDS: The Queer Paradigm

The mid-1980s saw a challenge to the insistent homosexualizing of AIDS: AIDS was "degayed" in the rhetorics employed in public, and homophobia was anxiously reproduced and dispersed by the increasing focus on anal sex. Fear of anal sex almost outstripped fear of "same" sex as U.S. society tried to rationalize away both these first "heterosexual" cases as caused by "anal intercourse." From popular women's magazines and male pornography to the *New York Times,* everyone wanted to talk about anal pleasures and paranoias. The old anxious linkage between male homosexuality and straight men's fears and fantasies of being made into a sexual object "come out" in rather transparent ways in AIDS discussions; anal sex as a symbol of homosexual desire becomes an obsessive topic of interest in discussions about safe sex. The conviction that anal sex is somehow at the root of AIDS enables heterosexuals to avoid thinking about making changes in their practice of vaginal intercourse. In addition, the insistence that AIDS is somehow a mark of perversion transforms infected persons into "queers," regardless of their exposure route, a phenomenon I have called the "queer paradigm."[14]

It is remarkable that the first cases labelled "heterosexual AIDS" were those in nice, middle-class people who adamantly denied any risk factor. In fact, there had long been heterosexuals with AIDS—Haitians, male and female drug injectors, blood product consumers—who could or did transmit HIV to their "opposite sex" partners. There were also bisexual men who transmitted HIV to their female partners, but these women did not count as heterosexuals because their infection was attributed to the "homosexuality" of their male partner. Transfusion recipients, who were represented in the press as aged and as having no sexual identity, although there were cases here of transmission to "opposite sex" sexual partners. And, there were, of course, children and adolescents who had been perinatally infected or infected through blood products, but since non-adults are represented as having no sexuality, these individuals were not counted as heterosexual (and certainly not as homosexual). None of these people were considered "real" heterosexuals (even if they were non-homosexuals); the illegal drug or unconventional sex behaviors of drug injectors and bisexual men, and social stereotypes which feminized men with hemophilia and desexualized anyone old enough to receive a transfusion during surgery already marked these people as sexually feminized, unmasculine, not fully heterosexual. These individuals' status as heterosexuals was insufficient to normalize their deviant behavior or socially marked relationship to a medical condition once they received an AIDS diagnosis: they became honorary queers.[15] In addition to whatever individual prejudices non-gay people with AIDS had, they were also subject to a backhanded homophobia due to their association with a disease apparently inextricably marked as "gay." From 1985 on there was concerted effort from several quarters to "degay" AIDS. People who were not gay recognized the importance of making people aware that there was risk through behaviors engaged in by people who did not identify as gay. The gay community helped degay AIDS in order to stem the tide of increased discrimination and violence resulting from the perception that all gay people (including lesbians) had AIDS. AIDS organizations also helped degay AIDS by asserting that their group served anyone with AIDS and were not "gay" political or social organizations.

The degaying of AIDS in 1985, while strategically important in separating gay-based discrimination and AIDS-based discrimination and in forcing public discussion of AIDS in general, only further complicated discussions of hetereosexuals with AIDS. An evolving set of terms were used to talk about HIV infection outside the gay male community: heterosexually acquired HIV (the best, but still problematic term, since it is intercourse, largely, which facilitates HIV transmission, and both anal and vaginal intercourse place the receptive partner at much high risk than the insertive partner), heterosexual AIDS (a totally inappropriate term implying that this is somehow a different syndrome than regular, that is, "gay" AIDS), and heterosexuals with AIDS or HIV (a term which is useful in discussing the problems affecting a class of people, but of no use in defining exposure route).

5.8 Anal Pleasure

Homophobia is a holograph of fears: fear of a different subculture, fear of forbidden male-male desires, and fear of anal penetration. Symbolically, AIDS has collapsed gay sexuality and straight sexual anxiety under the sign of anal sex. Somewhere deep in our representational scheme, the anus is constructed as the quintessential forbidden organ of male-male desire, calling into question the sexuality of straight afficionados of anal sex.[16] Strangely enough, although anal sex has surely been a pan-cultural, transhistoric form of sexual pleasure, the anus is not understood as a sexual organ,[17] although the vagina, another multipurpose orifice, is intrinsically sexual, at least from the vantage point of phallocentric culture. The anus's forbidden status both in Freudian auto-erotic terms and as a symbol of dirt combine with the anus's lack of gender reference. Thus, desires centering on the anus cannot infallibly be stabilized to produce "heterosexuality" and anal sex becomes a key site of (hetero)sexual danger through loss of gender reference. If a straight man wants to have anal sex with a women, or a woman wants a man to anally penetrate her, it calls into question the man's sexuality. If he can fuck a female asshole, what is to prevent him from fucking a male asshole? And if he fucks a male asshole, *that* man might also want to fuck him. In order to relieve this male anxiety, anal sex among heterosexuals must be explained away as a form of birth control, as an uncivilized "mistake" about where to put "it," or as a kinky pleasure engaged in only with "prostitutes." Forms of sex for which men pay are exempt from the queer paradigm; the act of payment carries such a connotation of heterosexual male power that it is sufficient to overshadow any other symbolic construction of the act bought.

The guilty pleasure of actual anal sex and the fears of homosexuality in unenacted anal desire confused AIDS researchers and confounded educational efforts. Rarely are gay men imagined to do anything *other* than anal sex; that a gay man is *not* infected is popularly viewed as a matter of luck, not as an indication that he engaged in little or no anal sex. Even in current epidemiology, gay men with multiple exposure routes (gay hemophiliacs, gay drug injectors, gay transfusion recipients) are counted as "gay" without regard to their particular sexual practices. The ideological association between AIDS and anal sex also creates paradoxes for heterosexuals: anal sex as birth control collides with vaginal sex as HIV control, an inaccurate, but widely believed "safe sex" notion among heterosexuals. But within the heterosexual logic, denial of anal desire constructs a double safety: they do not practice this risk behavior nor do they possess the queer desires that lead to it. Because AIDS discussions have focused attention on anal sex, heterosexuals seem more likely to frame their anxieties about sex in general as specific questions about HIV transmission, rather than directly confronting their own same-sex sexual desires, anal desires, or discomfort with the perceived demands of heterosexuality. Personal anxieties about lust for the guy in the locker room are displaced into questions about HIV transmission and anal sex.

5.9   AIDS, Sexuality, and Essentialism: "The Test"

Many of the conflicts in AIDS education result from the de-essentializing of homosexuality and the degaying of AIDS, which in itself essentializes AIDS. The existence and promotion of "The Test" mediates this contradiction and shores up societal belief that the reality of a virus produces a homogeneous experience.

We argue that homosexuality is fluid, socially constructed, historically contingent, but we say that AIDS and HIV antibody positivity are fixed, essential, objective. Because science can isolate a virus, AIDS and HIV are "real" states, not identities or roles to be negotiated. The antibody test is constructed as the moment of fixing the reality of AIDS for the individual: you either have "it" or you don't. The assumption that positivity or AIDS diagnosis have a set and common meaning distorts the immense variety of experiences of HIV and AIDS as physical and psychological health phenomena.

AIDS essentialism creates the person living with AIDS as a voiceless "victim." AIDS essentialism denies the power of individual and community attitudes to resist AIDS repression and to mediate our confrontation with pain and early death. The symbolic notions of health and sickness have everything to do with how the infected or diagnosed person understands him or herself, and how others understand her or him. Thus, while HIV is a "real" virus, and the symptoms of ARC or AIDS are painfully real, the way the experience of HIV infection is understood, symbolized, and policed is a social process of enormous importance.

The relationship between identity—especially gay and drug-subcultural identity—and HIV is highly unstable at present. For some people, HIV antibody positivity is another factor in their health and relationship decisions; for others, it is the focal lens through which all other experience is now understood. For people in the latter group who are already familiar with the "coming out" or "telling your story" models from gay liberation and Alcoholics/Narcotics Anonymous, respectively, HIV antibody positivity becomes a new and critical aspect of identity which is important to speak about publicly. The relative importance of HIV antibody positivity in relation to other aspects of identity or shared oppression varies within ethnic or sexual minority communities, and varies when HIV antibody-positive people organize as such and create their own group definitions, their own newsletters and books.

6

Power and the
Conditions of Silence

The linguistic turn in current critical practice has produced a crisis in what is often called identity politics—the mix of new left and minority analyses which characterize the organizing efforts of groups making claims for cultural autonomy and community self-determination. On the one hand, the foregrounding of cultural symbolic processes has aided in understanding why economic changes over the post-war decades failed to liberate ethnic minorities or women, or why class status has lost its power to insulate some gay men now that we are confronted with AIDS. But paradoxically, groups organizing around cultural practices are often viewed as not properly political. This may in part be due to the current trend in social philosophy toward a complex but ultimately liberalist hermeneutics; Richard Rorty, Thomas McCarthy, or, more complexly, Jean-Francois Lyotard, seem resigned to a kind of intellectual relativism grounded in an emotional foundationalism that perceives the world getting better through mutual understanding. This quest to "keep the conversation going" and the faith in the ability of discourse, as presently constructed through postmodern power relations (or perhaps, metaphors), seem prematurely and anxiously to foreclose as impossible a political practice based on deconstructive methods.

Deconstruction appeared initially to be an intriguing methodology with radical political potential. But increasingly it is charged with elitism, with eroding the basis for political judgment, and even, within academic research, of rendering critical inquiry too unstable to be emancipatory. The presumption that deconstruction's apparent skepticism cannot generate a political agenda despite the cultural activism of black British and Euro-American gay movements raises important questions about what— and whose—issues count as politics.[1]

What counts as properly political depends on assumptions about the relationship between power and the public grounded in the Enlightenment notion of the individual as unique agent with a will. Power is seen to exist in the play between the individual (or collections of individuals) and society; politics is defined as the activities of the individual in relation to society enacted in the social, i.e. public, sphere. That which is private is not political.

What is left out in this definition of politics is the relationship between power and language. Feminists and black and gay activists in particular have put tremendous energy into reconstituting native languages of sorts—women's discursive practices, camp, rap—and into criticizing the ways dominant language usages elide their voices and structure their experience. Each of these movements argues that people are oppressed by historical processes to which they are made to consent through identification with figures of power in the culture. The role of language and symbols is seen as crucial in a denial of identity that produces an inability among oppressed individuals to organize; at the same time, it is viewed as a key to the construction of identity and the formation of community that enables resistance. Thus, women's ways of talking, camp, and rap each function first as a closet code linking the members of the emerging community, then become a source of identity and expression within the ghetto culture. Race and sexuality function in structurally similar ways—both are cultural continua pressed into a socially constructed pair of opposites. In this context, the idea of passing (acquiring the signifiers of the normative category), of claiming "Black is beautiful" or "gay is good," and the increasing visibility of "racially mixed" persons and "bisexuals" constantly function to call into question the lines of demarcation between socially constructed opposites.

Feminism, by contrast, though also influenced by deconstructive analysis, functions with a pair of opposites rarely called into question; although Monique Wittig and French cultural activists reliant on her analysis propose to speak from a range of complex gender positions, most feminist work is designed to downplay the importance of the distinction between male and female, rather than proposing that there may be multiple genders.[2] The feminist concern with pornography, too, is a striking (and troubling) example of the conviction that texts—speech acts constitutive of social identity—can not only accompany and inspire acts of violence, but are in themselves discursive assaults on the self of subordinate persons. The Dworkin/MacKinnon ordinance, though not yet enacted into law, attempts *not* to censor—though this would undoubtedly be the way it would be used—but to create a torts structure where people harmed by the text (pornography) could engage in legal speech in the public arena of the courtroom in order to obtain a remedy. Under the proposed terms of the ordinance, a claimant would be required to demonstrate the influence of a particular text read by or used in the course of an assault by the perpetrator, even if the text is carried only in the imagination. The perpetrator of a crime which imitated or referred to that particular text, or even simply evidenced that she or he had internalized the patriar-chal sex structuring of the text, would meet the criteria of the ordinance. Exactly how such linkages would be made in court is not explained.[3] What *is* clear is that, like the proposed national hate crimes bill (which would require reporting of crimes in which physical and verbal assault was based on race, ethnicity, gender, religion, or sexuality), the Dworkin/ MacKinnon ordinance attempts to place the words people say and even the semiotics of their acts within the purview of the judiciary. While such a listing has short-term utility in enabling minority groups to document their oppression in terms defined by legislators, the law fundamentally conflates status issues (the "being" of blackness, femaleness, Jewishness, gayness) with the cultural ideologies which make violence against a range of "Others" justifiable through a variety of complex logics.

There is clearly an inchoate recognition in both these cases, not only that reality is socially constructed, but that texts and their symbolic links to socially repressive institutions are uniquely powerful. The harms al-leged to arise from the social power of texts include the following: physi-cal violence, the restriction of access to jobs, to health care, to housing, to transportation, and/or to security. Each of these is articulated as a "civil right" only in societies that construct power as a relation among individuals, administered by the summation of individuals called the state. These harms come to be of public, political concern in the context of the belief that individuals have identities that fall into coherent pat-terns. An attack on "one" becomes a symbolic threat to all others in that identity group. This is the basis of calls for legal intervention, but what is ignored here is the way in which the law as public discourse organizes repressive institutions which actually incite, define, and legitimate hate/ identity-based violence. Where identity categories are obvious (black, female) or presumed (gay), laws in fact create patterned social control over the subordinate group, through such practices as selective enforce-ment (the prosecution of assault by blacks on whites, but not whites on blacks; the prosecution of sex workers, but not pimps; charges of libel, but not prosecution of racist name-calling), or the mitigation of criminal charges according to the type of person assaulted (largely un- or under-prosecuted are wife battering, gay- or black-bashing, and rape).

When the marginalized confront these strange rules of social control, what they come to see in themselves is identity. What appears initially as random or individualized attack is eventually perceived as systematic repression based on a core element common to a class of persons. Thus, in the course of the 1960s, groups whose culture had been systematically denied found words to speak of their experience; they went beyond their closet languages, their rap, their camp, their female vernacular, and constituted themselves within the body politic as rich, culturally coherent subgroups. Yet, once they emerged in identifiable collectives to confront hidden, systematized repression they became subject to the overt systematic controls associated with colonial administration—police raids on community meeting places, arson, bashing. Identity politics are a resistance to and at the same time a reinstatement of the underground side of a public politics grounded in the threat of sheer coercion.

Conceptions of identity and its relation to the social (and therefore the political) are not uncontested, however. For example, the argument over whether the 1985 riot at the University of Massachusetts was "racial" or just happened to be between blacks and whites is symptomatic of attempts, on the one hand to recognize the power of identity representations, and on the other, to retreat to the idea that violence is essentially not differentiated or mediated by patterned codes of dominance and submission.[4] When the attempt in identity politics to achieve a cultural space for "minorities" loses sight of institutionalized oppression, the ability to situate the responsibility for terrorist tactics is in jeopardy. The right-wing rhetoric of terrorism asserts that violence is undifferentiated, and attributes that violence to particular individuals: the terrorist, the black radical, the communist fringe. The left, by contrast, has yet to develop a suitably compelling rhetoric of the subtle, highly mobile, and sophisticated repression that is the lived experience of daily terror for the marginalized.

6.1 Power: Two Competing Metaphors

In theorizing power, two competing metaphors emerge. The hegemonic representation is one of power as a contained unit, with simple arithmetic properties. In this conception, the rhetoric of power includes game metaphors, with nations, interest groups, or individuals seen as competitors or teams.

Unitary power is managed publicly as the game of politics, but it is administered privately through discursive control over the construction of identities. The identity politics of minority groups is an attempt to gain access to power outside the public arena (i.e., in private, in *culture*), not only by articulating the "authentic" subjective experience of oppression—by "speaking out," "coming out," "telling it like it is"—but also by using the community constructed on that identity as a base of block power.

Deconstructive critics have, however, suggested that the initially constructionist impulse behind identity politics has collapsed into a new essentialism, albeit one constructed on the margins of the unitary power discourse. In the U.S., that problem arose as the cultural formations of identity politics came to be used as platforms for vote-based minority organizing. On the one hand, the formation of vote-based constituencies tends to essentialize material difference in its requirements for membership (men can't be feminist, nor whites a real part of black politics); on the other hand, and simultaneously, socially constructed expressions of resistance (effeminacy or negritude, for example) come to be equated with transcendent subjectivities. The balance is not to be found in moderating tactics, but in understanding the interplay between one form of resistance and the changing formation of identity.[5] The Rainbow Coalition has had some success in welding together identity politics groups in a bid for electoral-level block power; yet this politics had to be articulated on a platform of "economic justice," suppressing marginal individual identities in order to be visible as a public political force.

By contrast, the deconstructionist conception is of power as network, a multiplicity of practices at play on intersecting and disjunctive sites. This notion of power suggests a political praxis of insistent de-essentializing, most often through "cultural politics" or artistic interventions. A politics of this kind attempts to deconstruct current discursive practices by signaling their complicity in covering up the more subtle aspects of the play of power, and by suggesting points of resistance. In practice, this involves not speaking from any particular place, or speaking from shifting subject positions in order to make apparent who is subjected to repressive practices and where the reader sits in relation to those systems of power. Though these critiques cannot cancel out the effects of power in unitary forms, they can de-essentialize power metaphorized as epistemological center, thereby opening up space for marginalized voices and subversive, local practices of resistance.

It is important to recognize unitary power and network power as coexisting metaphors, each generated by and appropriate to the critique of particular kinds of control. The representation of crude violence as an effect of military power is compelling and probably we *do* want to intervene most immediately and most overtly here. But the confrontation of violence with violence results in subtler, subterranean forms of control, pogroms of a highly administrative sort, and it is equally critical to understand power in this "network" form. Foregrounding power as unitary and public defers grappling with power in its fluid, administrative form. Our conception of these forms in terms of a hierarchy of political business (the unintended effect of documenting "hate crimes" as forms of violence will be that only the kinds of "crimes" already accepted as such will be monitored: militaristic rather than insidious psychological ones), one important and real, the other trivial and changeable, serves the interests of those who have a better language of coercion, well-established rhetorics, or open violence. Military dictators and our own far right have much to gain from a politics which collapses the subtleties of cultural resistance into claims for unitary power, and their own rhetoric of shrill feminists, germ-dribbling homosexuals, and psychotic blacks fundamentally undermines the attempts of these cultural groups to speak into the public power discourses. The right defines acts of cultural resistance as assault: women demanding unisex bathrooms, queers committing murder by sneezing, black music tearing at the fabric of Western culture. Within this discourse, there is no space for cultural difference.

But to understand unitary and network power as opposite, exclusive, or even exhaustive metaphors (as they seem to be understood in debates over the viability of deconstruction) is to miss the force of resistance that arises in the interplay between these fields. Increasingly, non-deconstructionist philosophers summarize the deconstructionist argument as "power is universal." This is to mistake metaphors which seek to describe the structured interplay of force and power, as representations of an essential thing in itself. In the postmodern period, a great deal hangs on the rhetorics deployed in the service of social control. "Power" is the grounding metaphor, along with notions of the "self," by which people negotiate their resistance and their politics. The political and cultural resistances which have surfaced around the AIDS epidemic provide a rich field for understanding the relationship between unitary and network power, and the explosions of other forms of power that are ultimately suppressed for want of a viable, culturally understandable rhetoric. Although many on the left would now agree that less unitary understandings of power are more "radical," even this discourse obscures voices from outside the discursive spaces we currently recognize. It is these voices I will be exploring in the rest of this chapter.

6.2 "Silence = Death."

No gay person needed to have explained the meaning of this stark black poster with an inverted pink triangle and white lettering,[6] which first appeared on Manhattan walls in 1986.[7] It was war zone graffiti, produced as a slick, tasteful poster warning anyone in a position to understand that this was our war. The poster needed no attribution: we needed no author for this message. The poster spoke an international, closeted language. It was multivocal and polysemic, but also anonymous and with a *single,* urgent meaning: this was a rallying cry to no place in particular—no march, no meeting, no group. A notice to a community of camouflaged guerrillas that "AIDS"—as a contemporaneous stencil graffito said—"is not over."

This was a strange war: literally and metaphorically, the battlefield was our bodies. Our armies were the lingering bits of an immune system we could not see and a splintered community that was difficult to locate. We needed the doctors' tests to tell us if we were winning or dying. Hidden antibodies lived in hidden bodies. Dysfunctional antibodies in functional anti/bodies.[8]

This closet war exploded into the popular imagination in 1985 through the body of Rock Hudson, beautiful Rock Hudson, public figure disfigured publicly. The "before and after" pictures of the gaunt or kaposi's-sarcoma-covered person with AIDS[9] became *de rigueur* and continuous across scientific and journalistic AIDS discourses.[10] AIDS marked bodies already marked out by medical and popular discourse. The pretty-faced homosexual, the ritually scarified African, the needle-tracked drug user—bodies "naturally" marked different were now branded unnatural through the somatic revelations of AIDS symptomatology.

Rock Hudson had always performed a dangerous tightrope act between the public and the private. Now this hidden life was revealed through a hidden virus. Rock Hudson epitomized the fear of fluid sexuality which epidemiological risk categories were supposed to shore up. Rock Hudson, the closet gay/screen heterosexual personified the fearful paradox: AIDS was a gay disease and anyone could get AIDS. Neatly sidestepping the obvious conclusion that anyone might be gay (or bisexual), Rock Hudson's death proved what everyone knew; despite *public* hysteria about casual contagion, "getting AIDS" required a private act, required "taking it," required feminization.

Rock Hudson was queer and he had to die. His death prompted the heterosexual AIDS panic: the screen idol had become a screen for the hidden homosexual desires of American males.

Silence = Death

When I first saw this poster I believed it said "Science = Death." I had no doubt that this was what I had read. When the poster became a button, a T-shirt, the key symbol of the anarchic resistance to a pogrom masquerading as a disease, I was sure that the slogan had been changed. It was only when I went back to Manhattan that I saw I had misread the original poster, now tattered and nearly lost under layers of newer posters. But the dyad silence/science was no mistake. Straight people find this slip funny. Gay people do not. Silence/science has dogged our very existence—once the closet, now media blackouts; once psychiatry, now internal medicine. The twin threats are oblivion and diagnosis.

And it is no surprise to any gay person that death holds down the center around which the sliding signifiers of AIDS discourse swirl; for centuries in the West, death has been held out as the penalty for homosexual acts. All of the discourse of AIDS has encoded the homosexual Other. Even HIV has been swept into homosexual coding; in a *New York Times* article a top U.S. researcher explained that HIV is not contagious because it is a "wimpy virus." In fact, no event in the AIDS crisis has been a surprise—not the relentless deaths, not the years of invisibility, not the sudden and promiscuous speaking about AIDS once sexual anxiety could be repressed and rearticulated as "public health."

But who decides what is public?

Paradoxically, the privacy of HIV antibody test results is not protected by law; instead, the status itself defines "the public." If you test negative, your test result is private, unreported, nobody cares (except you and your loved ones). If you "are" positive this information is public, scrutiny of your acts comes under state policing, and you are legally accountable for engaging in sex acts which, if performed by a person who tests negative would in no sense render her/him legally liable.[11]

Who decides who has health?

It is a devastating historical accident that HIV was first noticed among well-cared-for gay men; AIDS, a diagnosis of early death in the previously healthy, could only be recognized in a group on the verge of achieving the social status of "healthy." AIDS went unrecognized in the late 1970s in the "junky pneumonia" epidemic in New York City; no one was surprised that junkies were dying, no one took much notice. But AIDS could not occur in people whose ill health was already manifest: AIDS needed the implication of willful degradation to make possible the assignment of social blame and to allow the disease to go unchecked as if it were a divine, and therefore, supernatural happening. Despite the official definition of AIDS as the occurrence of certain opportunistic infections in a "previously healthy person," anyone who "gets AIDS" relinquishes any claim to prior healthiness, prior normality. Thus AIDS diagnosis increasingly qualifies as grounds for non-payment under "pre-existing condition" (homosexuality? HIV infection?) clauses in health insurance policies.

Public speech has always been terrifying for homosexuals; the speech which has often removed us from oblivion has been returned to us as diagnostic matter. Now the HIV antibody test provides a new coercive technology of confession. If we could once refuse to speak of our desires—at whatever cost to our psychic well-being—we cannot refuse our blood. The AIDS diagnosis, represented between the poles of somatic marking (kaposi's sarcoma) and disappearance (wasting syndrome), is the ultimate state takeover of homosexuals' inability to speak and to retain the protective camouflage of silence. Our bodies will give us away.

The narrative of AIDS overdetermines the virus, HIV. The narrative, AIDS, needed HIV and its test—HIV does not exist *outside* the test—in order to legitimate the social repression occurring through AIDS as a medical rather than political phenomenon. AIDS had first and everywhere to ground the discourse of science by constraining the public speech and scrutinizing the private acts of people subject to HIV.

AIDS precedes HIV. The system was already in place which held deviance in check through managed ill health: surveillance, but not prevention, of sexually transmitted diseases or unsterile needle use. The conditions for covert transmission were created in a system which forced drugs and sex underground. At the same time methods to identify and register those likely to be deviant were built into the record-keeping of VD and methadone clinics, in contact-tracing laws, in the ghettoization of marginal people and their localized state-run care facilities. Only when the conditions for transmission and identification were in place could HIV produce its epidemic AIDS. The virus must spread unseen until it can be publicly counted. Nowhere in the plan of international public health officials is the desire articulated to prevent the continuing march of the AIDS epidemic, only to sculpt its path and cover over the system's complicity with death.

. Silence: the never spoken, the yet to set itself into language, the unique, the individual, madness, the unrepresentable, the space of that which is not to be represented, the closet.

Silence: the unspeakable, the perceived but best not said, the ignored, the space occupied by that which is ignored, the hidden, the safely tucked away, the camouflaged, the safety of camouflage.

Every gay person can perform this deconstruction—it is written on our bodies. Indeed, as Eve Kosofsky Sedgwick's *The Epistemology of the Closet* suggests, every person oppressed under a metaphorized "identity" which both inscribes and regulates the "self" understands the fragile safety of invisibility. Identity is visibility, a textual production, the condition of both community and annihilation. The closet and its occupant the homosexual are merely a trope of the administrative state, the product of a convenient repressive ideology with a mobile class of bodies which can readily, easily, and publicly be humiliated, taunted, beaten, arrested, electro-shocked, driven to madness, murdered, made into the spectacle of AIDS.

Science: rationality, objectivity, certainty, above politics, the expert, the panoptic gaze microscopized.

Science: savior, transcendent language, the rules of the game, the game itself, the witness to life, the categorizing of differences.

Every gay person can also tell you this: our bodies are written by science. From at least the mid-nineteenth century we were scrutinized for visible difference—first our genitals, then our desires, our hormones, our genes, our perceptual apparatus, our moral capacity. This series of scientific moves always occurred in tandem with the elusive search for the essential quality of the "female." Homosexuality (and femaleness) stabilized the edge of an unstable heterosexuality, masculinity. Male homosexuality *preceded* heterosexuality (literally, in medical terminology, homosexuality arises first in the nineteenth century)[12] and was incorporated and contained so as to define and stabilize masculinity. Female "inversion" still threatens to destabilize masculinity, as the recent increases in murders of lesbians suggest.[13]

Can these homosexual bodies speak out of their silence and into the discourse of science? Can we speak about our experience of AIDS?

Speaking into scientific discourse, the person living with AIDS—especially the homosexual—produces an illusion of confession, a public representation of hidden desires. The HIV antibody test in particular speaks for the homosexual body, and the person with AIDS speaks for the virus, becomes the talking virus. Science asserts its certainty with the test, but the test after all relies on confession for interpretation. According to government guidelines, the test counselor is first to determine, through subtle questioning, whether the person is at high or low risk for exposure. If the person is perceived as "high risk," a positive result goes unchallenged. If the person is believed to be "low risk," the positive result is said to be a potential false positive.[14]

In the first few years of the epidemic before the representation of Rock Hudson as a person with AIDS (though Hudson himself never spoke publicly of his illness), people living with AIDS spoke often and well into the black hole created by the refusal of the mainstream press to report on the epidemic. Science needed the speech of people with AIDS and their friends in order to unlock the "mystery" of AIDS—a Nobel-prize winning task. Many men (and some women) willingly gave evidence of their illness and of their lives, describing symptoms and answering long epidemiological questionnaires about the intimate details of rich and complex sex lives. But once science had its information it could no longer tolerate the speech of people living with AIDS. People living with AIDS wanted some information back: When would a cure come? What would the treatment be? What would it cost? But once the disease had been wrested out of the discourse of people living with AIDS, once HIV was discovered and could be made to perform in the laboratory without homosexual bodies,[15] science no longer wanted to hear that discourse.

But people living wih AIDS would not stay quiet for long. Their discourse shifted to a critique of the oppression of early death and unnecessary infections resulting from treatments delayed and education denied. Then the media stepped in to coopt the new discourse by transforming the lived experience of people with AIDS and their friends into human interest stories which performed the pathetic absolution necessary to a society complicit in wholesale slaughter (and that performance is not unique to AIDS). The valiant victim and the selfless volunteer were lauded in the media. But the person with AIDS died neverthe-less, and this too was necessary; people with AIDS must in the end always be silenced, their words given over to an expiating hermeneutic.

They were all queers, outcasts, and they would not shut up, so they had to die.

But AIDS activists relentlessly pursued their speech. They confronted the paradox that while silence equals death, public speech—speech seek-ing remedy from repression—is impossible for those most harshly af-fected by AIDS precisely because of the systems of information control and the politics of scientific knowledge. Their words are only allowed as data, pathos, selfish complaints, politicizing demands for civil rights, and at the alleged expense of public safety. This was a situation in which any kind of speech recognizable as operating within the discourses of unitary or of network power was captured by science, the media, the politicians. The only remaining form of speaking was that which fell between the legitimated discourses, something approaching the discourse of art, but an art of the body in resistance.

Science, or rather, the governance of the political by scientific dis-course, equals death for people living with HIV. Silence, or rather, educators' failure to speak for fear of inciting the body to acts of pleasure that are now defined as "risks," prevents specific classes of people from obtaining information—about safe sex and needle hygiene—that will save their lives. And this can only be described as death by disinformation.

** ** ** ** ** ** ** **

The AIDS narrative exists as a technology of social repression; it is a representation that attempts to silence not only the claims of identity politics, but the people marginalized by AIDS. AIDS activists know that silence equals death, but we also know that this cannot be *said*, it must be *performed* in an anarchistic politics that sometimes coincides with and supports the political action of our allies working within the unitary power system, but sometimes contradicts it, or seems simply mad in the traditional public realm. The insight that "silence equals death" has spawned an international agitprop activism that circulates around the meanings elided in the legitimated discourses of science, media, public politics.[16] Not candlelight marches of commemoration and pathos—though we attend these, too—but throwing our blood at insurance com-panies, setting up illegal AIDS drug counters in front of the Federal Drug Administration, holding die-ins at hospitals and drug companies. There is no logical relationship between these events and the actions of the FDA, hospitals, and drug companies in changing some of their policies. But they do change their policies, and not only to shut up the militants and suppress their messy performances. Somewhere in the fissures of scientific discourse are lodged the elided meanings of, can we say it? justice? humanity? Somewhere in their practices the administrators see that silence equals death, and that they are the cool, if uneasy executors of the discursive death squad.

Notes

Acknowledgments

1. His gay liberation imbued collection of poems, *These Waves of Dying Friends*, New York City: Contact II Publications, 1989, is, for me, the most resonant artistic contribution to creating a public history of epidemic.

Chapter 1

1. The statement of purpose of the National Coalition of Black Lesbians and Gays (NCBLG) reads as follows: "As a national organization, we are committed to building solidarity between Black Lesbians and Gays, Transpersons, and with our heterosexual Sisters and Brothers, with the understanding that an end to the oppression of Black people requires the full participation, dedication, and commitment of us all." See especially "Homecoming" in the 10th anniversary edition of NCBLG periodical *Black/Out*, II:1, Fall 1986.

2. There was extensive fiction and non-fiction written by gay people of color, especially lesbians, in the early 1980s describing the difficulties of living between two communities. Along with local groups of lesbian and gay people of color, the National Coalition of Black Lesbians and Gays (formed in 1978) has actively critiqued existing gay groups, worked within communities of color to raise awareness of their longstanding membership, and pursued an autonomous political agenda which has been particularly evidenced by a range of publishing endeavors, including Kitchen Table Press (women of color), the Other Countries writing collective (gay/bisexual men), and *Black/Out*. See especially Alma Gomez, Cherrie Moraga, Mariana Romo-Carmona, eds., *Cuendos: Stories by Latinas*, Latham, NY: Kitchen Table Press, 1983; Aurora Levins Morales and Rosario Morales, *Getting Home Alive*, Ithaca: Firebrand Books, 1986; Dirg Aaab-Richard et al., *Tongues Alive*, London: Gay Men's Press, 1987; Joseph Beam ed., *In the Life: A Black Gay Anthology*, Boston: Alyson, 1986; Gloria Anzaldua, *Borderlands/La Frontera: The New Mestiza*, SF: Spinsters/Aunt Lute, 1987; Cherrie Moraga and Gloria Anzaldua, eds., *This Bridge Called my Back: Writings by Radical Women of Color*, Latham, NY: Kitchen Table Press, 1981; Barbara Smith, ed. *Home Girls: A Black Feminist Anthology*, Latham, NY: Kitchen Table Press, 1983.

3. Bell Hooks, "Homophobia in Black Communities," in *Talking Back: Thinking Feminist, Thinking Black*, Boston: South End Press, 1989, pp. 120–126. See also Cindy Patton, "The International Gay Movement," *Zeta Magazine*, October 1988, pp. 100–104; Judy Grahn, *Another Mother Tongue: Gay Words, Gay Worlds*, Boston: Beacon Press,

1984; Paula Gunn Allen, "Lesbians in American Indian Cultures," and Lourdes Arguelles and B. Ruby Rich, "Understanding the Cuban Lesbian and Gay Male Experience," in *Hidden From History*, ed. Martin Bauml Duberman, Martha Vicinus, and George Chauncey, Jr., New York: New America Library, 1989; Walter L. Williams, *The Spirit and the Flesh: Sexual Diversity in American Indian Culture*, Boston: Beacon Press, 1986.

4. In several cities—Washington D.C., Atlanta, Los Angeles—there are sizable and often autonomous African American or Latin gay communities with highly articulated economic infrastructures and public social venues. In other cities, there are smaller subgroups or networks of gay people of color who socialize and discuss political issues in fraternal or sororal groups, through the church, the workplace, or other cultural institutions which exist within the communities of color but are not specifically identified as gay or lesbian. However, the publicly identified gay movement—both in terms of the movement's leadership and especially in terms of the media representation—is visibly white. When gay people of color are represented, they are generally shown as advocates for the special issues of gay people of color and not as leaders of the movement as a whole. This is symptomatic of the problem of accessing political power through the "minority" framework at this time in the U.S.: public political power is read through a primary allegiance and "differences" are considered secondary, part of the internal agonistics of party-building. The innovation of the Rainbow Coalition was to unite identity, class, and issue-focused groups into a third-party voting block with a coherent new left agenda. Typically, the Rainbow Coalition pushed candidates at the level of Democratic party primaries, and then negotiated more progressive platforms in the final elections.

5. Dennis Altman, *The Homosexualization of America*, New York: St. Martin's Press, 1982. Dennis Altman, "AIDS and the Reconceptualization of Homosexuality," *Homosexuality, Which Homosexuality?*, Amsterdam: Uitgeverij An Kekker/Schorer, 1989, pp. 35–48. Barry Adam, *The Rise of a Lesbian and Gay Movement*, Boston: Twayne, 1987.

6. In safe sex education, there have been interesting debates about the importance of embracing some kind of identity with respect to sexual practice. Studies in Australia and a multi-city study in the U.S. suggest that it is indeed the relationship to an organized gay community which allows the maintenance of safe sex behavior. It is difficult to determine whether this is a product of information flows or whether it reflects the dynamic group process of community norm formation and mutual support for changes. Further, neither study analyzes the role of communities of color in enabling normative shifts for members occupying homosexual social roles, but not identifying with a sexual community. That is, there have been identified a number of social roles which would generally be occupied by homosexuals in a wide range of cultures, although members might not circulate in any large gay community. This would include religious leaders in both African American and Afro-Brazilian culture, to mention only two. Safe sex organizing work among these men must relate to their allegiance to their cultural community rather than a potential sexual community, as their homosexuality is defined in the context of their social role in the African American or Afro-Brazilian community. In fact, an organizing project among Afro-Brazilian priests in Sao Paulo has been undertaken and appears to be very successful in changing sexual practices in the context of support of the religious sect. This suggests, then, that pursuing behavior change might work best if community or micro-group norms can be addressed and if it is recognized that male-male sexual practices always have some larger social significance, even if it is not articulated in sexual terms comparable to those in contemporary Anglo-European gay communi-

ties. See also Bell Hooks, op.cit.; Gary Dowsett, Macquarie University AIDS Research Project, presented October 1989, Second International Symposium on AIDS Information and Education, Yaounde, Cameroon; Gill Shepard, "Rank, Gender and Homosexuality: Mombasa as a Key to Understanding Sexual Options," in *The Cultural Construction of Sexuality*, ed. Pat Caplan, New York: Tavistock, 1987.

7. For a recent critique of this legacy and some reflections on conflicts between the new social movements and post-Marxist French theory and praxis, see Cornel West, *The American Evasion of Philosophy: A Genealogy of Pragmatism*, Madison: University of Wisconsin Press, 1989.

8. For a case study of the emergence of a specific institution, the AIDS Action Committee of Boston, see Larry Kessler, Ann M. Silvia, David Aronstein, and Cynthia Patton, "Call to Action: A Community Responds," in the *The New England Journal of Public Policy*, Winter/Spring 1988, IV:1, pp. 441–453.

9. In Europe and Africa, community organizing centered around HIV infection: where the U.S. first developed PLWA groups, Europeans and Africans first developed "body positive" groups. This is in part because the U.S. had a high density of AIDS cases before a virus was identified and testing was widely in use. In addition, however, private insurance systems tend toward diagnostic categories that correspond to the intensity of services. This has kept the U.S. focused on AIDS rather than shifting toward an HIV-spectrum definition.

    "Body positive" organizing in the U.S. emerged after and in relation to the organizing in Europe. The U.S. organizing assumed that HIV-Ab+ (antibody positive) people have different issues than PLWAs, and for the most part, members feel that their issues are not dealt with by PLWA groups. This unconsciously constructs PLWAs as having a *terminal* illness and inscribes the AIDS diagnosis as the line crossed on the way to the place of medical Other. Body Positive groups are more oriented toward early treatment and social adjustment to the indefinite health status of seropositivity.

    By contrast, the European people with HIV organizing views asymptomatic antibody positives and PLWAs as having roughly similar issues, a position which unconsciously constructs HIV antibody positivity as a kind of diagnosis. The fact that most European countries have some form of socialized medicine means that diagnoses have fewer dispersed negative effects; however, the nearly complete coinscription of public health policing and service delivery under socialized medicine means that all HIV-Ab+ people are susceptible to blanket state decisions—for example, quarantine is effectively easier under socialized medicine and there are fewer medical alternatives and resistances available if the state limits care.

    Interestingly, the "body positive" groups in the U.S., unlike those in Europe, tend to be very locally oriented. Only the PLWA movement has organized in the U.S. on the national level. Finally, HIV-Ab+ groups, especially in the U.S., tend to become fragmented by demographic groups, except in very small towns. In this sense, the issues of HIV-Ab+ people *become* different from those of PLWAs insofar as AIDS is viewed as a "leveler" of difference. This tendency toward differentiation of concerns stems from the dramatic differences in how women, people of color, drug users, hemophiliacs, and gay men discover their antibody status.

10. PWAs at the 1983 lesbian and gay health conference held in Denver issued the "Denver Principles," the "founding statement" of people with AIDS/ARC movement. In extract, the statement reads: "We condemn attempts to label us as 'victims,' which implies defeat, and we are only occasionally 'patients,' which implies passivity, helplessness, and dependence upon the care of others. We are 'people with AIDS.'

... We recommend that health care professionals ... always clearly identify and discuss the theory they favor as to the cause of AIDS, since this bias affects the treatment and advice they give.... We recommend that people with AIDS ... *form* caucuses to choose their own representatives, to deal with the media, to choose their own agenda, and to plan their own strategies. ... People with AIDS have the right ... to die and to *live* in dignity." *Surviving and Thriving with AIDS: Collected Wisdom, Volume II,* ed. Michael Callen, New York: People With AIDS Coalition, 1988, pp. 294–295.

11. Harlon L. Dalton, "AIDS in Blackface," *Daedalus 118,* summer 1989, pp. 205–227; Ronald Braithwaite and Ngina Lythocott, "Community Empowerment as a Strategy for Health Promotion for Black and other Minority Populations," *JAMA,* 261:2, 13 January 1989; Melvin Delgado and Denise Humm-Delgado, "Natural Support Systems: Source of Strength in Hispanic Communities," *Social Work,* 27, pp. 83–89, January 1982.

12. Nick Freudenberg, "Social and Political Obstacles to AIDS Education," *Siecus Report* 17:6, August/September 1989. Nicholas Freudenberg, Jacalyn Lee, and Diana Silver, "How Black and Latino Community Organizations Respond to the AIDS Epidemic: A Case Study in One New York City Neighborhood," *AIDS,* 1:1, Spring 1989.

13. *Narcotics Anonymous,* Van Nuys, CA: World Service Office. See especially chapter four, "How it works," pp. 15–22: "1. We admitted that we were powerless over our addiction, that our lives had become unmanageable ... When we admit our powerlessness and the inability to manage our own lives, we open the door to recovery... Our inability to control our usage of drugs is a symptom of the disease of addiction. We are powerless not only over drugs, but our addiction as well. We need to admit this in order to recover. Addiction is a physical, mental and spiritual disorder, affecting every area of our lives ... 2. We came to believe that a Power greater than ourselves could restore us to sanity ... The First Step has left a vacuum in our lives. We need to find something to fill that void. This is the purpose of the Second Step... We have a disease: progressive, incurable, fatal. ... At some point we realized we needed the help of some Power greater than our addiction. Our understanding of a Higher Power is up to us. No one is going to decide for us. We can call it the group, the program, or we can call it God. The only suggested guidelines are that this Power be loving, caring and greater than ourselves."

14. On the social construction of "addiction" see David T. Courtwright, *Dark Paradise: Opiate Addiction in America before 1940,* Cambridge: Harvard Univ. Press, 1982, especially chapter 5, "The Transformation of the Opiate Addict."

15. This term was settled on by 1989, and is used internationally to distinguish non-government groups focused solely on AIDS from other non-government organizations (the Red Cross, International Federation of Planned Parenthood, etc.) who are also working on AIDS issues. Once again the term articulates a tension between an exclusive AIDS-focus and an add-on approach to AIDS work.

16. The AIDS Action Committee in Boston probably perfected this idea, organizing the multi-community walking event "For All Walks of Life," which in 1989 netted just over $1.5 million, about half of which went to three national groups, including the National Association of People with AIDS (NAPWA) and the National AIDS Network (NAN, which provides technical assistance to AIDS groups), and to two dozen small community groups which were chosen from project proposals. These included Fenway Community Health Center (one of the major HIV clinics in Boston), AIDS Project Worcester, Latino Health Network, Haitian Multiservice Center, Roxbury

Comprehensive Clinic, and Mattapan Family Center. In addition, FAWOL served as an important media event in legitmating AIDS volunteerism and promoting social compassion for people living with AIDS. There were 8,400 registered walkers and at least another 1,500 unregistered walkers. About half the walkers were women. Several major corporations sponsored walk contingents and paid for parts of the day-long event, including the Bank of Boston, the Bank of New England, the Lotus Corporation (which was the first and only sponsor in the walk's initial year), the Digital Equipment Corporation (which raised the most money of any single corporation); many smaller corporations encouraged their workers to participate.

17. Mary Douglas, *How Institutions Think*, Syracuse: Syracuse University Press, 1986.

18. Phillip M. Kayal, "Doing Good, Doing 'Dirty Work': The AIDS Volunteer," presented at the Annual Convention of the Eastern Sociological Society, Boston, 1 May 1987. This is a survey study of Gay Men's Health Crisis (New York City) volunteers. When asked if their motives were political or altruistic, respondents said "altruistic." However, more extensive questioning showed that respondents pursued work not for some greater abstract good, but because they saw a direct relationship between their volunteer work and community-building work toward the political goals of the gay movement, and because they felt less hopeless and more personally engaged through their work. Thus, far from the right wing ideological use of altruism as unself-interested "good work" for some abstract higher purpose (God, spirituality, "helping others," etc.), respondents showed concrete political and self-interested reasons for their involvement. This suggests that there is at least a latent "political consciousness" or "minority identification" among many ASO volunteers which may be at odds with the media representations of AIDS volunteers.

19. The idea of "thought style" derives from Ludwig Fleck, who may have been influenced by the German language work of sociologist Karl Mannheim. Fleck was a research scientist who, in the 1930s, wrote a sociology of scientific knowledge and proposed a novel way of understanding the relation between the spheres of the expert and of popular knowledges, between what he calls exoteric and esoteric knowledges. Fleck's line of analysis was not further developed until the 1960s, because he was encamped by the Nazis, and because his style of writing falls outside that of most sociology of science. The publication in 1978 of an English version of his sole sociological work—*The Genesis and Development of a Scientific Fact* (his voluminous additional work includes laboratory technology and testing monographs and several textbooks) has sparked an interest in his schema from anthropologist Mary Douglas and renewed interest in his work among historians of science. I owe my own discovery of the book to Meurig Horton, and the development of our mutual conceptualization of AIDS discourse in Fleckian terms to many hours of conversations with Mr. Horton and several other British collegues for whom Fleck's work seemed to hold a vital key to understanding AIDS research paradigms. While I cannot pretend to have more than a rudimentary knowledge of debates within the history and philosophy of science, I can say that the parallels between the Jewish Fleck's grappling with syphilis ideologies in the years preceeding Hitler's accession—during which syphilis became a linchpin in the Nazi medical imagination—are chillingly like the attempts of AIDS activists to reconstruct medical ethics and research paradigms today. Chapter Three expands the Fleckian analysis to HIV research.

20. For a discussion of the forces in play in the first four years of the epidemic, see Dennis Altman, *AIDS in the Mind of America*, NY: Doubleday, 1986 and Cindy Patton *Sex and Germs: The Politics of AIDS*, Boston: South End Press, 1985. Both relate the initial organizing efforts to the historical formations of the gay communities in New

York and San Francisco (Altman) and Boston (Patton). Randy Shilts' controversial *And the Band Played On*, NY: St. Martin's Press, 1987, covering the same timeframe, presents a very different view of the early years in New York and San Francisco. Shilts' book is typical of the genre of journalistic "you were there" histories which take considerable historical licence while simulating authenticity through narrative devices like direct reporting of conversations which could not possible have been recorded or remembered with such precision and detailed descriptions of scenes at which the author could not have been present. Shilts at once distances his authorial voice from his actual involvement in many of the events and insists in the accuracy of his view. Shilts' view of this timeframe is at odds with Altman's and my own precisely because Shilts ignores the structural and historical features of gay community formation. Shilts treats the evolving epidemic and its social formations as a contest between opposing forces and casts the story in terms of actual persons, though the latitude he takes in his depictions has become the subject of much controversy within the gay communities.

21. Dirk Johnson, "Broad AIDS Law Signed in Illinois," *NY Times* Section II, page 7, 22 September 1987: "CHICAGO, 9/21—Gov. James R. Thompson today signed a broad package of bills aimed at fighting AIDS, including one that requires marriage license applicants to show proof they have both been tested for infection with the AIDS virus, but does not ask for results . . . The couples need not divulge the results to anyone other than each other. People infected will thus not be prevented from marrying; the authors of the measure say the aim is to protect an unwitting partner."

22. This was, of course, not the only political project of the new social movements, and there were complex debates and splits about the relationship of basic civil rights to projects aimed at gaining cultural power and political power outside the federal and state government structures—local community-building, cultural development, political critique, education, etc. The gay movement also contained tensions between the civil rights approach and cultural strategies. In general the gay movement, especially insofar as it could mobilize the power of its members within the white middle/upper classes, had far more cultural power than civil power, as would become obvious as the epidemic unfolded.

23. By the advent of the first identified cased of AIDS in 1981, there were several nationally distributed newspapers and magazines from the gay community, dozens of stable local or regional newspapers and magazines, dozens more "bar rags" which came and went with the economic interests of their owners, and probably a hundred or more newsletters of specific gay organizations, including several national gay organizations. There was in existence a gay press association of several years' standing and the gay community had been constructed as a "market" by a range of national and local advertisers. The extent and significance of the merging of this "community" and "market" is a topic for further study. However, one particular product *is* of significance in our context. The hepatitis B vaccine, tested and developed on gay men, was marketed, coincidentally, at the same time the AIDS epidemic was becoming accepted as a real phenomenon by the gay community in about 1982. The extent to which these ads—which depicted a very sick gay man in a hospital bed— became the paradigm for the early images of gay men with AIDS (as patients and as a potential market for medicine) would make a fascinating study. Debates about these images, which were variously seen as offensive and as shaking men out of complacency, foreshadowed debates about representations of people with AIDS. At any rate, many of the men and their stored blood samples from the hepatitis B studies in San Francisco would continue as research subjects when their cohort became an

HIV study. The role of the hepatitis B vaccine trials in effecting the ideology of medical research and community support for experimentation may be a factor in why San Francisco has responded differently to AIDS politically. Few people perceive San Francisco as the site of a bizarre study of a minority population reminiscent of Tuskegee; however, the changing political climate and perceptions about medical efficacy and medical ethics suggest that such a case could certainly be made.

24. The 1980s also witnessed the emergence of a new identity for the "addict," which was rapidly picked up by AIDS educators and service providers. This allowed for only a partial and highly pathologized identity which could succeed only in pressing for more *treatment*, and not for civil and political rights for drug users. Claims for these rights would come to the extent that drug users were members of ethnic or racial groups already identified under civil rights rhetoric. That needle sharing was a significant problem among Native Americans on reservations did not become part of these efforts largely because Native Americans are in a different legal and cultural relation to civil rights law and because the U.S. government has used public health policing on reservations as if reservations were already quarantine camps.

25. It may be significant that at the time AIDS began, the group consensus was that the community identify as "black" and not yet "African American." Michael Omi and Howard Winant discuss the changing meaning of race in the context of evolving models for community organizing in the U.S. in their *Racial Formations in the United States: From the 1960s to the 1980s*, NY: Routledge and Kegan Paul, 1986.

26. See the "Facing AIDS" issue of *Radical America* (Boston) 20:6, November/December 1987, and especially the introduction:
    "The question seems to hinge on whether the enormous amount of rage in the gay male community will ever find a political form... The recent organizing for October's Gay and Lesbian March on Washington is also a forum where the growing political consciousness of gay men is emerging. We have been struck by the fervor and intensity among them, many of whom were previously apolitical. The June arrests of AIDS demonstrators by Washington police wearing yellow gloves have become a symbol, triggering discussions of more militant actions." (p. 6)
    See also the *Radical America* editorial, "The AIDS Movement and Its Challenge," in the 21:2–3, November/December 1988 issue, which reads:
    "1988 marked the beginning of a new national grass roots movement, an AIDS movement. Spearheaded by the direct-action, treatment-focussed group in New York City, ACT UP (AIDS Coalition to Unleash Power) formed largely from the gay community in 1987, similar groups have sprung up in more than 30 cities creating the national ACT NOW network (AIDS Coalition to Network, Organize and Win)."
    These types of analysis of AIDS activism deny not only the immediate response of the gay male community to the AIDS epidemic in the early 1980s, but erase even more of the historical involvement in AIDS work of gay liberationists. Although not as damaging as the Randy Shilts book, *Radical America*'s implication that gay men sat around doing nothing but being "in rage" until 1987 ignores the radical roots of many of the current ASOs, and the radicalism of people working inside what has become "the system." This is not to underestimate the differences and conflicts between ACT UP and the ASOs, but outside observers and increasingly, activists who have been told nothing of the early days of AIDS organizing, misunderstand the important place of each in the fight against AIDS. One reason for this rapid revision of AIDS organizing history is the reality that many of the early organizers are now dead. In addition, these analyses demand that political action take a certain form (direct action) before it is counted as "political."

27. I use these terms in quotes and not as a depiction of how people living with AIDS, AIDS activists, medical workers, or service providers may refer to themselves. Indeed, much energy has been expended since the beginning of the epidemic in preventing people from referring to people living with AIDS, ARC, or HIV as "victims" or "sufferers." When I use the term "victim" I mean to say that the industry, whatever rubric it uses for its objects—clients, people with AIDS, the acronym PWA—essentially considers them as "victims" unable to speak for or about themselves, unable to determine policy because of their biased status. Similarly, "volunteer" is a special category of those people who received the appropriate training/indoctrination and work with "victims" in the proper fashion, with the proper emotional attitude. They also are not helpful policy makers because they are too close to the biased "victims" and anyway are supposed to be acting out of pure, not selfish or self-empowering (i.e. political) motives. Only the "experts," who may indeed be members of "high risk" communities, are allowed to suggest policy, and then only through the proper channels and with the proper pedagogy and view of what AIDS service means.

28. Veneita Porter, "Minorities and HIV Infection," in *The AIDS Epidemic: Private Rights and the Public Interest,* ed. Padraig O'Malley, Boston: Beacon Press, 1988, pp. 371–79. See especially p. 374.

29. In response to an early statement of this position, Jeffrey Weeks argued that altruism is essential to any just society and further that national health care is based in this concept. While I appreciate the importance of creating societies in which mutual concern is valued, historical and cross-cultural data would suggest that basic cooperative impulses become socially structured and symbolically constructed in vastly different and mutually contradictory ways. My argument then and now is for the need to deconstruct the revitalized rhetoric of altruism which reappears in the context of Reaganism after nearly two decades in which new social movements have preached community- and self-empowerment. This new, rightist altruism has engendered social policies common to Thatcher's Britain and to Reagan/Bush's U.S.: privatization of formerly social welfare practices. This maneuver relies on free market economics that presuppose notions of individualism and competition, an implicit evolutionism which undercuts analyses of systemic disenfranchisement of racial/ethnic minorities, and in the late 1980s equated volunteerism with female leisure activity. The considerable summer 1989 press coverage of Barbara Bush's volunteer efforts reinscribed a pre-Second-Wave-feminist division of social (and moral) labor. Any progressive idea of altruism, such as Weeks' important contribution, is overdetermined by these rightwing social constructions. In addition, the slippage between social altruism and the genetic altruism of sociobiology unconsciously reinforces precisely the pattern of service delivery now written into AIDS work. A progressive recoupment of "altruism" seems highly problematic in this context. For the original statement of these two positions, see Cindy Patton, "The AIDS Industry: Construction of 'Victims,' 'Volunteers,' and 'Experts,'," pp. 113–126; and Jeffrey Weeks, "AIDS, Altruism, and the New Right," pp. 127–132, in *Taking Liberties,* ed. Erica Carter and Simon Watney, London: Serpent's Tail, 1989. See also Mary Douglas, op.cit., for an interesting discussion of how moral logics become embedded in institutional practices.

30. In New York City in 1988, for example, Gay Men's Health Crisis had a $10 million budget and a staff of about 75, while the Minority AIDS Task Force (MATF) had a budget of $1 million and staff of 8. Half the cases of AIDS in New York City were people of color. Many of these people were gay or bisexual men, yet GMHC had been criticized for failing to reach gay and bisexual men of color.

31. It is difficult to get sexual orientation breakdowns of female volunteers, but in raising this issue with AIDS organizers nationally—with the possible exception of San Francisco—and with organizers from Australia, Britain, and Canada, it is my impression that, until recently, there were few lesbians working in the major AIDS groups as altruists; rather, they have a political commitment to self-help and understand AIDS as an attack on their and other communites. At least some of these lesbians have begun autonomous organizing around women-with-AIDS issues and around attacks on sex workers. The fact that prostitutes and poor women—major objects of concern by first wave feminist altruists at the turn of the century—have not been deemed good "victims" by the AIDS service industry can probably be attributed to the sexism in an industry that prevents women volunteers from setting organizational agendas. The fact that straight women have not pressed their gay male comrades to target safe sex education at straight men—they ought to be able to relate to each other on the level of masculine problems—is equally suggestive of institutionalized sexism.

Chapter 2

1. The widely offered ELISA and Western Blot "tests" detect antibodies to Human Immunodefiency Virus (HIV), the virus generally believed to render the immune system incapable of fighting the relatively common opportunistic infections which become fatal in AIDS. Although research has demonstrated a high correlation between presence of HIV and presence of antibodies, ELISA and Western Blot do not test for the virus, do not tell who will progress to clinical AIDS, and do not predict appearance of symptoms. The correlation between antibody status and an individual's ability to infect others is unknown. The "window" time between infection with virus and production of antibodies varies from six weeks to eighteen months, and in some cases lasts years. The effective knowledge gained from the test is quite small and qualified.

   Thus, HIV and AIDS are *not* synonymous: HIV is a virus with a wide range of possible outcomes—from no health-altering changes to AIDS. Researchers do not know why some people show no symptoms with HIV infection, others show some chronic, mild, or moderate symptoms, and others die as a result of immune system collapse. The media's persistent collapsing of HIV and AIDS (for example, by using the incorrect term "AIDS virus" instead of HIV) works together with the common belief that "testing positive" on the HIV antibody test (HIV-Ab+) means you will soon "die of AIDS," an unnecessarily pessimistic landscape in which to negotiate health decisions and make sense of what is at stake in unsafe sex and sharing of needles. Simon Watney's *Policing Desire* (Minnesota, 1987) provides an excellent case study of the British media's confusing coverage of AIDS, especially the conflation of HIV and AIDS. On test takers' perceptions of test meaning, see M. Gold et al, "Counselling Seropositives," in *What to Do About AIDS: Physicians and Health Care Professionals Discuss the Issues*, ed. L. McKusick, Los Angeles: University of California Press, 1986.

2. Acquired Immune Deficiency Syndrome is, as the name says, a *syndrome*, not a single disease. AIDS is a definition: it describes an advanced state of immune system breakdown in which a person is progressively less able to fight off common, treatable infections, and can no longer keep in balance the bacteria and yeasts that are normally a part of the body's ecosystem. AIDS is widely believed to be the result of infection with a newly identified virus—in fact, a newly identified *form* of virus—Human Immunodeficiency Virus (HIV, a so-called RNA or retro-virus). "AIDS" and most

of the opportunisitic infections which are its symptoms are *not* communicable. Strictly speaking, most of the opportunistic infections are not communicable to people who do not have suppressed immune systems. However, other immune suppressed people may be more susceptible to each others' infections.

HIV is communicable through specific routes, but is not contagious (i.e., it is not easily "caught"). HIV has most commonly been transmitted through receiving infected semen into the vagina or anus, through injecting infected blood, or perinatally. AIDS is diagnosed when one of a set of twenty or so unusual opportunistic infections becomes uncombattable by the person with HIV infection. Many of these OI are treatable until very late stages of immune system breakdown. Although there is not yet a way to completely halt HIV replication once a person shows severe immune system breakdown, the idea that there is "no cure for AIDS" is somewhat tautological: if the definition of AIDS is, in essence, irreversible immune system failure, and thus, death, then "AIDS" precludes the idea of "cure" in the traditional sense. Given that untreated HIV infection extends as many as ten years from infection to "AIDS" diagnosis, and two to five years or more from AIDS diagnosis to "death" (depending on the OI—people with kaposi's sarcoma have a better prognosis than people with PCP, although pentamidine and bactrim prophalaxis are changing these projections), then HIV might better be viewed as a chronic, but manageable disorder, which may decrease lifespan, but is not rapidly and immediately fatal. AZT and other experimental drugs may further slow viral progress, suspending or extending immune system breakdown for many more years. With improved early treatment, the entire course of HIV illness, if fatal, may extend to twenty or thirty or more years from time of infection. In addition, a variety of known drug therapies, holistic measures, and nutritional supplements dramatically improve the quality of life. Increasing general access to health care, especially in poor and disenfranchised communities, and better coordination of HIV care will also improve the overall prognosis for those currently infected. *The New England Journal of Public Policy* Winter/Spring 1988 issue contains several excellent overviews of the medical aspects of HIV.

3. Nearly 6,000 scientific papers were presented in full or in abstracts at the Fifth International AIDS Conference in Montreal, June 1989, but this was the first year that newspaper accounts admitted that there was little "new" among the scientific reports.

4. F. Barre-Sinoussi, J.C. Chermann, F. Rey, et al. "Isolation of a T-lymphotropic retrovirus from a patient at risk for AIDS." *Science*, 1983, 220: 868–871. R. C. Gallo, S. Z. Salahuddin, M. Popovic, et al. "Frequent detection and isolation of cytopathic retroviruses (HTLV-III) from patients with AIDS and at risk for AIDS." *Science*, 1984, 224: 500–501.

5. The "effects" of media coverage are complex, fragmented, and contingent, as decades of media-effects research demonstrate. While specific correlations between particular stories or kinds of representations can sometimes be demonstrated, surveys, "exposure" to media in experimental situations, self-reports on the importance or use of media, and even the broadest trend surveys of general attitudes in relation to media content are all problematic research methods, especially if a "postmodern" critique of information is taken seriously. I cannot rehearse the exhaustive debates on media effects or on postmodernity here; however, my own position is that media are more like a landscape of potential "information" units which are interpreted in contexts which are partly socially-interactive (something like interpretive micronetworks or interpretive communities) and partly idiosyncratically reproduced and

incorporated or "owned" as knowledge. Thus, some parts of media reports become "meanings" to be circulated and reinterpreted in social contexts, while some parts are simply ignored or incorporated into "knowledge" as if they were not subject to interpretation. The latter are what are "known" as "facts." My discussion of the media here and later is intended to trace convergences between popular mediations of science presented as "new" and older cultural notions. Events in which policy or attitudes seem directly correlated with media reports are not to be interpreted as "media effects," but rather as symptoms of the convergences between two or more discursive formations.

6. In a course on representations of AIDS, taught at Amherst College in the fall of 1989, I assigned extensive readings from self-help books by people living with AIDS. The students remarked that these had challenged their perception of AIDS as rapidly fatal. In addition, many said they could relate the life skills advice of the PLWAs to their own experience in other areas—dealing with sensitive issues with their families, disappointing their friends, coping with physical differences and fears. The "ordinariness" of the lives described by PLWAs was the most striking difference between the view of AIDS the students had formed from media accounts and the sensibility they discovered in the PLWA literature. Certainly, the social context of "reading for school" affected their interpretive and incorporative processes.

7. See especially, B. Henricksson, "Social Democracy or Societal Control: A Critical Analysis of Swedish AIDS Policy," Institute for Social Policy, June 1988, also presented at the Fourth International AIDS Conference in Stockholm, 13–16 June 1988.

8. Don Des Jarlais and Samuel Friedman, "HIV infection among intravenous drug users: Epidemiology and risk reduction," *AIDS*, No. 1, 1987.

9. Dr. Edward Brandt, head of the National Institutes of Health until late 1984, pressured medical journals to speed up their review processes so that AIDS-related research could be more quickly available and critiqued. This decision—though controversial—was considered important because of the severity of the new epidemic and because no research paradigm against which to evaluate projects had stabilized. This freeing up of the market place of ideas, while probably necessary at the time, was only the first of many changes in the long-standing internal checks on the quality and reliability of research. Brandt discussed his decision at the First International AIDS Conference in Atlanta, 15 April 1985, in a plenary paper, "Health Policy Implications of AIDS" and again at the Public Responsibility in Medicine and Research Conference on legal and ethical aspects of AIDS, held in Boston, 24–25 April 1985.

10. Henricksson, op. cit.

11. Olna A. Selnes, presenting data from a multi-cohort study conducted by the Centers for Disease Control in the U.S., at the Fourth International AIDS Conference in Stockholm, June 1988.

12. Henricksson, op. cit.

13. David Ostrow, et al. "Drug use and sexual behavior change in a cohort of homosexual men," at the Third International AIDS Conference, Washington, D.C., 1987, and David Ostrow, "Antibody testing won't cut risky behavior," *American Medical Association News*, 5 June 1987.

14. For example, of the $542 million spent on AIDS by the U.S. federal government in 1986, 6% went to education, 45% to research, and the rest to blood screening and testing programs.

15. The 1988 MAC data was not picked up by the mainstream media until April of 1989, and then the study was reported as a preview of the Fifth International AIDS Conference, as if this data had not previously been available.

16. Presented at the Fourth International AIDS Conference in Stockholm, June 1988. See similar Australian data: Gary Dowsett, "Reaching men who have sex with men in Australia," plenary paper at the Second International AIDS Information and Education Conference, Yaounde, Cameroon, October 1989.

17. Steve Wolgar and Bruno Latour's *Laboratory Life*, Princeton: Princeton University Press, 1986, provides an excellent case study of the process of identifying and creating technologies to study biochemical substances.

18. Centers for Disease Control cost assessment and new counselling protocols for HIV-antibody testing, 30 April 1987.

19. David Silverman, "Making Sense of a Precipice: Constituting Identity in a HIV Clinic," in *AIDS: Social Representations, Social Practices*, ed. Peter Aggleton, Graham Hart, and Peter Davies, Philadelphia: Falmer Press, 1989.

20. See Michael Gross, "HIV Antibody Testing: Performance and Counselling Issues," *New England Journal of Public Policy*, Vol. 4, No. 1, Winter/Spring 1988.

21. The statistical projections for false positives and false negatives are useless caveats for individual test seekers. A deep irony is embedded in the test interpretation process—many individuals simultaneously claim (or are told by counselors) that they are not at risk or low at risk based on their reported behaviors, and yet they demand to be tested anyway. Clearly, the deep ambivalence about sexuality in our culture and the ambiguity about terms like "safe" and "sex" creates an intense anxiety that renders many people unable to believe that the particular sexual activities in which they have engaged have not placed them at risk, even though they feel guilty about engaging in any sex at all. Alternatively, whatever gay men, prostitutes, drug users, and people of color do or don't do is immediately suspect because they are already inscribed as "risky people."

22. This view stemmed from data suggesting that HIV was endemic but non-fatal in Rwanda and from unwillingness to abandon the earlier hypothesis that gay men and injecting drug users were suffering from immune depletion caused by sexual and drug practices which left them prey to various illnesses ordinarily benign. There are still a minority of practitioners and some people living with AIDS who do not believe HIV to be sufficiently or at all causal. I will not detail these debates here, as they have been well-rehearsed in the *New York Native* and in several books on alternative theories of AIDS. What is important to recognize here is that at the time of instituting Alternative Test Sites, the scientific community was considerably more divided than it is today about the prevalence and significance of HIV. Many viewed HIV as requiring co-factors, either environmental or pathological. Only with the compilation of test data on Army recruits did it appear that HIV was indeed a rare virus.

23. The alternative testing sites, funded and supervised through state and federal programs, were set in place in late 1985 after the antibody test became available in spring of that year. The test was designed for screening blood donations. Before a virus was identified and a screening test was available, blood banks asked donors at high risk to refrain from donating. A check list and pamphlet were given to donors, who were expected to self-assess their risk or ask questions. Blood banks agreed that voluntary donor deferral was highly successful and screening would further reduce donation of blood by people who didn't realize or understand their risk. Gay activists argued that blood testing positive—which included a large number of false positive

units—should be destroyed but that donors should not be put on any kind of register which might open them up to discrimination. Blood banks finally rejected this idea and decided that they had a moral obligation and legal liability to notify those whose blood was rejected that they had tested positive for HIV antibody and should seek additional counselling or medical advice. The blood banks feared that if it became widely known that testing was available at donation sites, high risk people might come in for testing and some HIV infected units might slip by undetected, since there is also a small but significant number of false negative tests. Thus, the decision to notify donors of their test result meant that donating might be used for self-testing, necessitating, apparently, the creation of sites where anonymous testing could take place. These were called alternative test sites—alternative not in the leftist or progressive sense, but alternative to seeking HIV antibody status knowledge through blood donations.

24. In conversations with AIDS Action Committee Hotline Coordinator Ken Smith, one of the longest tenured hotline people in the U.S., it became clear that asking for the test is the most common route to obtaining other kinds of information, especially risk reduction information. Most hotlines now seem to pursue with the caller why they want to be tested and urge the caller to begin practicing safe sex and needle hygiene whether or not they pursue testing.

25. The strange-bedfellow exceptions which do test are West Germany, Japan, Cuba, and South Africa. Sweden is considering limited testing proposals and the gutter press in Britain as well as the fascist National Front advocate mass testing.

26. Since it takes six weeks to 18 months from infection to production of antibody—seroconversion—a 2% rate in early 1987 means that significant changes had already taken place in the years before. The seroconversion rates for HIV must be considered in this long-term perspective, unlike rates for syphilis or gonorrhea, which reflect infections occuring in previous weeks to months.

27. Gerald Soucy et al, "Two key studies: 'Comparison of recreational drug and alcohol use among homosexual and bisexual men who are HIV antibody seropositive, and subsequent PWAs,' and 'Effects of HIV antibody disclosure upon sexual behavior and recreational drug and alcohol consumption by homosexual and bisexual men'," paper presented at the 1987 National Lesbian and Gay Health Conference and the Fifth Annual National AIDS Forum, Los Angeles, 26–29 March 1987.

28. Mr. Leather, a gay man chose through regional and later national "leather" contests, is nonetheless still mandated by the organizations that support him to spend his year doing safe sex education.

29. See also Paula Treichler, "AIDS, Homophobia, and Biomedical Discourse: An Epidemic of Signification," in *AIDS: Cultural Analysis, Cultural Activism*, ed. Douglas Crimp, Cambridge: MIT Press, 1988.)

Chapter 3

1. Benjamin Freedman, of McGill University and the Jewish General Hospital in Montreal, has been the most vocal and clear critic of proposals either simply to abandon or to maintain placebo-controlled trials. His arguments about the nature of the scientific agreement necessary to the assertion that neither the placebo nor the drug is "known" to be better are an implicit critique of the rise of scientific facticity. He and others, notably Kathleen Nolan, at the Hastings Center, an ethics think tank in

Briarcliff, NY, propose more complex evaluations of the ethical and scientific value of placebo controls. Nolan argues that a valid null hypothesis in clinical trials (i.e., the hypothesis that there is no difference between placebo and trial drug) must not only be judged against a placebo but also against other clinical interventions. This would require designing multiple investigational tracks within the single study, thus, making the research conditions and controls comparable. Freedman argues that the nature of scientific agreement on what is "better" is complex, involving "etiologic rationale" (i.e., theory of cause), "functional/clinical effects" (i.e., what will count as a "difference"), "undesired side-effects," "compliance, availability, mode of administration, and cost." Kathleen Nolan, "The Ethics of Placebo-Controlled Trials of Therapy for HIV Infection," Abstract W.F.O.6., Fifth International AIDS Conference, Montreal, June, 1989; Benjamin Freedman, "Ethical Point on Placebo and Treatment Controls in HIV Drug Trials," Abstract W.F.O.5., Fifth International AIDS Conference, Montreal, June, 1989; Benjamin Freedman, et al., "Nonvalidated Therapies and HIV Disease," *Hastings Center Report*, May/June 1989, pp. 14–20; Benjamin Freedman, "Equipoise and the Ethics of Clinical Research," *New England Journal of Medicine*, 317:3, 16 July 1987, pp. 141–5.

2. *You Can Do Something About AIDS*, (1988), ed. Sasha Alyson, Boston: The Stop AIDS Project, a free book collaboratively produced by the publishing industry, contains a section called, "Volunteering for a Study" (pp. 97–99). Physicians Lawrence Deyton and John Killen, Jr., who, we are told, "are both involved in AIDS research at the National Institute of Allergy and Infectious Diseases," write that "eventually, every promising drug or treatment must be tested in the population for whom it is intended. . . . The main requirement for volunteers in AIDS drugs tests is a commitment to stay with it even if the results aren't immediately promising. Many people with AIDS, understandably, won't feel comfortable making such a commitment. But for those who do there are benefits: not only the opportunity to help in the race to find a cure for AIDS, but the possibility that you will be among the first people to be helped by a new medication that proves effective."

3. *Surviving and Thriving With AIDS*, ed. Michael Callen, New York: PWA Coalition, 1988, contains many sections arguing for and against a variety of treatments and offers advice on getting access to clinical trials and underground drug networks. Written for and by people living with AIDS, the collection stands as an important indication of the evolving attitudes and rhetoric of the most vocal self-help activists. State departments of public health sponsoring clinical trials publish updated lists of available trials and inclusion/exclusion criteria. In addition, the American Foundation for AIDS Research (AmFAR), a highly respected and sometimes combative non-profit group, founded through the fundraising efforts of Liz Taylor, publishes a directory of trials. Local and national newsletters of PWA and HIV-Ab+ persons groups also include information on the prospects of treatment trials.

   A new concept has been proposed to cope with the uncertainty about lack of full consensus on the effectiveness and safety of current drugs, notably AZT. "Clinical equipoise" situates HIV/AIDS trial ethics in a situation in which, because so many trials are conducted concurrently and under different assumptions about HIV, it is no longer clear whether there is an established treatment (AZT) against which other treatments should be measured, thus eliminating placebo controls. Classically, placebo controls should only be used in situations in which there is no clear preferred treatment. See: Benjamin Freedman, 1987, op cit.

4. The several "get the facts" campaigns say more than they intend about *who* should get facts and why. The controversial U.S. Surgeon General booklet said, in English,

that a Spanish version was available on request. Great Britain's 1985 "Don't Die of Ignorance" campaign left much unsaid about *whose* ignorance (gay men's? scientists'?) about what (facts? sex?) was "responsible" for "death."

5. Dr. Jonathan Mann and a host of other researchers and policy makers say over and again, "education is our only vaccine," and scientific reports frequently end with some statement to the effect that "we need to know more."

6. See Patton, *Sex and Germs: The Politics of AIDS,* Boston: South End Press, 1985, for more extensive discussion of the forms of and differences within new right rhetoric. The most widely available rightist assessment of AIDS is Gene Antonio, *The AIDS Coverup? The Real and Alarming Facts About AIDS,* San Francisco: Ignatious Press, 1986. He begins calmly enough: "The public has a right to know all the pertinent information about this dangerous contagious disorder. Practical strategies for stopping this devastating epidemic must be based on objective data, not emotionalism" (xii). Of course, the practical, objective strategy is to "intransigently abide by Biblical standards of sexual morality" (199).

7. David L. Kirp, *Learning by Heart: AIDS and School Children in America's Communities,* New Brunswick: Rutgers, 1989.

8. Internationally, studies show that people understand that HIV is largely spread through sexual intercourse. Whether there are other perceived routes is an issue of great variation: many people still believe that HIV can also be spread through toilet seats and mosquitoes. Thus, arguments about whether people are well or poorly informed about AIDS depend on which is considered more important: knowledge of the actual routes of transmission, which enables people to control their exposure (via safer sex and safer drug use), or knowledge of routes which are not plausible, which may cause heightened fears. In any event, these knowledges are only haphazardly related to long-term changes in behavioral norms. Norman L. Webb, "Gallup International Survey on Attitudes Toward AIDS," Global Impact of AIDS Conference, 8–10 March, 1988, London.

9. The 1960s and 1970s saw attempts to remove the bodies of "racial minorities" and sexually different people from the total control of the existing medical system, both through control of local clinics and through understanding medical phenomena in their community context. See Barbara Ehrenreich and John Ehrenreich, *The American Health Empire: Report of Health/PAC.* New York: Vintage, 1971.

   In addition, Foucault talks about the medicalization of both sexuality and race. He argues, correctly I think, that in particular, the confessional system (confessing to one's supposed essential desires, or to the existence of supposed racially differentiated blood) banishes to the "inside" (via "desire" and "blood," respectively) traits once viewed as external differences ("behavior" and "color," respectively). He argues of both sexuality and raciality that they become subject to medical categories deployed to subject a "population" to surveillance, and then naturalized, in order to allow social power to take on the particular discipline/self-discipline structure it exhibits in the post-Victorian era. See M. Foucault, *Discipline and Punish,* and *The History of Sexuality,* esp. pp. 26, 54, and 149–151.

10. Fleck argues compellingly that laboratory science does indeed turn up technologies that "work," but by accident, skill, and intuitions which practitioners can't fully explain. Fleck argues, and I extend his argument here, that it is in the "forgetting" of mistakes and in the narrative revision of scientific reports that laboratory work is made apparently consistent with its supposedly scientific method. Ludwig Fleck, *The Genesis and Development of a Scientific Fact,* Chicago: University of Chicago Press, 1979.

11. I am alluding to Baudrillard's work on simulation. He argues that it is characteristic of post-modern society to lose the sense of origin/copy and instead experience a constancy of repetitions which shifts concepts of time, history, space, uniqueness. In addition, he suggests that previously distinct realms collapse into mutual metaphors—strikingly, medicine and communication. See Jean Baudrillard, *Simulacra and Simulations*, New York:*Semiotexte(e)*, 1983; and *The Ecstasy of Communication*, New York: *Semiotexte(e)*, 1987.

12. "Dissident vernaculars" seems to be a better term than "culturally sensitive" as it moves us away from the model of pristine scientific ideas which need "translation" for people lacking in the dominant culture's language skills or concepts. "Dissident vernaculars" also suggests that meanings created by and in communities are upsetting to the dominant culture precisely because speaking in one's own fashion is a means of resistance, a strengthening of the subculture that has created the new meaning. The idea of dissident vernaculars also places the health educator in a much different role, perhaps that of a technician rather than a translator.

13. The 1986 federal funding was very political and confusing. On the heels of the 1985 First International AIDS Conference in Atlanta the Centers for Disease Control issued requests for proposals in several categories, including community-based demonstration projects and innovative projects. The demonstration projects (initially Seattle, Denver, Houston, and Albaby) were primarily cohort studies of behavior changes in relation to antibody testing. The cities to receive innovative project grants (initially, Los Angeles, New York, Houston) were announced in July 1985, but for the rest of the year there was dispute about whether and how these small (roughly $100,000 grants) would be monitored. In January, 1986, the guidelines discussed above were released, although the full amount of $1.9 million allocated in the 1986 budget was not released. About $11 million went to state public health agencies under the same budget. See the *National Coalition of Gay Sexually Transmitted Disease Services Newletter*, February/March 1986, Vol. 7:3, pp. 12–15.

14. I flag the term "minority communities" because it bears a certain essentialist heritage that locates the bond of community in some transcendent trait like race, country of origin, and in recent years, sexuality. The term is Eurocentric in its refusal to recognize that, on a global scale, the white administrators are in fact a minority. The inscription of the term "minority" glosses over the historical processes through which race and ethnicity are formed, and through which Euroamerican and white become central reference points in Western culture.

    Nevertheless, the term "minority communities" has resonance for a range of micro-networks of resistance defined by their oppositionality in terms of race, gender, sexuality, culture, shared history of oppression. The idea of "minority community" tends to unite across class people whose perceived impediment to power is a cultural or social trait rather than strict economic disadvantage. In the post-war era, claims to being a minority were a major route to social power in the U.S. These claims were based in a model which suggests that power inheres within a group, is comprised of units in a zero sum game. This notion of power tends to run at odds with a more Foucaultian concept of a multiplicity of powers grounded by knowledge formations, with unique and local resistances.

    For now, I will continue to employ the term "minority communities," although the idea of micro-networks of resistance—drawn from Foucault and Deleuze and Guattari—is more consistent with the discussions in the last section of the book, and suggests a very different relationship between power and vernacular.

15. This story was reported widely and sensationally in the gay press from 1985. What is significant is less whether Gallo "stole" the virus, but the way in which scientific

competition was inscribed into the scientific narrative of the epidemic from the beginning. It is not insignificant that the October 1988 issue of *Scientific American* contains the first public jointly authored article on "the virus" by the two men who are viewed as rivals. Reporting on Montagne generally depicted him as a kindly, good-natured altruist, while Gallo was depicted as a villain out to make a name for himself. To some extent, differences in cultural attitudes about homosexuality in France and the U.S. account for the perceptions that Montagne is a good guy. However, Montagne's insistence on claiming that "AIDS began in Africa," despite no valid evidence or critical understanding of the social versus scientific meaning of locating origins, suggests that he is also largely influenced by cultural stereotypes. A new and rather sensationalist book details the medical and ethical aspects of the "who found the virus" controversy. See: "U.S. Government Attempts to Suppress Book about Gallo," *The New York Native*, 2 January, 1989. Randy Shilts' *And the Band Played On*, New York: St. Martin's Press, 1987, uses the good guy-bad guy tropes to weave a story of egotism and government inaction.

16. See: John Lauritsen "On the AZT Front, Part 2," in the *New York Native*, January 16, 1988, pp. 16–17. Lauristen critiques the November 25, 1987 *Journal of the American Medical Association* report on the "compassionate release" AZT trials, entitled "Survival Experience Among Patients with AIDS on Zidovudine (AZT)," which includes charts showing that 1120 or 23% of the people were missing from the final report overall and 734 of the 1043 people enrolled in the original September 1986 cohort were "lost." Lauritsen criticizes their use of a statistical model which "summarizes" the missing patient's data as if they are a cross-section of the accounted-for patients and criticizes the controls on the study in general, given the unusually high number of people researchers lost track of in a study of such short duration.

17. Bactrim and pentamadine prophylaxis against *Pneumocystis Carinii pneumonia* early emerged as the most successful ways to lower HIV morbidity; however, pentamadine was already known to be effective against PCP. In fact, the monitoring of disparate requests for pentamadine was one of the initial routes to identifying the original people came to be counted as people who had died from AIDS-related pneumonia. Many very sick people with AIDS could not tolerate pentamadine when intervenously administered, but researchers and manufacturers were very slow to develop aerosolizers for pentamadine, and the units were very expensive. The anti-bacterial Bactrim has also proven effective at preventing or decreasing the severity of PCP, effectively decreasing mortality from PCP, which is the major killer of people with AIDS. These innovations occurred largely outside the major, virus-oriented research paradigm, even though they significantly effect the lives of many, many people with symptomatic HIV infections. Some would count AZT as a successful anti-viral agent; however, its long-term benefits and effects are still the subjects of considerable controversy.

18. I perused numerous college libraries for introductory books on immunology and virology. I have chosen as fairly typical the following: Robin Nicholas, *Immunology: An Information Profile*, Bronx, NY: H.W. Wilson Company, 1985, which offers an overview of the history and workings of immunology as a profession for the college science major; and *General Virology*, a textbook from John Wiley and Sons, 1967. An "insider's view" of the controversies within immunology is Melvin Cohn's foreword to Rodney E. Langman's *The Immune System: Evolutionary principles guide our understanding of this complex biological defense system*, San Diego: Academic Press, 1989. In addition, I rely on the presentation of immunology contained in the National Institutes of Health pamphlet £88–529, *Understanding the Immune System*, by Lydia Woods Schindler, July 1988, widely distributed to AIDS service organizations.

19. On one hand, the use of "gay" rather than "homosexual" was an acknowledgement of this community's preferred designation. However, "gay" is considered to be an identity label. Calling the emerging syndrome "gay-related" suggested that it was something acquired by proclaiming one's identity, or through some feature of the "gay community" or "gay lifestyle." The term "homosexual" would have been similarly problematic, and indeed is problematic among epidemiological categories. The term "homosexual" does not correlate with any of the many biomedical or psychological indexes in 1960s–1980s research seeking a cause of homosexuality. In addition, homosexuals are not found to differ from heterosexuals on any psychological measures, and indeed, even if anal sex is chosen as a mark of differentiation, not all homosexual (males) practice anal intercourse, and many heterosexual men do. Even object choice is not consistent over a lifetime (as it is equally not for heterosexual males). Thus, from the outset, sexuality-oriented paradigms were problematic: two early theories of immune malfunction, for example, were system overload and sexual transmission, neither of which is exhaustively correlated with homosexuality.

20. AIDS refers to effects observed as dysfunctions of the immune system and evaluates "health" and "disease" in relation to an established norm of immune function. "AIDS" tends to construct diagnosis around symptoms suggestive of serious immune system failure, hence the use of PCP, Kaposi's sarcoma, and other opportunistic infections as the diagnostic markers of AIDS, to be confirmed by HIV testing. HIV disease refers to a causative virus and its sequential effects, regardless of whether these are experienced as harmful or uncomfortable to the individual. Here, presence of the virus is itself diagnostic of "disease," which is defined as the presence of a potentially harmful external agent. "Health" is considered a subjective state which does not correlate well with the progress of the virus, except in the late stages—that is, except in "AIDS."

21. Nicholas, op. cit., recounts how the "discovery" of antibodies, more correctly called immunoglobulin, enabled immunologists to visualize a concept which had been under debate for some time. This then allowed immunologists to describe in micro-terms the intricate series of events that had long been recognized in the effects of immunization and allergy. The description and visualization process established the "fact" of immunology's unit of study, thereby creating the conditions for the formation of a separate discipline. Virology's instantiation was less controversial, since the existence of bacteria had already been accepted, and viruses were perceived to be simply another form of parasitic life. Nevertheless, until the visualization of viruses, "microbes" were lumped together, as were the biologists who studied them.

22. I recall my own childhood terror resulting from having confused images from a Disney movie about "The Living Desert" and from another cinemascopic documentary film about the tiny creatures living in and on our bodies with the many Japanese space invader and monster films I watched early Saturday mornings while waiting for my parents to get up. Having nearly exhausted the exotic in the far reaches of the globe, *National Geographic* had pictoral essays of this new frontier: the internal geography mapped the space of white blood cells with such technical specificity that it seemed nothing could evade the eye of science.

23. Lay as well as scientific literature uses endless war metaphors. The cover of the National Institutes of Health AIDS pamphlet, op.cit., sports a stylized body outline with a circular inset depicting sepia-tone medieval jousters.

24. The paper, originally presented at the Fourth International AIDS Conference in Stockholm, began receiving extensive coverage in the gay press in April 1989,

beginning with the often sensationalistic *New York Native,* which has long been intent on questioning the HIV-AIDS link.

25. Even as late as 1988, much of the data on the success of single or multiple immunomodulator therapies derived from the first clinical experience with AIDS before a viral model was definitively accepted and HIV's workings well-described. Only in 1988 did the biomedical research community widely acknowledge that combination antiviral and immunomodulatory therapies would be likely to offer the most successful treatment of people with HIV (Oberg, Karolinska Institute address to the Fourth International AIDS Conference, Stockholm). Nevertheless, most clinical trials continued to research the particular effects of anti-virals, rather than beginning to model and research combination therapies. The AmFar *AIDS/HIV Experimental Treatment Directory,* December 1988 update, lists about twenty immunomodulator trials, about 20 combination trials of immunomodulators and anti-virals (all AZT), close to 60 other anti-viral trials, about 20 AZT trials (with specialized types of patients), and another dozen trials of AZT plus a toxicity reducer.

26. A recent reevaluation of the statistics on AIDS cases found that because the CDC list people with multiple risk factors in the exposure category with the highest incidence of cases, a person who was both homosexual/bisexual and had a hemophilia/coagulation disorder would be listed only in the first category. Adding back in those people who had multiple risk factors but were in a different exposure category increased the number of persons with hemophilia/coagulation disorder and AIDS by 16%. The CDC is now listing reported AIDS cases according to single versus multiple mode of exposure. This is critical information because people have varying degrees of identification with their "risk group" (in the former rubric, still used in the media) and/or have become socialized into receiving medical care in relation to these categories. It makes a difference to the social reality of a gay man with hemophilia whether he is treated as someone exposed "unwittingly" through use of a blood product or held responsible for his "reckless" behavior. Further, his ability to get both sensitive medical care in relation to his coagulation disorder *and* social support from his gay community depends on breaking down social phobias in both groups.

27. Thanks to Paula Treichler for pointing out the authors' caveat and the ambivalence about "representing transmission" which it represents.

28. The first social science and humanities presentations at an International AIDS conference were during the noontime sessions entitled "The Face of AIDS" in Stockholm, 1988. Ironically, because these were noontime sessions, most people watched the "faces" on television monitors in the dining areas. Another "face of AIDS" was the 10 August 1987 issue of *Newsweek,* "The Face of AIDS: One Year in the Epidemic," which featured on the cover the photographs of twenty-four people and then about two hundred more inside, placed high-school-yearbook-fashion. Although the issue was moving and covered people from all ages, ethnic, and professional groups, the effect was to create a cathartic distance from the life conditions faced by these "real (but now safely dead) people."

29. These are, of course, the "stories" science and society tell about science. Kuhn's analysis *does* seem to conform to how contemporary scientists describe their own work. M. J. Mulkay, "Some aspects of cultural growth in the natural sciences," *Social Research* 36:1, 1969; and M. J. Mulkay, *The Social Process of Innovation,* London: Macmillan, 1972. However, there is reason to doubt whether this accurately describes scientists' actual behavior and values. Using a variety of methods, other sociologists of science have described the rise of particular scientific facts, in terms which suggest that science is more literary and metaphoric than scientists themselves, or the society

which depends on scientific products care to admit. See especially Fleck, op.cit., and Wolgar and Latour, op.cit., and also Bruno Latour, *The Pasteurization of France,* Cambridge: Harvard University Press, 1988; and Karin D. Knorr, "Producing and Reproducing Knowledge: Descriptive or Constructive," *Social Science Information* 16:6, 1978; Karin D. Knorr-Cetina, *The Manufacture of Knowledge: An Essay on the Constructivist and Contextual Nature of Science,* Oxford: Pergammon, 1981; Karin D. Knorr-Cetina, "Scientific communities or transepistmic arenas of research? A critique of quasi-economic models of science," *Social Studies of Science,* 12, 1982. I am not arguing below that scientists are trying to "hide" their actual ways of working, or that the peculiar paradoxes within AIDS research are part of a plot. Rather, I propose that science is less "scientific" than we make it out to be, and considerably more involved in and created by cultural ideologies. Again, this does not diminish the usefulness of the products and knowledge of science, but demands that we ask a different set of questions about the interests science serves.

30. In his contribution to the "What Science Knows About AIDS" issue of *Scientific American,* jointly authored with Luc Montagnier, Gallo claims that retroviruses were actually first discovered early in this century, a rhetorical maneuver which outwits paradigm shifts. Gallo rewrites as a discovery the early observation of something which much later turns out to be "true" when technology improves, but which could just as easily have been proven "wrong" (either never visualized, or actually falsified by another "discovery"). This anchors the retrovirologic thought style as a long and scientific quest. It is however absurd to argue that the concepts surrounding the original hypothesis are the same as those in existence when a fact is finally established; countless theoretical, social, and technological conditions have changed the mode of inquiry and interpretation.

31. A number of methodological approaches seem attractive for such analyses, and the next chapter will draw on a number of these. Utilizing a Foucaultian method, one might be able to extend this analysis by locating the "epistemic" foundations of science across various eras. These "epistemes" would be seen to create the basic logic of, or narrative constraints on the elaboration of cultural ideas about science, and determine what must be explained in order that knowledge be transferred from the scientific world into the practical world—by the workings of what Foucault calls "technologies." See especially Michel Foucault, "The Politics of Health in the 18th Century," in *Power/Knowledge,* New York: Pantheon, 1980. Foucault's work on the organization of modern thought provides the basis for an alternative understanding of the politics and radical potential of "AIDS education," as will be suggested in the chapter on teaching about AIDS.

   Eve Sedgwick's work on the non-dialectical relationship between essentialist and constructionist logics for the construction of "subjectivity" in narrative forms suggests that science does not proceed by a battle between the fittest explanatory schemes, but works out narratives which reconcile fundamentally conflicting schemes utilizing available cultural metaphors. *Epistemology of the Closet,* Berkeley: University of California Press, 1990. This suggests that the intermittent "gaying" and "degaying" of AIDS discourse is a foregrounding/backgrounding maneuver rather than a pendular or dialectical movement.

32. By prefigurative logic I mean the assumptions so implicit in a discipline or a thought style that they are no longer available for question. These are the ways of thinking that are so fundamental to a particular thought style that when questioned, one is greeted with answers such as, "that's just how you do it." Prefigurative logics are fragmentary structures of thought which compel participants in the thought style to

approach problems in a particular way by reflex. It is not possible to think totally freed from some prefiguring logic, but it is possible to critique the assumptions and patterns of problem-solving they produce. I have taken the term "prefigurative logic" from the coordinated management of meaning (CMM) method, which uses the concept on a more micro-level to explain what individuals bring into a conversation. See W. Barnett Pierce, *Communication and the Human Condition,* Carbondale: Southern Illinois University Press, 1989.

Chapter 4

1. This essay is an expanded version of my earlier "Inventing African AIDS," *City Limits,*London, no. 363, September 1988, pp. 15–22. I also thank Profs. Doris Sommer and Andrew Parker for asking me to present an earlier version at their Nationalisms/Sexualities Conference at Harvard University in June 1989, and Eve K. Sedgwick for hosting a mini-conference around this work at Duke University in September 1989.

2. I am of course using M. Foucault's periodization in *The Order of Things,* New York: Random House, 1970. V. Y. Mudimbe's excellent *The Invention of Africa: Gnosis, Philosophy, and the Order of Knowledge,* Bloomington: Indiana University Press, 1988, argues that movements parallel to those of Foucault and other twentieth-century French philosophers have been occurring in African philosophy, and in fact, that some of these philosophers have begun the epistemic break Foucault struggled to imagine. Mudimbe also provides an excellent review of twentieth-century developments and problematics in African philosophy with careful attention to local and international historical/political developments. For other works on AIDS and Africa from a cultural/critical perspective, see Paula A. Treichler, "AIDS and HIV Infection in the Third World: A First World Chronicle," in *Remaking History,* ed. Barbara Kruger and Phil Mariani, Seattle: Bay Press, 1989; and Simon Watney, "Missionary Positions," in *Critical Quarterly,* Autumn 1989.

3. Although I am heavily indebted to M. Foucault's work on *episteme* (in particular, *The Archaeology of Knowledge*), I have found it difficult when analyzing texts produced now, and especially when assessing the "genealogy" of practices which have substantially evolved during the short time of the AIDS epidemic, to identify coherent discursive formations.

4. Bruno Latour, noting his debt to Jacques Derrida, makes much of the literary quality of laboratory science. Indeed, AIDS also involves endless inscription or discovery of inscription, not only the blots on HIV antibody tests and the markings on the body of the diagnosed (both Kaposi's sarcoma lesions and the wasting syndrome which reveals the markings of the skeletal interior structure of the body), but also the way in which AIDS and non-AIDS are mediated by the category of "risk groups," which produces the possibility of AIDS deferred. See Latour, *Laboratory Life, The Social Construction of Scientific Facts,* Princeton: Princeton University Press, 1986.

5. See James H. Jones, *Bad Blood,* New York: Free Press, 1981.

6. See Richard Chirimuuta and Rosalind Chirimuuta, *AIDS, Africa and Racism,* Burton-on-Trent, U.K., 1987 for an exhaustive review of the problems with early AIDS/HIV epidemiology in Africa.

7. In *Social Science Medicine,* Vol. 28, No. 12, pp. 1211–1220, 1989. Rushton was a Guggenheim Fellow while completing this work.

8. For a more detailed discussion of the silencing effects of science as conceived during the colonial era, see Mudimbe, op.cit. Treichler, op.cit., takes this in a different direction to demonstrate the rhetorical maneuvers that leave only the tiniest space for African contributions to discourse *on* Africa.

9. We now know that HIV has a long incubation period; however, the identification of all of these first cases in roughly the same timeframe of about six months still tells us little about when these first individuals may have been infected. The time it takes for information about a new disease to move through international research channels, and for researchers and clinicians to review mysterious cases and determine whether they fit with the evolving case definition of the new epidemic, creates the illusion that the "first cases" are essentially similar. Differences in treatment and care, especially in the context of HIV disease, substantially change the time from infection to symptoms to death. That AIDS was first labelled "gay" and was defined, essentially, as unexplained death in a very healthy population slowed identification of similarities in cases from very different populations, with different health profiles and different expectations of healthiness. However, at the time, the diseases which served as analogues for AIDS—hepatitis B and syphilis—suggested that there would be much less time from infection to symptoms. Given the models from which epidemiologists were working, it was sheer supposition and not *science* which generated the belief that the Haitian and Zairean cases had not been infected in their new countries. That this guess turned out to be correct is not a basis for arguing that AIDS started in Africa.

10. The International AIDS Conference is the major annual AIDS conference and attracts medical and social science researchers from around the world. The Montreal conference, held in June 1989, had over 10,000 attendees.

11. Christakis presented a paper entitled "Ethical Aspects of the International AIDS Agenda." However, I have taken the above quote from his published work, "The Ethical Design of an AIDS Vaccine Trial in Africa," *Hastings Center Report,* June/July 1988. The chief other published sources of debate on the ethics of AIDS vaccine trials are as follows: Wendy K. Mariner and Robert C. Gallo, "Getting to Market: The Scientific and Legal Climate for Developing an AIDS Vaccine," *Law, Medicine, and Health Care,* 15:1–2, Summer 1987, pp. 17–26; Nicholas A. Christakis, "Responding to a Pandemic: International Interests in AIDS Control," *Daedalus,* 118:2, Spring 1989, pp. 113–134; Wendy K. Mariner, "The Trouble with Immunization," *The Harvard Medical School Health Letter,* X:11, pp. 3–5; Wendy K. Mariner, "Why Clinical Trials of AIDS Vaccines Are Premature," *American Journal of Public Health,* 79:1, January 1989, pp. 86–91. Mariner, an Associate Professor of Health Law at Boston University, presented "Vaccine Testing: An Important Legal Question" on the panel with Christakis in Montreal.

12. The Chirimuuta critique provides a brief history of the conflicting reasons for the early cooperation of African governments and researchers with Western AIDS researchers, as well as explaining why several countries broke off relations with Western AIDS researchers and reporters.

13. A 1984 World Bank study, cited in Mudimbe, p. 54. The forms of Christianity are multiple, sometimes syncretic with longstanding local religious beliefs and practices, sometimes virtually supplanting them. Nevertheless, it is quite bizarre to construct radical difference between Western and African worldviews as if centuries of evangelism and colonialism have not left Africans well aware of the curious workings of a Western ethics supposedly designed to "protect" unwitting "Others."

14. I learned what the "ethical space" is, and that it cannot be "objective," when I served as a theologian and a "community" (i.e., "gay") person on an institutional review board for local, Boston-based AIDS research from 1983–1985. The nature of negotiating that specific conditions be met, particularly regarding the content of informed consent, takes on an agonistic quality that is, and in AIDS treatment trial debates consistently has been, interpreted as political. The rise of community research initiatives—where community-based scientists and activists conduct their own trials under review board supervisions—are a stage in this process.

15. The first conference held on AIDS in Africa, actually sited in Europe, was boycotted by most of the African researchers and some of their Western colleagues. Colin Norman, "Politics and Science Clash on African AIDS," *Science*, Vol. 230, 6 December 1985, pp. 1140–42.

    It is not unusual now for presentations by Africans to be pulled from the International Conferences at the last minute, as economic and political conditions change. The first major international conference on AIDS held in sub-Saharan Africa was an education conference held in October 1989 in Cameroon.

16. This can be overcome in early trials by performing more costly viral tests. However, the problem becomes substantial in the proposed Phase Three vaccine trials, in which thousands of people are to be vaccinated. Trials conducted to determine the vaccine's effect on already infected people (and there are such Phase One trials now) constitute a much greater risk than trials on non-infected trial subjects, since an HIV-infected person's condition might worsen from the effects of some forms of vaccine. See both Christakis and Mariner/Gallo, op.cit.

17. There is uncertainty about what would constitute a successful vaccine, and a variety of approaches are currently implemented. Some attempt to prevent HIV infection from occurring at all. Others try to disable the virus once it has attacked certain cells. Still others aim to prevent HIV replication or slow it down enough to lengthen the time it takes for the immune system to be functionally affected. For a good review of current approaches, see Thomas J. Matthews and Dani P. Bolognesi, "AIDS Vaccines," *Scientific American*, 259:4, October 1988, pp. 120–128.

18. Donna Haraway's "Situated Knowledges: The Science Question in Feminism and the Privilege of Partial Perspective," *Feminist Studies*, 14:3, Fall 1988, pp. 575–599, grapples with the inextricable need of science for bodies (and vice versa) by proposing an epistemology of partial and consciously subjective knowledges which paradoxically produces a new kind of objectivity by locating the observer, rather than positing "him" as outside the field of study.

19. This includes the possibility that the vaccine won't work and that people who become infected through vaccination, not having been aggressively educated about safe sex, will increase the total number of infected people. Further, the belief that a vaccine is around the corner may decrease people's willingness to practice safe sex. There are also probable social effects: because widespread vaccine trials will confound testing programs, border regulations may discriminate against Africans. Popular claims about having been vaccinated (like the folklore about men claiming to be sterile and therefore not needing to use condoms) may, on the micro-level, thwart the safe sex education programs that will have to continue to take place until the entire world is vaccinated. There is an additional problem with the placebo controls: since it may be quite easy for trial subjects to get antibody testing, the placebo control subject will be able to easily find out whether she/he has been vaccinated or not, which may change her/his behavior and will certainly compromise the *scientific validity* of the trials. A key standard in Western biomedical ethics is that trials *must be* able

to yield valid scientific data; the impossibility of placebo-controlled vaccine trials being fully blind should be enough to render them unethical. Further, the ethics of researchers and the ethics of educators conflict. In the Western context, testing is perceived to be a critical component of risk reduction education. Preventing trial subjects from knowing their serostatus as a condition of participation runs counter to previous debates in the U.S. about withholding or requiring self-knowledge of HIV status. Currently, antibody testing counselors are only to deny testing if the individual seeking the test is believed to be at risk of suicide. In the U.S., despite substantial data to the contrary, the knowledge of serostatus is believed to promote behavior change. Of course, denying serostatus knowledge is internally consistent with the logic of the vaccine trial, since some number of subjects must be subsequently exposed to HIV if any data is to be obtained.

20. One example of many is the June 1988 *Vanity Fair* article, "In Search of the Source of AIDS," by Alex Shoumatoff, which describes the source as follows: "The heart of Africa is stricken. The 'AIDS belt' is spreading, and the disease that has already claimed the lives of thousands of men, women, and children will claim millions more."

21. John Dixon of the British Columbia Civil Liberties Association has coined this term. See Fifth International AIDS Conference abstract Th.F.P.11, "Catastrophic Rights." This concept entered HIV/AIDS treatment trial debates in response to demands by HIV-Ab+/PLWA activists to speed up trials. Dixon argues that the catastrophically ill may have a justifiable claim to have government drug control policies relaxed. The concept hinges on the idea of "an enhanced right to therapeutic self-determination." Several AIDS-related drugs have been "fast tracked" and allowed into human trials before completing the usual round of preliminary trials. Several drugs, including AZT, were widely released before completing trials, and data was collected on those people who took the drug. These are referred to as "compassionate release" trials, and they result in data that is uncontrolled by traditional standards.

22. The last two years of International AIDS Conferences have seen a dozen or more reports on the success of condom campaigns, especially among prostitutes, who are now organizing self-help and peer education projects in many of the major cities throughout Africa.

23. It is common in medical practice in developing countries to frequently transfuse for malaria during pregnancy; for severe anemia, including that during pregnancy, during severe malaria, and sickle cell; and for low-weight or sick infants and children. Alan F. Fleming, "Prevention of transmission of HIV by blood transfusion in developing countries," Global Impact of AIDS Conference, London, 8–10 March 1988.

24. In addition, the early years of the HIV epidemic coincided with the discovery of the serious hygiene problems of and possible cross-infection through smallpox vaccination. A detailed understanding of the value and errors in the efforts to wipe out smallpox in Africa is only now emerging.

25. Alan Whiteside, "Migrant Labor and AIDS in Southern Africa," Global Impact of AIDS Conference, London, 8–10 March 1988. Whiteside is sympathetic toward both the migrant miners and their home governments whose economic stability in part depends on the taxes and currency exchange that miners provide. He has worked with unions and the Chamber of Mines to maintain non-discrimination rules concerning the migrant and South African miners in the face of government pressures to institute actions both economically injurious and in violation of human rights. I chose Whiteside's presentation not to criticize his work, but because it exemplifies the

terms of South African AIDS discourse. His work is clearly better than that of the government, not coincidentally because the South African mines' economic interests are best served by more liberal policies. Homosexual relationships at the mines have long been tolerated by mine officials even in the face of government and Christian reform attempts because those relationships are useful to mine discipline. Details of miners' male-male relations come from a study by T. Dunbar Moodie, "Migrancy and Male Sexuality on South African Gold Mines," in *Journal of South African Studies*, 14:2, January 1988, pp. 228–56.

26. This baffling assertion is contained in the Panos publication *Blaming Others*, ed. Renee Sabatier, London: Panos Publications, 1988. See especially the section on "Sex and Race."

27. The African National Congress has, in the late 1980s, begun to recognize and embrace the work of gay liberationists within the anti-apartheid movement. The arrest of ANC and gay activist Simon Nikoli brought the anti-apartheid and gay movements in the West together, and the work of Alfred Machela within the International Lesbian and Gay Association has politicized both that group and the other largely white South African gay organizations. See the BBC broadcast on South Africa in the "Out on Tuesday" series edited by Mandy Merck and screened in 1989 for an excellent overview of the changes in the ANC concerning the status of gay people.

28. See Fleming op.cit.

29. There are a number of studies comparing male-to-female and female-to-male transmission in heterosexual couples, but see especially Isabelle Vincenzi and R. Ancelle-Park working for the European Community Study Group, "Heterosexual Transmission of HIV: A European Study, Part II: Female to Male Transmission" (Abstract Th.A.O.20., from the Fifth International AIDS Conference, Montreal, June 1989), which considers a variety of factors including the history of STDs.

30. Francis Allan Plummer, et al., "Effectiveness of Condom Promotion in a Nairobi Community of Prostitutes," abstract T.A.O.25.

31. Lenni W. Kangas, et al, "The Supply of, and Demand for, Condoms to Prevent HIV Transmission in Developing Countries," abstract W.A.P.98., Fifth International AIDS Conference, Montreal, June 1989.

32. "Work of the Rand Gay Organization," Homosexual Identity Before, During, and After HIV, Conference, Stockholm, June 1988.

Chapter 5

1. Annick Pruier, "Reasons for Practicing Unsafe Sex," presented at the Homosexual Identity Before, During, and After HIV Conference, Stockholm, June 1988.

2. No one, to my knowledge, actually used this phrase, but it captures the gist of the original educational material.

3. The emergence of safe sex information in rap music, and the insert in Madonna's "Like a Prayer," are some hopeful signs that youth may be able to generate or find information that respects their cultures.

4. *New York Times*, "AIDS Threat Brings New Turmoil for Gay Teens," 21 October 1987; Ralph J. DiClemente, "Prevention of HIV Infection Among Adolescents," *AIDS Education and Prevention*, 1:1, Spring 1989.

5. See Jan Zita Gover, "Reading AIDS," in *AIDS:Social Representations, Social Practices,* eds.AIDS as Emergency P. Aggleton, G. Hart, and P. Davies, Falmer Press: Philadelphia, 1989.

6. Ian Warwick, Peter Aggleton, and Milary Homans, "Young People's Health Beliefs and AIDS," in *Social Aspects of AIDS,* ed. Peter Aggleton and Hilary Homans, Philadelphia: Falmer Press, 1988; Stephen Clift, David Stears, Sandra Legg, Amina Memon, and Lorna Ryan, "Blame and Young People's Moral Judgements About AIDS," in *AIDS: Individual, Cultural, and Policy Dimensions,* ed. Peter Aggleton, Peter Davies, and Graham Hart, Philadelphia: Falmer Press, 1990.

7. Some ideas on AIDS education in the classroom.

The AIDS epidemic is a major international event at the end of the twentieth century, cutting across disciplines and serving as a focus for vast policy and moral reinterpretation. Students need not only practical information and suggestions about the effects of the epidemic on social and political life, but they need critical skills to continue understanding the epidemic and its effects as medical information and policy trends change. Teaching about AIDS—for a single class period or an entire course—involves relating AIDS to other kinds of subject matter and to students' immediate concerns. How AIDS should be incorporated into the curriculum will change as time goes on, but the following are some suggestions:

1. Avoid using the AIDS 101 format.

Facts spawn facts, which become contradictory, leading people to be skeptical about any "answers" and reinforcing their preexisting prejudices and logics, which may not be useful tools for understanding AIDS. Stimulating discussions which foreground their own experiences, concerns, and methods of thinking through sex and drug choices helps people begin to determine what facts make a difference and to locate credible answers to their questions. Before giving an "answer," try to encourage group discussion of *how* such information addresses their real issues and concerns. It is unethical to allow students to believe that facts will determine their attitudes and behavior when this is clearly not the case: it is a disservice to reinforce belief in a fully objective science instead of teaching the interpretive skills needed to utilize scientific information. As students openly discuss the validity, usefulness, and political commitments of "facts" they will develop a capacity for thinking about AIDS policy and HIV transmission.

2. Use a variety of media as a focus of discussion.

Pamphlets and alternative media of the right are especially useful for stimulating discussion. These contain in blatant form the underlying logics and tropes of AIDS discourse. Do not be afraid that students will "believe" everything they read; simply getting them to apply the far out logic of the right to their own lives will begin to raise their critical skills. Students who cut their critical teeth on highly rhetorically charged material will quickly see the hidden problems and logics which they uncritically accept in more reasonably sound sources. This is an especially helpful process to use in the discussion of public policy issues.

3. Use outside speakers to provide a variety of points of view.

If time and scheduling permit, have students discuss what kind of outside speakers they feel will help them address their issues. Encourage students to read widely about AIDS, from scientific and public health reports to self-help manuals by people living with AIDS and analyses by activists, from the novels and plays about the lived experience of the epidemic to the right-wing policy recommendations. Speakers should move students beyond the existing material, not substitute for failing to "do their homework." Avoid overuse of doctors or medical "experts" who reinforce students' view that "facts" rather than critical thinking will solve their anxieties.

Instead, use hospice volunteers, activists, writers, lawyers, people living with HIV/AIDS, parents, lovers, or friends. Most people who do regular speaking are thoroughly familiar with any "facts" that might be necessary to a discussion. Showing that lay people can easily become fluent in the necessary "scientific" information empowers students' own lay research. Playing on the authority of personal experiences challenges the assumption that facts and science can conquers the AIDS-related social problems. Be aware of the different subject positions and rhetorics used by a range of speakers and help students understand the congruences and conflicts in AIDS discourse as rhetorical and political rather than as a legitimacy battle between politically neutral experts and social interest groups.

    4. Teach "practical deconstruction."

AIDS and the discursive practices which vie to "explain it" will be around for a long time. The ability to "read AIDS" in critical daily practices—reading newspapers, pamphlets, watching television, engaging in ordinary conversation—is important if HIV transmission and AIDS-related social backlash are to be stopped. But students must also understand the textual quality of life in the post-modern era in which their practice and interpretation of daily life is creative of and formed by texts. Such a daily practice of reading will help students to understand their relation to the "object" of AIDS discourse, which is both a real virus and a set of knowledges increasingly administered by media, medical, and sociological "experts." Students must evaluate the status of *their own* knowledge about AIDS, and understand the implications of feigned ignorance. Critical, *interventive* reading will impel students to read themselves *into* the AIDS episteme, will not allow them to fatally position themselves outside of or in a place of exemption from the discourses of safe practices and social equity.

8. Judith Schwartzbaum et al., "Physician Breach of Patient Confidentiality Among Individuals with HIV Infection: A Preliminary Investigation of Racism, Sexism, and Homophobia," presented at the Fifth International AIDS Conference in Montreal, abstract M.F.P.4. In a survey of 222 Tennessee physicians presented with case studies of infected individuals, physicians were almost ten times more likely to inform the partners of black males than those of white males. Physicians with increased levels of AIDS knowledge were fifty times more likely to inform the partners of black heterosexual males than black homosexual males. Interestingly, physicians who indicated confidence in their knowledge of AIDS were about sixty times more likely to report the cases of male heterosexuals to the public health department than female homosexuals, indicating their beliefs about the relationship between identity categories and exposure patterns.

9. This was literally the text of the major 1987–88 testing campaign in Sweden.

10. The responsibility for the entire social and cultural upheaval occurring in the context of AIDS is laid on those identified as "at risk" under varying rubrics and ever-changing logics.

11. J. Phillipe Rushton and Anthony F. Bogaert, "Population Differences in Susceptibility to AIDS: An Evolutionary Analysis," *Social Science Medicine*, 28:12, 1989, pp. 1211–1220. For a longer discussion of the problems in this argument see Chapter Five.

12. Ian Warwick, Peter Aggleton, Hilary Homans, "Young People's Health Beliefs and AIDS," in *Social Aspects of AIDS*, ed. Aggleton and Homans, Philadelphia: Falmer Press, 1988.

13. An excellent review of early U.S. strategies to gain political and social equality for lesbians and gay men can be found in Toby Marotta's *The Politics of Homosexuality*, Boston: Houghton Mifflin, 1981.

14. See Cindy Patton, "Heterosexual AIDS Panic: A Queer Paradigm," *Gay Community News*, 9 February 1985.

15. It was only in about 1988 that drug injection became identified by the press as the "source" of "heterosexual AIDS." This idea, and the notion of "African (heterosexual) AIDS" only broadened and spelled out the categories of denial for the "general public." By linking AIDS with drug use in white of Latin non-gay PLWAs, and hetero-*sexuality* with African/African American PLWAs, the general public could simply return to its "opposite-sex" partnering and be "hetero" while denying "sexuality."

16. Eve Kosokofsy Sedgwick's *Between Men: English Literature and Male Homosocial Desire*, New York: Columbia, 1985, is the best theoretical work on the anxiety of male desire and anality.

17. This oddity, while widely noted, is best explicated, in terms of Western sexual ideology, in *Policing Desire*, Simon Watney, Minnesota University Press, 1988.

Chapter 6

1. The work of the Sankofa film collective in England, of the now-defunct *m/f*, of the British quarterly *New Formations*, and of the U.S. AIDS Coalition to Unleash Power (ACT UP) are examples of groups intervening in cultural and political processes from using deconstructionist tactics. ACT UP also draws on cultural marxist and semiotic analyses to select specific sites and moments for intervention into political, medical, and legal decision-making processes.

2. Interesting divergences from this trend are Eve Sedgwick's work on male homosociality, her new work on gender and nationality, and the work of Liz Kennedy and the Buffalo (New York, U.S.) Women's History Project examining the identity constructions of butch/femme lesbians in the 1950s.

3. Interestingly, recent trends in product liability law in cases having to do with the fertility drug DES found that a claimant did not have to produce evidence of exactly which company's product they had used; rather, they applied to a single fund to which companies contributed in proportion to their market share of the drug.

4. The riots took place outside a huge, high-rise dormitory at the university, which holds tens of thousands of students in a tiny New England town. The event occurred after a New York City team beat the Boston team for the national title. The Boston team has long symbolized racism, with fans booing their own black players, and numerous contract disputes alleging racism. After the New York team's victory, several black students were chased and beaten by white students and a drunken riot involving over 100 students ensued. In preceding weeks, the right-wing student paper had published unusually racist and homophobic articles. After an investigation by the Massachusetts Coalition Against Discrimination, several white students were suspended. Anti-prejudice programming is annually held at the university for the anniversary week of the event.

5. See, for example, Foucault's criticism of the gay movement: "Homosexuality is secrecy and truth. What is the relationship we can set up, invent, transform through homosexuality? Homosexuality is not a desire, but a thing to be desired"; Omi and Winant's (largely Gramscian) critique of race politics in the U.S.; and Cornel West's critique of American pragmatism and identity politics. All propose moving the politics of resistance beyond claims for blocks of power. While these kinds of critiques are often read as giving up identity, their arguments are more practical; they propose

that we must do both traditional radical politics and deconstructive politics, that we must learn to strategize our reformisms more creatively. *Foucault Live,* New York: Semiotext(e), 1989; Michael Omi and Howard Winant, *Racial Formations in the United States: From the 1960s to the 1980s,* New York: Routledge and Kegan Paul, 1986; Cornel West, *The American Evasion of Philosophy,* Madison: University of Wisconsin Press, 1989.

6. This slogan first appeared on a poster produced by the Silence=Death Collective, a group of gay men who postered New York City for several months, and then attended the founding meeting of what became the AIDS Coalition to Unleash Power. The symbol has been used on posters, stickers, and buttons produced by ACT UP since spring 1987. For a history of this poster and other ACT UP graphic interventions see Douglas Crimp and Adam Rolston, *AIDS DEMO GRAPHICS,* Seattle: Bay Press, 1990.

    The poster uses an "inverted" pink triangle, a point-up version of the symbol the Nazis used to designate people interned for being homosexual. The point-up version is intended to signal active fighting back, a different tactic from the silent resistance associated with the original point-down version. The point-down pink triangle came into use as a code and symbol of resistance among the international gay movement in the mid-seventies. The "homomonument," a pink granite triangle set into a canal park in Amsterdam, memorializes homosexual repression under fascism past and present, and stands as a permanent reminder—if any symbol against fascism is permanent—that gay people everywhere in the Western world, especially now, are subject to a silent apartheid. The monument was completed in 1987 after several years' cooperation between the Dutch national and Amsterdam city governments, gay movement organizations, and the Anne Frank House.

7. ACT UP, especially the original New York City group which holds weekly meetings attended by hundreds of people, provides an interesting example of emerging postmodern political praxis using deconstructionist analyses and tactics. A number of the key people in the group are artists or intellectuals with deconstructionist politics. To many people actively involved in gay and now AIDS anarchist politics, deconstructionist, cultural marxist, and post-structuralist methods and jargon are fairly familiar, whether coming directly from Derrida, Gramsci, or Foucault, or simply as part of a *zeitgeist.* In addition, particular postmodernist texts form the reading list of the ACT UP New York group, which holds discussions of the relationship between their particular praxis and their experience/politics.

8. Technically, the antibodies produced against Human Immunodeficiency Virus— HIV—are non-covering antibodies, that is, they do not kill the virus. Thus, a "positive" antibody test indicates exposure but not immunity to HIV illness, unlike positive tests for antibodies to other illnesses, which do indicate immunity.

9. I mean here the pictoral *representation* of the person—the body—who "has AIDS," as displayed in scientific and mass media. Of course, one does not "have AIDS," but has an AIDS diagnosis and any of a range of other expressive illnesses which are symptoms of the immunological lack which is by definition AIDS. Thus, the before and after picture of the "person (body) with AIDS" is a multiple army of misleading metaphors—the body as self, the symptom as illness, the disease as person, representation as possession.

10. Simon Watney, Stuart Marshall, Meurig Horton and others have made this point in numerous publications; see especially Watney's *Policing Desire,* Minneapolis: University of Minnesota Press, 1987; and Marshall's three-part BBC series "Bright Eyes," 1986.

11. This is the lie implicit in the idea of neutral testing: explicit in Swedish law and implicit in recent lawsuits in the U.S. is the idea that if you know or should have known that you might test positive (i.e., you recognize yourself in the litany of risky people), your acts of intercourse subject you to legal control: medical detention in Sweden and the U.S., and in addition, financial liability in the U.S. Further, the protocol for administering the test in the U.S. states that the practitioner should ascertain whether the person is likely to be a member of a "risk group" or engaged in "risk behaviors" in order to decide whether a positive test is actually positive or a false positive. A U.S. gay man recently won a large suit for mental distress for having gone through two years believing he had tested positive when the test was in fact incorrect. By contrast, convincingly heterosexual, non-drug-using heterosexuals with positive tests are brought in for repeat testing and told their tests are among the small percentage of false positives. Thus, apparent "risk group" membership outweighs test result in the determination of whether one is brought into the public sphere of potential legal liability.

12. See Jeffrey Weeks, *Sex, Politics, and Society: The Regulation of Sexuality Since 1900*, London: Longman, Harlow, 1981; and Foucault's *The History of Sexuality, Volume 1*, New York: Vintage, 1981.

13. In 1989, in Ithaca, New York and on a Caribbean island U.S. lesbians were brutally murdered. These reported cases are only the more well-known of a more general upswing in anti-lesbian violence documented by gay/lesbian organizations in the U.S., central Europe, and Latin America.

14. See the April 1987 report from the Centers for Disease Control summarizing the effects of the Alternative Test Site program of the previous two and a half years. The report attempts to provide a cost/benefit assessment of the number of infected people found. The problem arises in estimating and calculating the social cost of false positive tests. The reporting, as is standard practice, falls back on the intuitions of the counselors.

15. Certainly, there were also female bodies, injecting drug users' bodies, etc.; however, gay men constituted the bulk of research subjects, not only because they constituted the largest category, though an artificially constructed one (a gay man who had another risk factor was counted only as gay), but also because class biases made doctors perceive gay men as ideal, pleasant, and compliant guinea pigs.

16. I have doubts that the spawning of ACT UP groups around the U.S., Canada, and England, represents the spread of a counter-resistance movement, though each group is important in its own locale. ACT UP New York is a very special phenomenon: a guerrilla theater that for all its work with communities of color and with women reads as "gay" because that is the only way we know how to understand such enactments in the streets of New York, streets in which gay people never had a domestic space. In an important sense, the insight "silence = death" must be rewritten for each city because the experience of gay people with respect to repression is unique in each place. Thus, ACT UPs now function as a vibrating, anarchistic assualt on unitary power whenever the groups meet *en masse* for a demonstration. But these demonstrations also show the very different ways of working of each group—from holding up watches at a particular time to symbolize "time is running out," to pulling the microphone, tactics of two different ACT UP groups at a speech by Food and Drug Administration Commissioner Frank Young in Boston, July 1988. As long as the symbols and actions continually reinvent the meaning felt by those in the gap between legitimated discourses, ACT UP will be a source of resistance, a form of transversal power of the sort described by Deleuze, Guatarri, and Foucault in differ-

ent non-systematic writings. The evolution of an "ACT-Out" group in Boston pursuing gay confrontation politics with AIDS actions as a subset, and of a national direct action coordinating group in Washington, D.C., "ACT-NOW," suggest that initial acts/events of speaking out of the void are inevitably pulled into other power/discourse formations, albeit progressive ones. The sensibility in New York City that produced the poster and the first ACT UP still exists, and the high participation of actors and artists, people with AIDS and people enraged by AIDS, enables the group to maintain its anarchist style. This local resistance cannot be cloned, and hopefully will not be overshadowed by grassroots organizations modelled after ACT UP, but inclined toward more recognizable new left protest. ACT UP groups do not protest or demonstrate; rather, they perform, and in their "actions" they identify the unspoken, inaudible linkages in the power system which are obscured by both the unitary notion of power ("get a government response") and the network notion of power ("decentralize"). I do not intend to sentimentalize ACT UP as it appeared in New York City, rather to point out the nature of politics now. The idea of local resistances, taken seriously and in specific contexts, means that coalition, especially geographically understood, is not a coherent idea. What the emergence of ACT UP through the silence = death symbols suggests is that sparks are given off through attempts to "unleash" power within the power/discourse gap. Resistance in other locales may be ignited by these sparks, but must spring from an analysis of the local situation, finding leverage points within the narrow space offered differently by different localities. The problem with coalition politics when they collide with identity politics, as Judith Butler points out in her *Gender Trouble*, (New York: Routlege, 1989), is the tendency to seek agreement on an increasingly totalizing critique, set of practices, or logic of identity. It has not seemed workable to construct hierarchies or matrices of identity when, say, HIV antibody positivity and gender or racial identity create tactical or community conflicts. None of us think persons situated at junctures of multiple identity/issue points should have to "choose" their allegiances, and yet, the tendency to totalization in coalition efforts practically boils down to just such painful choices. Butler suggests that we consider that coalition, and even agreement, may not be a desirable goal, but only a strategic or tactical moment in denaturalizing identities and the systems of power which construct them in order to control us.

Bibliography

Aaab-Richard, Dirg, et al. *Tongues Alive*. London: Gay Men's Press, 1987.

Adam, Barry. *The Rise of a Lesbian and Gay Movement*. Boston: Twayne, 1987.

Aggleton, Peter, and Hilary Homans, eds. *Social Aspects of AIDS*. Philadelphia: Falmer Press, 1988.

Aggleton, Peter, Graham Hart, and Peter Davies, eds. *AIDS: Social Representations, Social Practices*. Philadephia: Falmer Press, 1989.

Aggleton, Peter, Graham Hart, and Peter Davies, eds. *AIDS: Individual, Cultural, and Policy Dimensions*. Philadelphia: Falmer Press, 1990.

Allen, Paula Gunn. "Lesbians in American Indian Cultures." *Hidden From History*, eds. Martin Bauml Duberman, Martha Vicinus, and George Chauncey, Jr. New York: New American Library, 1989.

Altman, Dennis. *The Homosexualization of America*. New York: St. Martins Press, 1982.

Altman, Dennis. *AIDS in the Mind of America*. New York: Doubleday, 1986.

Altman, Dennis. "AIDS and the Reconceptualization of Homosexuality." Dennis Altman et al. *Homosexuality, Which Homosexuality?*. Amsterdam: Uitgeverij An Dekker/Schorer, 1989.

Alyson, Sasha, ed. *You Can Do Something About AIDS*. Boston: The Stop AIDS Project, 1988.

Antonio, Gene. *The AIDS Coverup? The Real and Alarming Facts About AIDS*. San Francisco: Ignatious Press, 1986.

Anzaldua, Gloria. *Borderlands/La Frontera: The New Mestiza*. San Francisco: Spinsters/Aunt Lute, 1987.

Arguelles, Lourdes, and B. Ruby Rich. "Understanding the Cuban Lesbian and Gay Male Experience." *Hidden From History*. Eds. Martin Bauml Duberman, Martha Vicinus, and George Chauncey, Jr. New York: New American Library, 1989.

Barre-Sinoussi, F., et al. "Isolation of a T-lymphotropic retrovirus from a patient at risk for AIDS." *Science* 220 (20 May 1983): pp. 868–871.

Bauldrillard, Jean. *Simulacra and Simulations*. New York: *Semiotext(e)*, 1983.

Baudrillard, Jean. *The Ecstasy of Communication*. New York: *Semiotext(e)*, 1987.

Beam, Joseph, ed. *In the Life: A Black Gay Anthology*. Boston: Alyson, 1986.

Berk, Richard A., ed. *The Social Impact of AIDS in the U.S.*. Cambridge: Abt Books, 1988.

Braithwaite, Ronald, and Ngina Lythocott. "Community Empowerment as a Strategy for Health Promotion for Black and other Minority Populations." *Journal of the American Medical Association* 261:2 (13 January 1989).

Brandt, Alan M. *No Magic Bullet: A Social History of Venereal Disease in the United States Since 1880.* Cambridge: Harvard, 1985.

Bronski, Michael. *Culture Clash: The Making of a Gay Sensibility.* Boston: South End Press, 1984.

Callen, Michael, ed. *Surviving and Thriving With AIDS.* New York: PWA Coalition, 1988.

Caplan, Pat, ed. *The Cultural Construction of Sexuality.* New York: Tavistock, 1987.

Carter, Erica and Simon Watney, eds. *Taking Liberties: AIDS and Cultural Politics.* London: Serpent's Tail, 1989.

Chirimuuta, Richard, and Rosalind Chirimuuta. *AIDS, Africa and Racism.* Burton-on-Trent, U.K., 1987.

Christakis, Nicholas A. "Ethical Aspects of the International AIDS Agenda." Montreal: Fifth International AIDS conference, abstract W.F.O 2, 1989.

Christakis, Nicholas A. "The Ethical Design of an AIDS Vaccine Trial in Africa." *Hastings Center Report* (June/July 1988).

Christakis, Nicholas A. "Responding to a Pandemic: International Interests in AIDS Control." *Daedalus* 118:2 (Spring 1989).

Clarke, Loren K. and Malcolm Potts, eds. *The AIDS Reader: Documentary History of a Modern Epidemic.* Boston: Braden Publishing, 1988.

Clift, Stephen, et al. "Blame and Young People's Moral Judgments About AIDS" *AIDS: Individual, Cultural, and Policy Dimensions* Eds. Peter Aggleton, Peter Davies, and Graham Hart. Philadelphia: Falmer Press, 1990.

Committee on Government Operations, U. S. House of Representatives, 98th Congress. *Federal Response to AIDS.* Washington: Government Printing Office, 1983.

Courtwright, David T. *Dark Paradise: Opiate Addiction in America before 1940.* Cambridge: Harvard University Press, 1982.

Crimp, Douglas. "How to Have Promiscuity in an Epidemic." *AIDS: Cultural Analysis, Cultural Activism.* Ed. Douglas Crimp. Cambridge: MIT Press, 1988.

Crimp, Douglas, ed. *AIDS: Cultural Analysis, Cultural Activism.* Cambridge: MIT Press, 1988.

Crimp, Douglas, and Adam Rolston. *AIDS DEMO GRAPHICS.* Seattle: Bay Press, 1990.

Dalton, Harlon L. "AIDS in Blackface." *Daedalus* 118:3 (Summer 1989).

D'Emilio, John. *Sexual Politics, Sexual Communities.* Chicago: University of Chicago Press, 1983.

Delgado, Melvin, and Denise Humm-Delgado. "Natural Support Systems: Source of Strength in Hispanic Communities." *Social Work* 27 (January 1982).

Des Jarlais, Don, and Samuel Friedman. "HIV infection among intravenous drug users: Epidemiology and risk reduction." *AIDS* No. 1 (1987).

Deyton, Lawrence, and John Killen, Jr. "Volunteering for a Study." *You Can Do Something About AIDS.* Ed. Sasha Alyson. Boston: The Stop AIDS Project, 1988.

Dixon, John. "Catastrophic Rights." Montreal: Fifth International AIDS Conference, Abstract Th.F.P.11, 1989.

Douglas, Mary. *Purity and Danger.* London: Routledge, 1978.

Douglas, Mary. *How Institutions Think*. Syracuse: Syracuse University Press, 1986.

Dowsett, Gary. "You'll Never Forget the Feeling of Safe Sex! AIDS Prevention Strategies for Gay and Bisexual Men in Sydney, Australia." Geneva: World Health Organization Workshop on AIDS Health Promotion Activities Directed Toward Gay and Bisexual Men, May 1989.

Dowsett, Gary. "Reaching Men Who Have Sex With Men in Australia." Yaounde, Cameroon: Second International AIDS Information and Education Conference, plenary paper, October 1989.

Duberman, Martin Bauml, Martha Vicinus, and George Chauncey, Jr., eds. *Hidden from History*. New York: New American Library, 1989.

Ehrenreich, Barbara, and John Ehrenreich. *The American Health Empire: Report of Health/ PAC*. New York: Vintage, 1971.

Fleck, Ludwik. *Genesis and Development of a Scientific Fact*. Chicago: University of Chicago Press, 1979. Fleming, Alan F. "Prevention of Transmission of HIV by Blood Transfusion in Developing Countries." London: Global Impact of AIDS Conference, 8–10 March 1988.

Foucault, Michel. *The Order of Things*. New York: Random House, 1970.

Foucault, Michel. *The Archaeology of Knowledge*. New York: Pantheon, 1972.

Foucault, Michel. *The Birth of the Clinic: An Archaeology of Medical Perception*. New York: Vintage, 1975.

Foucault, Michel. *Language, Counter-Memory, and Practice: Selected Essays and Interviews*. Ithaca: Cornell University Press, 1977.

Foucault, Michel. *The History of Sexuality, Volume 1*. New York: Vintage, 1978.

Foucault, Michel. *Discipline and Punish*. New York: Vintage Books, 1979.

Foucault, Michel. "The Politics of Health in the 18th Century." *Power/Knowledge*. New York: Pantheon, 1980.

Freedman, Benjamin. "Equipoise and the Ethics of Clinical Research." *New England Journal of Medicine* 317:3 (16 July 1987): pp. 141–5.

Freedman, Benjamin, et al. "Nonvalidated Therapies and HIV Disease." *Hastings Center Report* (May/June 1989): pp. 14–20.

Freedman, Benjamin. "Ethical Points on Placebo and Treatment Controls in HIV Drug Trials." Montreal: Fifth International AIDS Conference, Abstract W.F.O.5., 1989.

Freudenberg, Nicholas, Jacalyn Lee, and Diana Silver. "How Black and Latino Community Organizations Respond to the AIDS Epidemic: A Case Study in One New York City Neighborhood." *AIDS* 1:1 (Spring 1989).

Freudenberg, Nicholas. "Social and Political Obstacles to AIDS Education." *Siecus Report* 17:6 (August/September 1989).

Gallo, R. C., et al. "Frequent detection and isolation of cytopathic retroviruses (HTLV-III) from patients with AIDS and at risk for AIDS." *Science* 224 (1984): 500–501.

Gilman, Sander L. *Disease and Representation: Images of Illness from Madness to AIDS*. Ithaca: Cornell, 1988.

Gold, M., et al. "Counselling Seropositives." *What to Do About AIDS: Physicians and Health Care Professionals Discuss the Issues*. Ed. L. McKusick. Los Angeles: University of California Press, 1986.

Gomez, Alma, Cherrie Moraga, Mariana Romo-Carmona, eds. *Cuendos: Stories by Latinas.* Latham, New York: Kitchen Table Press, 1983.

Grahn, Judy. *Another Mother Tongue: Gay Words, Gay Worlds.* Boston: Beacon Press, 1984.

Grover, Jan Zita. "AIDS: Key Words." *AIDS: Cultural Analysis, Cultural Activism.* Ed. Douglas Crimp. Cambridge: MIT Press, 1988.

Grover, Jan Zita. "Reading AIDS." *AIDS: Social Representations, Social Practices.* Eds. Peter Aggleton, Graham Hart and Peter Davies. Philadelphia: Falmer Press, 1989.

Gross, Michael. "HIV Antibody Testing: Performance and Counselling Issues." *New England Journal of Public Policy.* 4:1 (Winter/Spring 1988).

Haraway, Donna. "Situated Knowledges: The Science Question in Feminism and the Privilege of Partial Perspective." *Feminist Studies* 14:3 (Fall 1988).

Henricksson, Benny. "Social Democracy or Societal Control: A Critical Analysis of Swedish AIDS Policy." Institute for Social Policy, June 1988.

Hooks, Bell. *Talking Back: Thinking Feminist, Thinking Black.* Boston: South End Press. 1989.

"Homecoming." *Black/Out* II:1 (Fall 1986).

Jones, James H. *Bad Blood.* New York: Free Press, 1981.

Kayal, Phillip M. "Doing Good, Doing 'Dirty Work': The AIDS Volunteer." Boston: Annual Convention of the Eastern Sociological Society, 1 May 1987.

Kessler, Larry, Ann M. Silvia, David Aronstein, and Cynthia Patton. "Call to Action: A Community Responds." *The New England Journal of Public Policy* 4:1 (Winter/Spring 1988).

Kirp, David L. *Learning by Heart: AIDS and School Children in America's Communities.* New Brunswick: Rutgers University Press, 1989.

Knorr, Karin D. "Producing and Reproducing Knowledge: Descriptive or Constructive." *Social Science Information* 16:6 (1978).

Knorr-Cetina, Karin D. *The Manufacture of Knowledge: An Essay on the Constructivist and Contextual Nature of Science.* Oxford: Pergammon, 1981.

Knorr-Cetina, Karin D. "Scientific Communities or Transepistmic Arenas of Research? A Critique of Quasi-economic Models of Science" *Social Studies of Science* 12 (1982).

Kuhn, Thomas. *The Structure of Scientific Revolutions.* Chicago: University of Chicago Press, 1962.

Johnson, Dirk. "Broad AIDS Law Signed in Illinois." *New York Times,* 22 September 1987, p. II:7.

Latour, Bruno. *The Pasteurization of France.* Cambridge: Harvard University Press, 1988.

Machela, Alfred. "The Work of the Rand Gay Organization." Stockholm: Homosexual Identity Before, During, and After HIV Conference, June 1988.

Mariner, Wendy K., and Robert C. Gallo. "Getting to Market: The Scientific and Legal Climate for Developing an AIDS Vaccine." *Law, Medicine, and Health Care* 15:1–2 (Summer 1987): pp. 17–26.

Mariner, Wendy K. "The Trouble with Immunization." *The Harvard Medical School Health Letter* X:11.

Mariner, Wendy K. "Why Clinical Trials of AIDS Vaccines Are Premature." *American Journal of Public Health* 79:1 (January 1989).

Marotta, Toby. *The Politics of Homosexuality.* Boston: Houghton Mifflin, 1981.

Masters, William H., Virginia E. Johnson, and Robert C. Kolodny, *Crisis: Heterosexual Behavior in the Age of AIDS*. London: Weidenfield and Nicolson, 1988.

McKusick, Leon, ed. *What to do about AIDS: Physicians and Health Care Professionals Discuss the Issues*. Los Angeles: University of California Press, 1986.

McNeill, William H. *Plagues and People*. Garden City: Anchor, 1976.

Moraga, Cherrie, and Gloria Anzaldua, eds. *This Bridge Called my Back: Writings by Radical Women of Color*. Latham, New York: Kitchen Table Press, 1981.

Morales, Aurora Levins, and Rosario Morales. *Getting Home Alive*. Ithaca: Firebrand Books, 1986.

Mudimbe, V. Y. *The Invention of Africa: Gnosis, Philosophy, and the Order of Knowledge*. Bloomington: Indiana University Press, 1988.

Mulkay, M. J. "Some Aspects of Cultural Growth in the Natural Sciences." *Social Research* 36:1 (1969).

Mulkay, M.J. *The Social Process of Innovation*. London: Macmillan, 1972.

Narcotics Anonymous. Van Nuys, California: World Service Office.

National Coalition of Gay Sexually Transmitted Disease Services Newsletter 7:3 (February/March 1986): pp. 12–15.

Newsweek. "The Face of AIDS: One Year in the Epidemic." Special issue, 10 August 1987.

Nolan, Kathleen. "The Ethics of Placebo-Controlled Trials of Therapy for HIV Infection." Montreal: Fifth International AIDS Conference, Abstract W.F.O.6., 1989.

Norman, Colin. "Politics and Science Clash on African AIDS." *Science* 230 (6 December 1985): pp. 1140–42.

O'Malley, Padraig, ed. *The AIDS Epidemic: Private Rights and the Public Interest*. Boston: Beacon Press, 1988.

Omi, Michael, and Howard Winant. *Racial Formations in the United States: From the 1960s to the 1980s*. New York: Routledge and Kegan Paul, 1986.

O'Reilly, Kevin. Stockholm: Fourth International AIDS Conference, June 1988.

Ostrow, David, et al. "Drug Use and Sexual Behavior Change in a Cohort of Homosexual Men." Washington, D.C.: Third International AIDS Conference, 1987.

Ostrow, David. "Antibody Testing Won't Cut Risky Behavior" *American Medical Association News*, 5 June 1987.

Ostrow, David, et al. "Disclosure of HIV Antibody Status: Behavioral and Mental Health Correlates." *AIDS Education and Prevention* 1:1 (Spring 1989).

Patton, Cindy. "Heterosexual AIDS Panic: A Queer Paradigm." *Gay Community News*, 9 February 1985.

Patton, Cindy. *Sex and Germs: The Politics of AIDS*. Boston: South End Press, 1985.

Patton, Cindy, and Janis Kelly. *Making It: A Woman's Guide to Sex in the Age of AIDS*. Ithaca: Firebrand Books, 1987.

Patton, Cindy. "The International Gay Movement." *Zeta Magazine*, October 1988.

Pearce, W. Barnett. *Communication and the Human Condition*. Carbondale: Southern Illinois University Press, 1989.

Porter, Veneita. "Minorities and HIV Infection." *The AIDS Epidemic: Private Rights and the Public Interest*. Ed. Padraig O'Malley. Boston: Beacon Press, 1988.

Pruier, Annick. "Reasons for Practicing Unsafe Sex." Stockholm: Homsexual Identity, Before, During, and After HIV, June 1988.

Radical America: "Facing AIDS." Special Issue, XX:6 (November/December 1988).

Richardson, Diane. *Women and AIDS.* New York: Metheun, 1988.

Rieder, Ines, and Patricia Ruppelt, eds. *AIDS: The Women.* San Francisco: Cleis Press, 1988.

Rushton, Philippe J., and Anthony F. Bogaert. "Genetic Variations in Susceptibility to AIDS." *Social Science Medicine* 28:12 (1989): pp. 1211–1220.

Sabatier, Renee. *Blaming Others: Prejudice, Race and Worldwide AIDS.* London: Panos Institute, 1988.

Schwartzbaum, Judith, et al. "Physician Breach of Patient Confidentiality Among Individuals with HIV Infection: A Preliminary Investigation of Racism, Sexism, and Homophobia." Montreal: Fifth International AIDS Conference, abstract M.F.P.4., June 1989.

Sedgwick, Eve K. *Between Men: English Literature and Male Homosocial Desire.* New York: Columbia, 1985.

Sedgwick, Eve K. *Epistemology of the Closet.* Berkeley: University of California Press, 1990.

Selnes, Olna. Plenary Address on Drug Research. Stockholm: Fourth International AIDS Conference, June 1988.

Shepard, Gill. "Rank, Gender and Homosexuality: Mombasa as a Key to Understanding Sexual Options." *The Cultural Construction of Sexuality.* Ed. Pat Caplan. New York: Tavistock, 1987.

Shilts, Randy. *And the Band Played On.* New York: St. Martin's Press, 1987.

Shoumatoff, Alex. "In Search of the Source of AIDS." *Vanity Fair,* June 1988.

Siegel, Larry, ed. *AIDS and Substance Abuse.* New York: Harrington Press, 1988.

Silverman, David. "Making Sense of a Precipice: Constituting Identity in a HIV Clinic." *AIDS: Social Representations, Social Practices.* Eds. Peter Aggleton, Graham Hart, and Peter Davies. Philadelphia: Falmer Press, 1989.

Silverman, David. "The Social Organization of HIV Counselling." *AIDS: Individual, Cultural and Policy Dimensions.* Eds. Peter Aggleton, Peter Davies and Graham Hart. Philadelphia: Falmer Press, 1990.

Smith, Barbara, ed. *Home Girls: A Black Feminist Anthology.* Latham, New York: Kitchen Table Press, 1983.

Soucy, Gerald, et al. "Two Key Studies: 'Comparison of Recreational Drug and Alcohol Use aomng Homosexual and Bisexual Men Who are HIV Antibody Seropositive, and Subsequent PWAs,' and 'Effects of HIV Antibody Disclosure upon Sexual Behavior and Recreational Drug and Alcohol Consumption by Homsexual and Bisexual Men'." Los Angeles: National Lesbian and Gay Health Conference and the Fifth Annual National AIDS Forum, 26–29 March 1987.

Starr, Paul. *The Social Transformation of American Medicine.* New York: Basic Books, 1982.

"The AIDS Movement and Its Challenge." *Radical America* editorial. XXI:6 (November/December 1988).

Treichler, Paula. "AIDS, Homophobia, and Biomedical Discourse: An Epidemic of Signification." *AIDS: Cultural Analysis, Cultural Activism.* Ed. Douglas Crimp. Cambridge: MIT Press, 1988.

Warwick, Ian, Peter Aggleton, and Milary Homans. "Young People's Health Beliefs and AIDS." *Social Aspects of AIDS.* Eds. Peter Aggleton and Hilary Homans. Philadelphia: Falmer Press, 1988.

Watney, Simon. *Policing Desire.* Minneapolis: University of Minnesota Press, 1987.

Watney, Simon. "AIDS, 'Moral Panic' Theory and Homophobia." *Social Aspects of AIDS.* Eds. Peter Aggleton and Hilary Homans. Philadelphia: Falmer Press, 1988.

Watney, Simon. "The Spectacle of AIDS." *AIDS: Cultural Analysis, Cultural Activism.* Ed. Douglas Crimp. Cambridge: MIT, 1988.

Watney, Simon. "Missionary Positions." *Critical Quarterly* 31:3 (Autumn 1989).

Watney, Simon. "The Subject of AIDS." *AIDS: Social Representations, Social Practices.* Eds. Peter Aggleton, Graham Hart and Peter Davis. Philadelphia: Falmer Press, 1989.

Watney, Simon. "Safer Sex as Community Practice." *AIDS: Individual, Cultural and Policy Dimensions.* Eds. Peter Aggleton, Peter Davies and Graham Hart. Philadelphia: Falmer Press, 1990.

Webb, Norman L. "Gallup International Survey on Attitudes Toward AIDS." London: Global Impact of AIDS Conference, 8–10 March 1989.

Weeks, Jeffrey. *Sex, Politics, and Society: The Regulation of Sexuality Since 1900.* London: Longman, Harlow (1981).

Weeks, Jeffrey. *Sexuality.* London: Tavistock, 1986.

Weeks, Jeffrey. "Love in a Cold Climate." *Social Aspects of AIDS.* Eds. Peter Aggleton and Hilary Homans. Philadelphia: Falmer Press, 1988.

Weeks, Jeffrey. "AIDS: The Intellectual Agenda." *AIDS: Social Representations, Social Practices.* Eds. Peter Aggleton, Graham Hart and Peter Davies. Philadelphia: Falmer Press, 1989.

West, Cornel. *The American Evasion of Philosophy: A Geneology of Pragmatism.* Madison: University of Wisconsin Press, 1989.

Williams, Walter L. *The Spirit and the Flesh: Sexual Diversity in American Indian Culture.* Boston: Beacon Press, 1986.

Wolgar, Steve, and Bruno Latour. *Laboratory Life.* Princeton: Princeton University Press, 1986.

Index